ESSEX

SHOWING THE PRINCIPAL PLACES
MENTIONED IN THE TEXT.

ESSEX PEOPLE
1750–1900

from their diaries, memoirs and letters

ESSEX PEOPLE
1750-1900

*from their diaries, memoirs
and letters*

by
A. F. J. BROWN

Published by
THE ESSEX COUNTY COUNCIL, CHELMSFORD
ESSEX RECORD OFFICE PUBLICATIONS No. 59

First published 1972

SBN   900360 14 3

Printed in England by
W. S. Cowell Limited, Butter Market, Ipswich

CONTENTS

PLATES

INTRODUCTION

The purpose of this book is to show how some representative Essex people lived, worked and thought at different times during the one hundred and fifty years prior to our own century, and thereby to add something to our understanding of Essex social history. For lack of suitable material, a few important aspects of local life and a few important groups of people are either inadequately represented or not represented at all. There are no farm workers among the writers to speak for that numerous but, unfortunately, inarticulate class, while only two women find a place because, surprisingly, very little suitable writing by Essex women has proved to be available. I also wish that there could have been more contributions from South Essex. Otherwise the range is a wide and representative one, including as it does two cloth-manufacturers, a silk weaver, a tailor, a miller, a watchmaker, two farmers, a doctor, two clergymen, a fifteen-year-old girl, a country gentleman and a country gentleman's wife, and among these there are Anglicans, Nonconformists, Tories, Liberals and a working-class leader.

The introductions to each section have generally been kept as short as possible. Where the writer himself tells what needs to be known for the understanding of what he writes, I have left him to tell his own story. Wishing to keep the notes to the minimum, I have rarely tried to elucidate references which the reader can investigate for himself. Those notes, which are given, deal mainly with such allusions to the Essex background as seem to require some explanation for those unacquainted with the county and its history.

In Sections II, V, VII and X, I have reproduced the manuscript almost as exactly as the printed word allows. Sections II and IX are taken directly from printed works. Elsewhere, in the interest of brevity or clarity, I have taken the following liberties in presentation, all of them quite minor and all calculated to leave unaltered the meaning and the flavour of the original. Where the manuscript urgently requires it, I have in a few places introduced additional paragraphing. Capitals have been changed to minuscules in nouns other than proper ones. Mistakes, which are obviously slips of the pen, have generally been corrected. I have in some places abbreviated the dates of entries or regularized the system of dating used by the writer. Some abbreviations not now in use have been replaced by the full word or the modern abbreviation. Omissions from the middle of sentences are generally indicated, but not omissions of whole paragraphs or of whole sentences which are self-contained in their meaning; however, from Sections VIII, XI, XIII, XIV much unimportant or repetitious material has been excluded, the omission of which it would have been pointless to indicate. Where a blank occurs in my transcript, it is a blank left by the original writer. The only aim pursued in presenting the material has been to convey accurately and effectively what the author wrote. For

Sections I and V it has not been possible to check my own transcript against the original text.

My thanks to the County Archivist, Mr K. C. Newton, to Miss Nancy Briggs and to other friends at the Essex Record Office; to Mr F. G. Emmison, former County Archivist; to the Colchester Borough Librarian and his staff; to the Curator of Colchester and Essex Museum and his staff; to my parents, Mr and Mrs A. J. Brown, among other reasons for reading my manuscript and advising on the relative interest of possible inclusions; to Miss P. E. G. Wood for help in connection with the Hicks memoirs; to Mr John Bensusan Butt for advice and information about the Carter autobiography; and to Miss Susan Corley for advice about the illustrations.

I

JOHN CROSIER, MALDON MILLER, 1753–78

Crosier's diary perhaps deserves publication in full, such is the variety and interest of its subject-matter and the jovial liveliness of its author. A large part of the original is published here, comprising almost all the Essex material but excluding some of his accounts of visits to places outside the county, though enough of the latter have been included to illustrate the holiday-making and sight-seeing which had so prominent a part in Crosier's social life.

The diary gives the main facts about its author's life up to 1788, so that no further comment is needed here. The date of his death is 1796. As historical evidence, the diary is valuable for the vivid picture it gives of middle-class life in eighteenth-century Essex, when Evangelical seriousness had not yet reduced the level of social gaiety. Though a miller and a farmer, Crosier took time to enjoy himself whenever opportunity offered him some interesting experience. Prices of food, drink and entertainment were rising less swiftly than the income of this substantial man of business in the prosperous agricultural county of Essex, so that he was able to indulge his appetite for travel without restraint. Movement had become easier, safer and faster. It is interesting, too, to observe how the urban and rural middle-class of the Maldon region felt themselves part of a wider south-east England society and were quite at ease not only in London and Brighton, but in Newcastle and the Netherlands, with both of which Maldon's trade in coal and corn helped to make them familiar. It should be remembered, however, that Crosier was a bachelor who perhaps spent relatively little time at home and that his diary apparently records all the events which he found exciting, so that an impression of sustained pleasure-seeking may be received from its pages that would probably have been modified, had more humdrum occurrences in his farming, milling or domestic life found a place in them.

One subject of minor interest, about which useful detail is given, is the constituency politics of Maldon borough. Something can be seen both of the working of the local political machines and of the type of candidate seeking a Maldon seat.[1]

The original manuscript seems to have been lost in recent years. Fortunately the late C. Willett Cunnington made a complete transcript, with a useful introduction, which Mr F. G. Emmison, when County Archivist, secured as a deposit in Essex Record Office [T/A 387]. This transcript has been of the greatest use to me in the preparation of this section and I have followed it in re-arranging entries in chronological order.

Further information about eighteenth-century Maldon may be found in A. F. J. Brown, *Essex at Work*, 1700–1815, Essex Record Office Publications, No. 49 (1969), 120–3.

MEMOIRS relative to the life of John Crosier, Junior; From the twenty sixth of February, one thousand seven hundred and fifty three, being the time of his birth; the account from that time to the year 1774 is imperfect as it's extracted only from memory and the relation of others. But an accurate narrative commences anno 1774.

My father originally came from Felsted in the County of Essex where his ancestors liv'd in the farming business, (most likely) for century's past. He was apprentice to Mr. John Strutt of Beeleigh Mills near Maldon in Essex. After which he took Hoe mill in the parish of Woodham Walter for a term of seven years; and married the daughter of Mr. Sooley, Surgeon and Apothecary of Maldon, by whom he had John, Eulalia, Jonathan, Ann and Elizabeth, and several others that died in their infancy. Old Mr. Strutt remov'd to Wickham Mills and the young one succeeded him at Beely, which buisness he carried on seven years; at which time my father's lease expir'd and he took Beely Mills. Mr. Strutt then went to Springfield Place where he resided some years and from thence remov'd to Terling Place which he purchas'd of Sir Matthew Fether-stonehaw. The old gentleman went to Bath for the recovery of his health and returning home died at Devizes in Wiltshire, was brought to Terling and buried in their family vault. He was a man of great abilities, independent and enter-prising in buisness, by which he acquired a considerable fortune.

I was educated at Felstead school under the tuition of the Rev. Mr. Drake, where I continued five years; from thence to Caldow's Academy in Witham; staid one year, came home to my father to learn his buisness in the year 1769.

The first remarkable event I can recollect was the taking down of the houses from London Bridge and rebuilding it with stone... My father in his buisness of mealman and merchant sold and dispos'd of his goods himself; it is the general custom for people in the corn and flour trade to employ commission'd factors to sell their commodities in London; they are people of great credit and property, and immense sums have been accumulated by this employment.

1769.   The first tour or party of pleasure was to Harwich with Mr. and Mrs. Fisher of Woodhamwalter, my father and mother. We left home in the morning early, breakfasted at the 3 Cups,[2] an agreeable well-accomodated inn, din'd at Mistley and arriv'd at Harwich about 5 o'clock, May, 1769. Spent our evening in walking about the town and places adjacent, which are very pleasing, having a view of the sea and the ships coming into the harbour, of the fort on the other side and several eminences. The town is not the most agreeable, a large seaport for ships of any burden, a King's dockyard where ships for both his and the India service are built. It's about 4 miles from the ocean; the Packet sails from hence to Holland. The town is barricaded with an immense quantity of timber, with two old Men of War, to defend it from the violence of the sea which sometimes sets into the harbour with great rapidity; and without these defences the town would be in great danger of being entirely wash'd away. The security of the place has always been very much fear'd.

The next morning went over to Languard fort (Governor Thickness), a tolerable fortification at the mouth of the Harwich river; it's utility rises from the command it has of the ships coming into the harbour being oblig'd to pass immediately by the mouth of the guns on account of the deep water being directly in that place... After reconnoitering the port and its environs we re-embark'd on board our long boat (lent us by Capt. Bridge of the Custom house), row'd down the river on the Suffolk side 2 or 3 miles, when we landed and went to the seat of — Collett, esq., a young gentleman of genteel fortune, handsome equipage, hounds and horses, and everything around him calculated for the enjoyment of a country gentleman. Mr. Fisher was steward to the lady to whom Mr. Collett was heir. He behav'd very polite and intreated us to dine with him; our engagements denied us the pleasure of accepting his repeated sollicitations.

We then proceeded to the town of Walton in the same parish, which affords nothing very remarkable except a market cross built of wood which has stood these 600 years according to the accounts of two antiquaries who reside there. They also give an account of a town which stood near the sea, some small distance from Walton; the ocean beating violently upon it in time destroy'd it; we saw the space where they told us it stood, and many acres of land have undoubtedly been wash'd away. This is all the authority I have for this assertion; therefore I rather believe it to be fabulous, but it is certain that, had it not been for the barrier of timber before the town of Harwich, it long ago must have shar'd the same fate.

We din'd the same day at the last mention'd place, left it the same afternoon and lay at Manningtree that night. Breakfasted the next morning at Mr. Beven's, steward to the Honble. Mr. Rigby, whose gardens we took a slight view of, are esteem'd very elegant and laid out with the greatest judgement and taste; the house was then rebuilding. Din'd at Colchester and arriv'd at Beeleigh that night.

September 3, 1769. Went up to London with my Father, from thence to Bristol. On Tuesday afternoon left town with two friends who accompanied us to Turnham Green where we parted and they return'd home. . . We din'd at Chippenham (the Angell Inn), a town noted for its woolen manufactory, etc. From thence to Bristol. Putt up at the White Hart in the old market place, a most infamous disagreeable place, the accommodations of all sorts very bad.

The next day we walk'd about the City and notic'd their trades which are very capital and extensive. There is a large navigable river call'd the Severn. The tide flows 20 feet perpendicular and admitts into several parts of the City ships of very great burthen. Some parts of the town is very dirty and indifferently pav'd; a noble bridge of stone and a tolerable exchange. They were improving the place in general and I doubt not but in a few years will become a most noble city.

Din'd with Mr. Ames Hellicar, merchant; in the afternoon went to his gardens and to Radcliff church, remarkable for its buildings, endowments, charities, etc, and embellish'd with some grand tombs and a very fine organ. We return'd to our Inn where we found Mr. Reed (a quaker), having met him upon 'change in the morning, a most generous hospitable kind of man I ever met with. He intreated us very much to go home with him but were oblig'd to refuse his civill offer. We parted with our friend and sett off for Bath, which we soon reach'd being only 12 miles. . .

The next morning went all over the City and see the Baths, the Abbey church, the pump room, the Circus, and the Crescent, then about half built, in the form of a half moon, having before it a pleasing vale with a river and extensive prospects besides. All the buildings are of stone and seem to vie with each other in grandeur.

We left Bath the same day and slept at Devizes (the Bear Inn), din'd the next day at Speckham Lands or Newberry, and the following day arriv'd at London. Did some business there and got home the next day.

The road from London to Bristol is very spacious and fine, both for travelling and the diversity of it's objects. One county abounds with wood, another quite open, one place the fields are parted off by ridges of dirt thrown up on banks, another by stone walls, which they dig in flakes from the pitts and lay them upon one another; the whole earth is of the same materials for many miles together. They mend their roads with it by beating it together with hammers and strewing it as we do gravel. As you ride along the road you see the progress of it, it is first chalk, then harder, and so on 'till it comes to a perfect stone.

Elizabeth Crosier was born in November, 1769, which my mother did not recover, but linger'd till February, 1770, when she died, aged 39 years, leaving John, Eulalia, Jonathan, Ann and Elizabeth to mourn for the loss of the most tender mother.

Soon after the rector of All Saints, Maldon[died] . . . A clergyman undertook the curacy. As he was an entire stranger, he found difficulty in procuring lodgings and was oblig'd to take up his residence at an inn for some time. A Capt. A . . . m, who liv'd in the same place, pitied his disagreeable situation and commenc'd an acquaintance with Mr. G . . . n, which from the Capt.'s easy manner and pleasing freedom was no difficult matter to do; he kindly invited him to his house for a few weeks 'till he could accommodate himself with lodgings elsewhere. This was a most desirable event to G . . . n, who immediately went home with Capt. and was introduc'd as a temporary boarder.

He was receiv'd politely, and the family promis'd themselves much entertainment from his interesting and agreeable company; he soon found out the disposition of Mrs. A. and her friend and adapted himself to their inclinations, and by the most insinuating arts endeavour'd to gain their favour and approbation. He was soon admitted into high respect and by giving himself up wholly to their amusements he became an essential to their happiness. He begg'd to be regarded by them as their brother, as this degree of relationship would admit him to many innocent familiarities and free them from some little restraint, which a more distant connection would make it necessary to observe. Upon this footing he was receiv'd, and became quite the object of their whole attention.

He past off some time for a batchelor, but somehow or other it came out that he was a married man and had a large family in Norfolk, but he thought it proper to have this conceal'd; therefore it was only whisper'd about.

Things went on in this manner and G . . . n seem'd to have taken his residence for life in the Capt.'s family. He devoted his whole life to his females, riding out with Mrs. A. and carrying her behind him upon a little horse which, with her extraordinary riding dress, made a very comical appearance. Sometimes they would loose themselves in the retirement of a wood or shady grove, and tying their horse to a gate wander about this sequester'd retreat absorbed in *platonic* love and friendship, forgetting the world's loud laugh which scarce the stern philosopher can bear. He was their companion and they his attendant; when his lethargic hour came on (which was always after dinner) he slept with his head reclin'd upon their laps or shoulders. Happy slumbers! Let beaus and macaronis envy!

Several months elaps'd in this delightful manner; at last the neighbourhood began first to whisper, then to talk strange and severe things. At last the Capt. began to be very uneasy, but Mrs. A., being then in a condition that call'd for the tenderest usage, on this account the injur'd Capt. suspended his remonstrance and smother'd his wrongs.

After Mrs. A.'s recovery the parson promis'd the ladies a jaunt to town; the too easy Capt. being willing to keep the peace suffer'd this serpent to take the ladies to London without the least opposition. In town he exerted all his abilities to make them as happy as possible. They went to a miniature painter's and made a mutual exchange of each other's pictures.

They return'd home, but their master received them with sullen and reserv'd looks, which made them a little more cautious in their marks of affection; but soon behav'd in a manner so as to exasperate the generous spirits of the Capt. and by that means make an opportunity for an elopement. The Capt. at last snatch'd an opportunity and follow'd his wife into her chamber, where he expostulated with her in the most tender stile, desir'd to know in what manner he had injur'd her, and why she should be so attach'd to a villain that, if possible, would ruin them both. "From this moment let everything be forgott, and no other concession do I desire than G . . . .'s immediately quitting my house." She flounc'd and turn'd from him with this unnatural reply: "No, Sir, terms of reconciliation are in vain; when Mr. G . . . n goes, I go too."

She then left him and was met by the gentle Mrs. C. who on her knees beg'd her to consider the consequences of so precipitate and rash an action. "Oh my friend," says she, "I know it all and am sensible that my place of assignment in the regions of eternity cannot be with you, but, if you will pitty your unhappy friend, I must be satisfied, for to return is impossible." Tears gave vent to the struggling passions for a few moments; the Capt. return'd again and renewed his conversation which grew rather warm.

At that instant she saw Gr . . n in the garden to whom she flew. "Will you protect me, Mr. G . . . n?", "Yes, Madam, now and for ever!" Upon which they walk'd arm in arm out of the house, took a post-chaise to an inn in the town and hurried to London.

The Capt. and Mrs. C. were in a state far better imagin'd than describ'd. Surrounded by the distresses of his family, urg'd by the strongest feelings of parental affection, he rous'd himself and had recourse to the advice of his friend, Mr. D . . . e of Colchester, who pursu'd Mrs. A. to town. He wrote to her and besought an interview, which she granted if the parson might be near. Mr. D. pleaded the cause of her injur'd husband and distress'd children; he bro't her to tears; he told her he came with terms of peace and reconciliation. She heard him and promis'd a meeting next day, which was not granted, but a letter dictated by G . . . n sent. To this purpose, that her exceeding agitation of spirits the preceding day had so affected her that she was incapable of waiting on him any more; that she never intended to return and insisted on a maintenance separate, and that not a scanty one, but agreeable to the fortune she brought. She thanked him for his kind interposition but it was in vain. Her too generous husband sent her money and her clothes, but she and the parson threaten the Capt. in black and white for the separate maintenance. But how this astonishing affair will end, time only can unravel.

The Capt. has transfer'd all his conjugal affection to her forsaken children and behaves to them with the greatest tenderness, and his faithful friend, Mrs. C . . . n, watches over them with maternal fondness and care.

1772. In July, 1772, went with young Mr. Hunt of Latchingdon to visit Mr. Savage of Ipswich. Set off early in the morning, breakfasted at Colchester, got to Ipswich by dinner, went to the races that and the following day. The town, I believe, can brag of nothing very singular unless a tolerable market-place. Mr. Savage's house and mills stand on the highest ground about the town; it presents to your view all the town and some distance beyond; also the river, which, when full with the tide, is one of the most pleasing I ever beheld. It's about ¾ of a mile broad with groves and pleasure grounds to the water edge, as far as you can see.

From thence we went to Walton in the Neys, where we spent two days agreeably at Mr. Richard Savage's. It happen'd at the time of the Fair, when there is two night's dance. All the country lads and lasses meet, with whom we join'd. I cannot say much as to the beauty of Walton, but it's society and neighbourhood compensates for every other deficiency. The Corporas House[3] we took particular notice of, and indeed it's very curious. It's a peculiar kind of earth which is found and gather'd on the sea shore; then laid thin and spread on a large space of ground under which are deep spaces for the reception of the liquor which drains from this earth. Then it's pump'd into coppers and boil'd; then let into cisterns where, as it grows cool, it candy's on sticks and is fit for use. It's of a beautiful transparent blue.

We left our Walton friends with some reluctance and got home by Saturday night after a very pleasant week's tour.

1773. My aunt, Eulalia Sooley, died of a lingering illness in March, 1773. Who left her estates to the enjoyment of Mr. and Mrs. Malden and, at their decease, £100 to be paid to each of the children of J. Crosier's and Mr. Malden's families (the eldest son of each family excepted). She did not even leave my father the least memorandum, not so much as a ring. He thought himself not so civilly treated as he expected, having always the most disinterested regard for her, and ever behav'd to her with unfeign'd freedom and generosity. Artifice and cunning, by it's insinuating ways, often imposes upon weak and honest hearts, under the specious pretence of serving a friend without the least interested or mercenary view.

By the death of my mother (as per marriage settlement) the 3rd part of an estate lying in the parishes of Little Dunmow and Felsted, being the eldest son, came to me; it's occupied by the widow Lawdon at £26 per annum . . . another small estate also comes to me, lying in the parish of Rayleigh.

1773. The morning after Miss Sooley was buried I embark'd for Rotterdam in the William and Mary sloop, for a large cargo of wheat purchas'd by Messrs. Pillans and Rose, wine and corn merchants there. We sailed from Maldon on the friday morning, came to anchor at Coe's Island where we spent the afternoon in going on shore and sporting the rabbits . . . the next day we return'd to our ship with fish and perriwinkles and dress'd our repast for supper.

Weighed anchor at 3 o'clock in the morning, wind due west, quite fair; lost sight of the English land about 2 o'clock in the afternoon.

The wind the same all night at sea and at 7 o'clock on the Saturday morning discover'd Goree church beacon, and soon after the Holland coast appearing white, which cut a pleasing appearance from sea.

We took our Dutch pilot at sea about 11 and at 2 arriv'd at the Brill harbour, the first town within the land. It's rather small, not very populous but well fortified. After paying the Custom house dues we went up the River Maze 12 miles to Rotterdam. The river is very broad and the banks, being adorn'd with regular planted lofty trees and summer houses all along, form a most beautiful sight.

At last by the winding of the river is presented to our view at once the city of Rotterdam which with nobleness of the quays, the houses, the canals leading up the streets, interspers'd with lofty elms, exceeded anything of the kind I ever beheld. We then proceeded to the merchant's house which we found in the wine haven, opposite whose door we moor'd our vessel to take in cargo.

I was civilly received by Mr. Pillans who with his son and another gentleman walk'd about the city and to the principal church; we soon return'd to his house where we found a party of Ladies and Gentlemen engag'd to spend the evening. They all talk'd English and were quite sociable and conversant. . .

On Monday after I arriv'd I amus'd myself in walking about observing the manners and customs of the people which are very diverting, being so totally different from our own.

On the Wednesday morning early I went to the Hague with Mr. Rose, son to Mr. Pillan's partner, in a chaise and pair. The Roses travel extraordinary well but the carriage uncomfortable, something like our old one horse chaise made 50 year's ago. . . In our journey we breakfasted at Delf, a very clean pretty place; there you would suppose the church was falling. I was very happy when I had pass'd it. . . The city of Delf is mostly employ'd in making a ware call'd by that name. After breakfast we proceeded on. The banks by the road side all the way are embellish'd with statues, summer houses and pleasure gardens innumerable. We reached the Hague about 10 o'clock; went to see young Mr. Anderson who was there for his education; his brother married Mr. Rose's daughter. It's the most elegant place I ever beheld; our time being short I saw but little of it. . .

We din'd at the Hague, after that took a ride to Schevling which answers to the description; I never rode three miles so agreeably in my life. We came back to the Hague, left our friend, Mr. Anderson, and from thence back to Rotterdam.

On the Thursday we loaded one vessel, finish'd her cargo the next day, and on the Saturday following took leave of my worthy friend Mr. Pillans and family, whose politeness and civility I shall ever acknowledge with the greatest satisfaction. Went down the river Maes in a hard gale of wind, came to anchor at the Brill, landed at the town the same day. . . The Monday morning was very fine. We weighed anchor about 5 o'clock and went out to sea with about 30 sail of ships. The sun rising upon the water, the noise of the sailors, with a beautiful shore on the right and left, and the ocean before us, at once offer'd the most beautiful appearance nature could afford and, out of sight, causes reflections replete with ideas most entertaining and agreeable.

The wind was fair all Monday night and continu'd so the next day and we arriv'd at Maldon on the Tuesday night after a quick and pleasant passage.

1773. In the same year my Father and the Rev. Mr. Shaw went over to Holland; they were a fortnight there. They went thro the most entertaining part of the country and to most of the towns and cities. They had a guide who shew'd them everything worthy of note. Our sloop, which they sail'd over in, being detain'd for the want of her cargo, oblig'd them to come over in the packet to Harwich. The widow and family of Mr. Pillan's partner, Mr. Rose, came over at the same time; the partnership being dissolv'd, they left Rotterdam and went down into Scotland to reside.

In June after my Father return'd he with Mr. Hewetson and Bendford of London went a tour into Derbyshire, Westmoreland, where Mr. Hewetson's Father lives. To Lord Scarsdale's, a noble seat; to Lord Pembroke's, remarkable for statuary, and a many other places.

About the latter end of July, in harvest, happen'd one of the largest floods I ever knew; it being a very hasty rain caus'd it to come with the greatest rapidity, and before we could get up our floodgates it run all round the house and through the Mill, but did no great damage to us. A vast deal of corn was carried entirely away.

In December died John Husk, esq.,[1] member for Maldon, in Paris. He contested the election with Bamber Gascoygne, esq., and Husk was return'd by a considerable majority. He paid his debts honourably and pleas'd the people much. At the next general election he contest'd it again with Bullock and Hennecar; the latter was not elected; 'twas said bribery and corruption bore a great sway. At his death he stood endebted to the people of the town a large sum of money for bills contracted at the last election. These bills never discharg'd.

Husk's vacancy was contested by Colonel Rainsford and John Wallenger, esq., of Hare Hall. Rainsford return'd by a majority of 221 votes.

This, I believe, was in general thought one of the most capital absurdities ever committed by Coe's[4] party, after the most eligible offer of a certain Lord it was confidently reported that Lord Ro . . . d offer'd to compromise the matter at the general election (which was only a year and a half) and return a man of each party, in case of no opposition to Colonel Rainsford. The old party veteran would not submit and oppos'd with all his might, tho' to little effect, and upon the whole affords a very laughable tale.

A certain tradesman of Maldon (whom I presume is more capable of bartering for tallow than raising candidates for an election) being employ'd to ride about in post chaises, ransacking the whole county, through offering the borough of Maldon to many, but none were weak enough to accept it. At the same time open'd houses on their own account and contracted debts to a considerable amount, £500.

They were now put to wit's last stake; and Lord W. and this tradesman took post chaises and went to Wallenger who came down immediately and canvass'd the town. The election was the next day which they told him was as safe as if the poll was struck in his favour. Elated with the certainty of success (as he suppos'd) fac'd his champion upon the hustings; between whom the greatest politeness pass'd and upon a closer conversation found themselves once valu'd friends in the same army.

He (Wallenger) soon suspected the deceit and in 3 or 4 hours time found the majority irrevocably against him, and desir'd the books to be shut and gave his friend, Mr. Rainsford, joy. Finding himself dup'd he honourably discharg'd the bills of the day and went off immediately, I dare say, without any intercourse with the old partisan and his agent. They were still in the sudds about the remaining debt; and 'twas said Mr. C[oe] drew on him for the said sum in the following words, viz: "Dear Sir, I have drawn upon your good self for £500 which I doubt not but you will duly honour, Yours etc.". Mr. W. returned him for answer: "I received your draft and I understand Maldon salt is very fine – and sells at a good price." Upon this Mr. C. sent him a barrel and enclos'd another draft as before, but W. never took the least notice of it, and I believe it was pretty well known Mr. C. paid it himself. This inconsistant behaviour enrag'd the other party so much that they were determin'd, at the general election, to bring in two men of their own side.

In March '74 there was a subscription assembly at the town hall. It cost 13s. 6d. apiece. It was very agreeable and extravagantly expensive.

In the same month young Jonas Malden came from surgeon Sharp's in the Old Jewry, London, into the county for a little recreation. He was at the ball, as to make it agreeable we were invited, to the several families of Mr. Cooche's, Mr. Malden's, Mr. Crosier's; and on the Saturday to Miss Marrett's at night, where we finish'd our festival week with a dance. On the Monday following Jonas return'd to Mr. Sharp's to finish his practice there in physic and surgery, in which he made a very great proficiency.

In the same month there was a company of strolling players came into the town; built up their scenery, etc., in the Friar's Barn where they acted three nights without controul. Then esqr. C[oe] sent them word that he insisted on their quitting the town immediately. This was, I suppose, to exercise (as he pronounces it) his authority, which was none in reality because any other man that chus'd to be so busy was at as full liberty to act as nominal Justice[5] as the worshipful Mr. C.

As this was the true state of the case 'twas in general look'd upon as a very shabby trick, to take advantage of a set of poor wretches after being at more expence than they could possibly recover in the time. Had he absolutely told them at first they should not act in the place, he would have acquitted himself as a gentleman and have been of great utility to the town.

An unfortunate affair happen'd to the daughter of a grocer in the town, who was a very singular character, secluding herself from the world and the society of the young people of the town. She married to a young decenting clergyman of Bocking, where he was exceedingly respected and esteem'd as an amiable, religious man. The pledge of their mutual love was a fine boy who came into the world too soon to save the conjugal credit of his parents. His infatuated congregation excommunicated him, and they were oblig'd to retire to some lonesome place for a considerable time to mourn the loss of the best of characters.

In April our sloop, the William and Mary, arriv'd from Sunderland after a long and tedious journey of a month.

About this time the chancel of All Saints Church in Maldon was painted and gilt by David Ogborne,[6] which most people suppos'd was the gift of Dr. Fortescue. But when the churchwardens settled their accounts 'twas observed in them £10.10 for Mr. Ogborne. Every parishioner thought this superfluous, as the church and chancel were lately repair'd in a very neat manner, and much more to the credit of a churchwarden than this ridiculous addition.

At the same Parish meeting (to their shame be it spoken) they made a motion for the expense of Cromwell[7] to be put into the rates; this is a well which

B

supplies the whole town with fine, clear water, and Mr. Argent who repair'd it could not collect about £5 of all the inhabitants to defray the expenses. They desir'd it might be put to the vote because they were sure of a majority, because the people of the town would certainly vote for it's being in the rates, which would take the expence in great measure off them and be levied upon my Father and several more out of the town, who could not possibly receive the least benefit from the water. My Father, discovering the mean intention, oppos'd it, and I believe it was never put in the rates at all, so how it was supported for the future I know not (but I believe by Mr. Coe); when our charter was in being it was paid for there.

Monday, 2nd of May. Went with a party to Lexden review of the North British Dragoons, commanded by Major General Preston. The men and horses were very noble and went thro their exercises very well and much to the satisfaction of a number of spectators. After it was over we adjourn'd to Colchester, at the White Hart din'd; afterwards went to see Mr. Great's curious Vandyke pictures, estimated at a very great value.

See the Assembly room which is a spacious room, a very good length and handsomely ornamented. See Porter's Garden of the High street, which exhibited a most beautiful shew of auriculas, part of the stock of the late Mr. Stow of Lexden; many other curious plants and a pretty greenhouse. This Porter fail'd in the King's Head, Maldon; there was no end to his extravagance of his taste for flowers, which I believe was the chief introduction to his ruin.

Being in London at the Jews' holiday I took the opportunity of going to the Synagogue in Duke's Place, where I heard Leoni sing, esteem'd at this time the best voice in the Kingdom. I really was surpris'd, his musick was melodious, clear and high. At the same time the ceremony of circumcising a child of distinction; the men sit and stand below, and the women in gallerys above rail'd in so that you can scarce see them. When the child seems better after the operation is over, which they know from the child ceasing to cry, they then set up a general shout, which is done in a moment as it were, and not expecting such a clamour I was actually startl'd. After this they read and sing something in a recitative way, then they all talk together, then read with everyone a separate book. Then all silent, only the High priest up at the altar who prays aloud and has a particular motion in bowing his head; and when he begins sets all the rest in motion.

May, 1774. On Monday set off for a journey into the Isle of Ely (to Wisbeach) with Mr. and Mrs. Creak and their son; the latter and myself went on horseback by Bury, the former in a post chaise by Cambridge. Two hours after we got from hom it rain'd hard; we got to the Horn at Braintree and were detain'd there 'till after dinner, when it ceased and we proceeded to Hedingham. Spent an hour in viewing the old castle which is worth looking over and commands a very extensive prospect. By the castle is the seat of Sir H. Horton. The house not worth observation, the gardens very pretty.

We then went to Sudbury to tea; from thence to Long Melford, a very pleasing place having a fine lawn presented to our view. By the road side the green very pleasant and terminates by the parish church, very neat and a lofty tower. There is a hospital also with many good endowments. From hence to Bury where we slept that night at the Three Kings on Angel hill, a very good inn and genteel accommodation. Breakfasted with Alderman Prettyman who behav'd very polite, shew'd us the Town Hall, a very convenient building having a court for to try their causes and a long dining room with several other apartments for the business of the Corporation.

After breakfast we left Bury and cross'd Brand Heath. . . We dined at the town of Brand which has, I believe, nothing remarkable in it but a very good inn. Din'd there and reach Lynn in Norfolk in the afternoon. Spent the evening agreeably with a relation of Mr. Creak's at the Duke's Head, a remarkable good one, civil and polite usage and everything very good. The next morning went over the town which I do not admire; the market-place is certainly very handsome and the buildings round it, noble; the rest of the town is compos'd of narrow streets and a bad pavement. There is a fine navigation for ships of great burthen. They trade very capitally in wines which are esteem'd very excellent and furnish'd the country round for a vast many miles. Their corn trade is likewise extraordinary great. They have a fine fish market and reasonable.

Went to Houlton Hall, the seat of Lord Orford, son of Sir Robert Walpole, minister to Geo. II. . . After viewing the noble edifice o'er and o'er we return'd to Lynn and din'd; left it about 4 o'clock in the afternoon, went over to Smee, it's about ten miles. . . We at last arriv'd at Wisbeach race ground where we found our friends Mr. Harrison and Mr. Creak. The ground is small in circumference and very even, convenient for the spectators and good running for the horses. There was a new stand finish'd that year. After the races were over we went to the town about 2 miles from the ground; found our friends at the play. We join'd them and were entertain'd very pleasingly in seeing "THE SCHOOL FOR WIVES" tolerably well acted. Afterwards went to Mr. Harrison's, slept there and din'd there the next day with a party of sociable friends.

On the Friday din'd at Mrs. Wormall's, a lady of genteel appearance, the widow of Mr. Wormall, surgeon and apothecary of the same place; supp'd at Mr. Tomson's, a man in great buisness as a rope-maker and signalis'd for his sense and ingenuity. On the Saturday paid a visit to Sir Philip Vavazor, a gentleman of character and fortune. He behav'd to us with the greatest politeness and civility, shew'd us over the house himself, which is well furnish'd, and his garden is laid out with pleasing walks, bowers and canals. He invited us to dinner but being engag'd were oblig'd to refuse. . . The same day we din'd at Miss Buxton's and drank tea. Spend the evening at Mr. Goddard's, a Quaker; he being absent we were entertain'd by his daughter and neice who, discarding the stiff veil of Quakerism, render'd themselves as agreeable as possible. The hours glided along in *Love and innocence*; we reluctantly left them and begg'd for another interview which they granted. The civility and politeness of these and the rest of our friends render'd our time there quite agreeable and made us leave Wisbeach unwillingly. . .

On Monday morning went from Wisbeach to Peterborough (20 miles). . . We din'd at Peterborough. . . From thence to Huntingdon; slept there, the town tolerably neat. The next day went to Kimbolton, a dull indifferent town, but the Duke of Manchester living there sometimes in the summer enlivens the place. We were treated very genteely by Mr. Welstead, his steward, who shew'd us over the house. . . Din'd with the steward whose hospitability and good behaviour made us quite happy. We left him in the afternoon and went to Mr. Collett's at Dean. . . A generous, independant man, and an agreeable family; we staid with them 2 or 3 days. Went to St. Neot's fair; din'd at a friend's of

Mr. Collett's and amus'd ourselves in seeing the humours of the country people.

Left Dean on the Friday and went to Cambridge accompanied by young Mr. Collett, where we met Mr. and Mrs. Creak. Saw the colleges, libraries and other places worth notice. On the Saturday morning Mr. Collett left us and we return'd home by night after a very pleasing fortnight's tour. June, 1774.

On the 15th July our vessel arriv'd from Rotterdam lading with wheat, after a long and dangerous passage, having sprang a leak in the Brill harbour, bound homeward. They were oblig'd to unship her cargo and search for the leak which was found to be a knot in her timbers. There was a great deal of the corn damag'd and sold at public sale, and upon the whole prov'd a very great loss.

Mr. Jonas Malden, junior, came from Mr. Sharp's and settled at Dunmow.

A brick bridge built at Wickham,[8] part by subscription and part by the county.

In October the Parliament was dissolv'd on account of the American contest. It put the people into great agitation as the election[1] writs were issu'd immediately, and on Saturday, 8th inst. it was contested by Lord Waltham, Hon. Mr. Nassau, and John Strutt, esq. The two last return'd by a great majority.

Lord Waltham, the Friday morning, declar'd himself candidate for the county of Essex, which astonish'd everyone and put them into confusion everywhere, no one suspecting such an attack and indeed from reason. For on the 14th of August there was a nomination held at Chelmsford, when the whole county met and unanimously agreed to support the two old ones, Conyers and Luther, Lord Waltham being then and there present and positively agreed to every proposition. By this unprecedented step he violated his honour, set the whole county at nought, and lost his election by above 1050 majority. He had not 4 gentlemen of the county to support him.

It was confidently said that a certain naval officer (who is more renown'd for his eloquence than his hon.ur) not having his demands satisfied from the min . . . . y, was determin'd to shew his inveteracy by giving the men in place as much trouble as possible and sacrific'd the reputation of a generous easy man, Lord Waltham, to his caprice and ill-nature. . .

As Mr. Brickwood and Harridance were going to Terling in October they were stopp'd by a highwayman who took from them about 40sh. Mr. Harridance escap'd with ten guineas in his waistcoat pocket; the man was never heard more of.

As Thos. Parmenter of our sloop the "William and Mary" was going over the plank leading to the sloop lying at Harrison's wharf, fell into the Thames and was drown'd. He left a wife and large family in very indifferent circumstances.

1775. In May went to visit Mr. Marshall of Jesus College, Cambridge, where I spent 4 days quite agreeably, in seeing the colleges, libraries, senate house and all that's in general notic'd. . . Newmarket races happen'd to be whilst we were at Cambridge, went 3 days and were highly entertain'd. . . We left Cambridge on Thursday afternoon accompanied by Mr. Lugar of Ardleigh and his friend. Slept at Acton Hall the same night (Mrs. Lugar). The next morning went to see Acton Place. . . Arriv'd at Beely the same night.

July. The Commissioners for the Land Tax of Maldon met, alter'd the collectors, dismiss'd Mr. Smart from the clerk's place and appointed Mr. Mitchell.

The house of John Conyers esq.,[9] was robb'd of his plate to the value of £1,500. The stratagem was brought about and executed by an old coachman who formerly liv'd in the family; just before this unwarrantable act his master rescued him from transportation. He and his accomplices were taken and executed at Chelmsford. It was very remarkable that the coachman (who was the principal in this matter) robb'd on Monday, apprehended on Tuesday, taken on Wednesday, tried on Thursday and hang'd on Saturday. Mr. C. recover'd all his plate.

August.   Went with Mr. Cooch in post chaise from Colchester to Misley; saw the house[10] and gardens of Richard Rigby, esq., one of the most engaging seats in the county. The house is rather small but completely built, having two wings containing only two single apartments, the one a dining room, the other a 'drawing room, both elegantly furnish'd.

Before it is a beautiful healthy lawn, the ground gradually descending for about $\frac{1}{2}$ a mile. Several objects in view of the house, viz: the church, a neat building erected by Mr. Rigby upon his own plan and allow'd for its size to excel as to beauty of the structure. The river running up to Manningtree and a landscape on the other side of the country for several miles along the shore. On the right and left is the park with hill and dales with trees rang'd not in formal but natural order; just over them you have a sight of a fine Dutch w.mill, erected by Mr. Rigby. Round the back part of the house for a mile and a half is one of the finest shrubberies in England.

From hence we proceeded to Harwich, din'd there, look'd the town over and return'd to Misley and drank tea at the Thorn inn. Went down to the quay, then building by Mr. Rigby, of brick fac'd with stone, very noble and convenient, with large granaries over it and on one side a dock for building vessels of small burthen. All this was constructed by the Duke of Bridgewater, noted for his ingenious and mechanical abilities.

Walk'd up to the kitchen garden, which is some distance from the house and is said to have cost £10,000. There is a hot house, green house, glass house and every article both entertaining and convenient.

Return'd to Colchester the same evening and were divert'd by Mr. Breslaw's slight of hand in the Assembly room at the White Hart. He is very clever; he had a man who perform'd the singing of birds very well. Slept there the same night and return'd the next day in a chaise with Mr. Cooch, to whom I am under the most indispensable obligations for his politeness and civility in treating me with this pleasing excursion.

August 29th. Died Mr. Thos. Tomas, apothecary in Maldon; the business was continued by his widow and an assistant from London (Mr. Kirby) who some time after was taken into partnership.

September 14th. Mr. Bullman of Harlow mill was accidentally kill'd by falling into a tub in his house, coming in when his family was in bed.

November.   Went up to London to Mr. Sharp's in the Old Jewry for a rheumatick disorder in my back, occasion'd by a cold got after a wrench; staid there 3 months and received some benefit from cupping, bathing, electrifying, etc. I must at the same time (with great satisfaction) mention the generosity and politeness of Mr. Sharp who, after a vast deal of trouble, was perswaded – tho' with much difficulty – to accept of five guineas, which I imagin'd must have been 20 at least.

A comic opera call'd "The Duenna" or Double Elopement at Covent Garden; wrote by Mr. Sheridan, who deserves singular praise for this humurous, witty and well tim'd piece. It's run for above 70 nights the first season bespeaks it's deserved applause.

An alehouse establish'd at Spittle, a little village within the precinct of Maldon. This was generally disapprov'd, knowing it was plac'd where it could be supported only by the labouring people. But all this was conniv'd at, and 'twas said a certain priest and churchwardens settled the buisness in a private way and declar'd, at the time the man petition'd the Justices for a licence, that it was quite the general approbation of the parish. Thus far I believe it was if silence gives consent, for there were not four people in the Parish (save those already mention'd) that knew anything about it.

Geneva merchants are too apt to sacrifice the good of parishes when they have in view the valuable acquisition of a country *alehouse*, to support trade and to keep up the vending of *choice spirits*.

Our churchwardens, having a qualm of pity come over their consciences (which I believe are allow'd to be pretty stretchable) for the support of religion and the better order of the Lord's Day, gave under their hands that no shops should serve in their several occupations on a Sunday on pain of paying the penalty. . . The alehouses (I believe) had only a gentle admonition verbally, not to keep it up too late of a Sunday night or kick up any violent dust in time of divine service; but that was not to be understood that a man was to be denied a drop of the good creature on a Sunday any more than another day. 'Twasnt even denied by the laws of God or the Gemm'n of the vestry.

These curious law-givers soon digested this qualm, and I think in a fortnight's time a man might get shav'd and dress'd, by a few plumbs for his pudding after ten o'clock; and if a man was distress'd he might purchase a bottle of cordial julep at one of the churchwarden's own houses, after the minister had declar'd his text.

Chipping Hill mill[11] burnt. . . Mr. Bretnall who held it lost his all, but by a public contribution he recover'd the whole sum. Mr. Bullman, who own'd it, and having the mill not above half insur'd, lost a considerable sum. It was rebuilt immediately.

1776.   My father left the Wind Mills, the lease of 7 years being expir'd, in the year '76.

Mr. Lawrence, coal merchant of Maldon, was drown'd by a sudden squall of wind in the Maldon river. He went afishing in his *washington* pleasure boat, to whose name and cause he was particularly attach'd, even to a degree of infatuation; and in opposition purely to the loyal party would make the most unwarranted speeches. A man who was govern'd entirely by his passion and when cool, not particular as to his abilities.

This said boat was as unfit for a gale of wind as it's master was for a commodore. It was open all but a small cabin and the ballast laid in the wrong place. Unfortunately Mr. Lawrence was alone in the cabin, in and out of which he could only creep; and, before he could get releas'd from it, the boat overset. There were several more people who with great difficulty sav'd their lives. Mr. Lawrence left a wife and family.

Francis lost his hoy going up to London, running foul of a sloop; Pudney lost his barge.

My father repair'd the flood gates and mill pond in May, 1776. This being a very expensive affair requires a memorandum to know when 'tis proper to do it again.

Garrick left the stage and retir'd with a large fortune.

An action at Quebec when the American General Montgomery was kill'd.

June. Mr. and Mrs. Esdale, Miss Malden and Miss Frost went over to Holland in his own pacquett; they took the whole tour and spent a very agreeable month.

July. Went to Ipswich where I spent 2 days among my friends; saw Othello, Moor of Venice, acted at the playhouse there, very well.

September. On Monday morning embark'd on board Capt. Watson's ship with Mr. James Quilter for a voyage to Newcastle on Tyne. Sail'd from Stansgate on the 2nd of September at 2 o'clock in the morning with a strong fair breeze which carried us into Yarmouth Roads by 4 o'clock in the afternoon. Sickness prevail'd so much that I believe both of us must leave the description of the voyage thus far until we return, in hopes on our passage home being inur'd to the sea, we shall be more ablebodied sailors. The same breeze held us to Dimlington 'till 6 o'clock on Tuesday morning. Then the wind tack'd about and carried us into Bridlington Bay . . . there remain'd, and went on shore at the town and din'd. . . On Thursday afternoon went to Flamborough, a small town about 2 miles from the shore, compos'd entirely of fishermen's huts, the very emblem of distress and poverty. . . On Saturday afternoon got into Shields harbour, a very capital one for colliers. . . On Sunday arriv'd at Newcastle. . . Got up to Newcastle quay about 2 o'clock in the afternoon; left the ship and adjourn'd to Capt. Watson's in the Close, which we made our home whilst we staid at Newcastle, finding the Capt. and his wife so very sociable and civil that we had not a wish to alter our place of residence.

On Monday we stroll'd onto the quay which is very large and a vast deal of business is carried on there. Look'd about the town which afforded us great entertainment; it is very large and some part of it stands very lofty. . . On Tuesday went to Sunderland and din'd at Mr. Chambers's, to whom we are much oblig'd for his civil entertainment. . . Return'd to Newcastle the same night. On Tuesday din'd at Alderman Baker's at his country house at Tinmouth, where we spent a day in magnificence join'd to the greatest hospitability I ever saw in my life. . . His house is *elegantly neat* and the dining room commands a view of the ocean and the ships coming out of the Shields harbour, the prettiest sea prospect I ever beheld. Return'd to Newcastle the same day; the road is very good and a stage goes twice a day.

On Friday went to see Willington colliery, the property of Matthew Bell, esq., and Co., 102 fathom deep or 612 feet perpendicular, and is said to have cost fifty thousand pounds before he receiv'd the least benefit from it, and the foul air has taken fire 2 or 3 times since, which generally carries great destruction with, and cost a large sum to repair the damage. The foul air blazes out of a funnel at top, like the fire of a furnace; this is reckon'd a great curiosity.

Din'd with some friends at Shields and spent the day very sociably. On Saturday walk'd about the town and saw the Barber Surgeon's hall. . . Din'd with Mrs. Boutflower. Went to the wheat market. . .

Sunday went to Morpeth, a very pleasant country all the way with handsome hills and vales. Din'd and went to Mr. Watson's at North Seaton. Return'd the Monday night to Newcastle, quite delighted with our two days excursion.

Went on Wednesday with Mr. Lewis to Throckler coal pit, 240 feet deep. We were let down on a rope coming from a large horizontal wheel turn'd by horses. The cavity, which is like a well, is dark and the water running thro' the pores of the earth and the people hollowing below make altogether a terrible passage. When you are at the bottom, the first object is a large furnace which draws the fresh air down. Then you see all blackness and a little glimmering light to conduct the men and boys in their work, who are also as black as the place. The echo of the hole, hollowing and singing, and altogether is the most horrid spectacle I ever beheld. . .

When you get to the bottom of the shaft (as they term it) or hole, there are lanes leading as the stratum or seam of coal runs, which is general, at least in our pit, about 4 feet thick and a third wide; there pick'd out by axes and hammers and put into a basket which stands on a sledge. An hobby is hook'd to it and draws it along these narrow lanes to the bottom of the pit; put onto the rope and goes up to the top. There are two ropes, one brings down an empty basket whilst the other carries up a full one. Then it's put into a cart, carried upon ways laid in the earth; the grooves of the wheels are made to these ways, of wood so that the four-wheel'd cart will run for a mile or two with very little assistance; and if there is a vale between the pit and the river, they build a wooden bridge over it and lay the wooden ways upon that, the same as in the earth. It's carried 'till it comes to a steath or coal shed, under which are the keels or barges, and by knocking the bottom of the cart out, the coals shoot directly into the keels which go down river and deliver them on board the ships.

The whole process of the colleries are very astonishing. To several of them there are fire engines to pump the water from the pits; the foul air is of so many different qualities that it becomes one of their most difficult affairs to know how to keep it from taking fire. It sometimes is so very sulphurous that they cannot work by candles and are oblig'd to contrive a wheel to be made with steel to strike flints and work by the sparks. There has been several instances of the foul air taking fire and the explosion has blown 20 men and horses out of a pit 500 feet deep.

A little beyond this pit there is one with a day hole to it, that is an hole cut thro' the earth 50 fathoms so that anyone may walk into the pit. This we walk'd down, being determined to see the whole.

We din'd with Mr. Brown, engineer and part owner; he treated us very politely and we return'd home the same day, quite happy to get clear of Pluto's dominions with a resolution never to enter them more.

Thursday. Went to see the glass houses; the whole process is exceedingly curious. There is large manufactorys here in every branch of it.

Din'd at Mr. Young's of Newgate Street, and in the afternoon went into the old castle built by William Rufus.

Friday. Din'd with Matthew Bell, esq., part owner of Willington and other collierys, a generous, high-spirited man, rather too liberal with his port but the best I ever drank in my life.

Wednesday. Went with Mr. and Miss Young to Morpeth races which were not the best I ever saw, tho' tolerably pleasing. . . Return'd to Newcastle the same evening after a very pleasant excursion.

Friday. Went up to Throckley with a few friends in a boat, cover'd and carpetted. Drank tea and return'd. . .

On Saturday went with our friends down the river and saw a ship launch; but unfortunately the stocks broke and damag'd her considerably.

Parted with our friends and got into the Capt.'s boat and row'd to our ship at Shields.

Sailed on the Sunday morning about 2 o'clock with a fine breeze; this, added to the moon's reflection on the sea, afforded a scene inexpressibly beautiful. The gale left us in a few hours and we were haunted by a calm for several days. We tided it almost to Yarmouth roads. . .

We arriv'd at Maldon on the Sunday after a tiresome passage of a week, tho' I cannot with justice complain much, as we were quite hearty and the mornings afforded us great pleasure when the sun arose.

I never spent a month more agreeably in my life; the place and the people deserve our warmest thanks and greatest praise; their hospitability and gentility none can surpass and few equal.

The rebels defeated in America.

A general fast on Thursday, Dec. 13. A form of prayer set for the purpose and great respect in general paid to the day; but a Mr. Lee, Bright and Kirby had the meanness to shew their dislike to the maxim by ordering dinner at Totham Bull alehouse, where they spent the day in a manner that did them no credit. . .

Mr. Parmenter came to Lanford[12] mill in Essex, pull'd it down and new built it under a lease from Nicholas Westcombe, esq.,

1777. March. Thos. Fytche, esq., of Danbury Place, died and left his estate, which was very large in landed property, to Thos. Dysney, esq., who married his neice; afterwards named Thos. Dysney Fytche, esq. This gentleman was not married and like most old bachelors had his peculiarities; he was very parsimonious and his generosity extended only to his tenants. He never rais'd their rent, which was easy, nor ever turn'd 'em out of their farms.

March died Mrs. North, spinster, remarkable for her great size and narrowness of disposition. Her brother . . . was a comical witty blunt kind of reverend, more celebrated for his oddities than his morality or piety.

Two remarkable hot days in the middle of March; the people worked without their coats, and two days after—it snow'd.

Padgett hanged at Chelmsford, who confess'd that they intended to rob Mr. Coe[4] of Maldon.

Mr. May, grocer in Maldon, died; a middle-aged man, remarkable for his corpulence, but by his abstemious living he became very moderate as to size.

Jan. Chelmsford jail bill concluded on; this is a matter, I believe, that did nobody any credit that was concerned in it; therefore the less is said the better.

My father purchas'd Beeleigh mills of J. Strutt, esq.

Mr. Bygrave purchas'd a farm in St. Peter's parish, Maldon, for 28 hundred pounds of Richard Comyns, esq. Thought very dear.

All Saints church repaired entirely; the whole shingling made good. There's an estate in Maldon left by Lady Wentworth to repair the chancel and maintain 2 or 3 poor boys, but 'twas generally allow'd her donation was embezzled.

Esq. Matthew, a West Indian born, seat at Felix Hall near Kelvedon, died in Lorraine.

May.   Mr. Hoare of Boreham[13] died; in the connexion of a capital banking house.

June, 1777.   Spent an evening at Vauxhall with an agreeable party.

Mr. Hance of Maldon Wick gave for 2 or 3 years a kind of Fete Champaitre; the young folks and most of his neighbours were invited and after tea in the house they danc'd in the barn, where fruit and other refreshments were partook of by the company, and every harmonious diversion prevail'd, and the day spent, in general, in the most pleasing manner imaginable.

At this time corn got high in price, but by chance or mismanagement the ports for Essex were not opened, on which account wheat rose to £17 per load; but at the latter end of August it declin'd.

In August my Father drew the floodgate hole and caught a very fine salmon of 8 lb, some large pike, carp, etc.; this is mention'd, on account of the depth of this water it was difficult to draw and so many fish were scarcely ever known to be caught and I believe a salmon trout was never known in our rivers above once or twice.

The Charter of Maldon was lost in the year[14]—from a long connivance or impropriety amongst the bailiffs and aldermen. At length the body corporate neglected to pay some compliment to one of their clan; he took umbrage (a Mr. Draper) and blow'd their plot, and Bamber Gascoyne, esq., long owing the people a grudge,[15] took up the matter and soon settled the business for them. The privileges were every non-freeman paid the bridge toll, an estate of marshes (They were mortgaged, I believe),[16] and a town key at the Hythe hill, which soon after fell into decay. The freedom of this place was acquir'd by 7 years apprenticeship and family connexions. A father free made his children also, and, in case a non-freeman marri'd a freeman's daughter, he became free.

Jonathan Crosier went to Mr. Taylor's of Terling apprentice for 5 years.

Went on board an East India ship lying at Blackwall; the cargo consists in a variety of bale goods, muslins, etc., teas. It's quite like a fair on board one of these ships when they arrive; every sailor has a kind of shop, where he vends his teas, canes, china, etc., being each of them allow'd a certain stock to bring home; and between their selling their wares, fiddling, dancing, singing, etc. becomes a very comical and diverting scene. This place is disagreeable enough in itself, but very pleasantly situated opposite Greenwich which, with its environs, are past description beautiful. The hospital, park, the observatory, Blackheath, are not to be equall'd anywhere.

My father purchas'd the Grange farm of the heirs who possess'd it after Dr. Fortescue. About 110 acres. Beely mill standing in the midst of this land, the purchase became an object of convenience, but was very dear, the land and the buildings in as bad a state as possible. The late occupiers, Mr. James and John Wright, having it on a life lease, spared no pains to drain it of every sweet, and it was said the former saved a great deal of money by it, and, in everything he was concerned in, luck plaid such a game for him; which with a great share of discernment and industry he acquired a considerable property, as well as the countenance and company of all the gentlemen round him. He built a very genteel house in Woodham Mortimer near Maldon, married Miss Evett of Colchester, kept his carriage and lived in a very respectable manner.

Mr. Shuttleworth of Maldon Hall bought the abbey at the same time.

A remarkable high wind in October, by which more ships (colliers in

particular) were lost on the Gunfleet sand, and others, than were ever known.
1778

Jan. 23. Mr. Quilter of Maldon died aged 70 years; a man indefatigable in his trade of a corn and coal merchant, by which he acquir'd some considerable property.

April. My Father bought the houses occupied by Knopp and Trusell in Maldon.

Lord Chatham died. . . He spent his fortune in his country's cause and died without riches.

May. George Fitch bound to my Father for 5 years at 66 guineas.

Warley Camp began to form. Went to London and back within the day and call'd there going and returning.

August. Rev. Mr. Holding of Maldon, a decenting clergyman, died; a man of learning, exemplary living, gentle and courteous in his manner. He publish'd several Paraphrases.

Left Beely mills in September, on which account I had my friends at my Father's, where we were entertained in a most agreeable manner, having our friends in the boat; and before we reach'd the Island a band of French horns, hautboys, flutes, being plac'd there, struck up, which had an admirable effect. Play'd whilst we stay'd there, and follow'd in a boat playing all the way back again. We drank tea, danc'd, and spent the whole afternoon and evening in a most harmonious manner, and I dare say, to the satisfaction of all the company. There were some bullocks in the field; directly as they heard, they came to the water's edge and seem'd highly diverted.

Went to London as a factor for my father and Mr. Richard Barnard of Hoe mills.[17] Took lodgings at Mr. Love's, silversmith, in Aldgate, who behaved in the most genteel manner possible the year I staid with him. He is a man attach'd to Mr. Wesley's tenets whom he follows strictly; and is a religious, sincere, moral, pleasant, agreeable man, above a mean action, and a gentleman in every respect.

There is an office near Maldon[18] where they make some of the first quality salt in England. They have the rock of salt from — by ships; it's put into baskets and steep'd in salt water. After laying there a stated time it's put into pans and boil'd till it comes to a proper consistency of fine flaky salt, and then fit for use.

About July Smyrna was destroyed by an earthquake.

My father, being oblig'd to sell out of the Stocks to pay for purchases, lost one thousand pounds by their falling.

October. The King and Queen went to Warley Camp; after parading thro' the ranks and receiving the compliments of the generals, officers, etc., were diverted with a sham fight which was conducted in a very masterly manner and gave entertainment to one of the most innumerable multitudes I ever saw. The King, Queen, and attendants slept at Lord Petre's and were entertain'd in the most magnificent style that this country could afford.

Din'd at Draper's Hall, Throgmorton Street, which is a new hall and one of the most elegant buildings inside and out that ever I saw. There was a sumptuous dinner and plenty of wine, punch, etc., and a very genteel company. This was on Lord Mayor's day.

Went to see the Bluecoat boys of Christ's Hospital sup in public in a large Hall for the purpose, in which is a pulpit and an organ, when one of the largest scholars reads prayers. They then sing a Psalm and the organ plays to them; after which they all walk round separately and pay their compliments to one of the governors who is seated on a throne at one end of the hall.

1779

David Garrick died in January.

Mr. Coe of Maldon[4] died in March. A merchant in coals, deal, iron, etc., and said at one time was computed to be worth two hundred thousand pounds. He died a single man and left his fortune, I believe, to Mrs. Bird, his sister, Mr. and Mrs. Pigott, and their son; and on the whole might amount to about forty thousand pounds. He kept his carriage and lived always in a close, genteely private manner; a man of very good knowledge but a good deal of austere pride. Always said from the first we never should conquer the Americans.

Lord Waltham of New Hall (who married Mr. Coe's neice with whom he had ten thousand pounds) by some means wanted to borrow some cash, got into Chelmsford jail for a very little time, by getting into the hands of swindlers to whom he gave notes, for which I believe he never received the value. On their being due he was arrested and suffer'd what is mentioned. But I have heard he was very ill used in this business.

This gentleman's abilities consisted merely in good nature; he was a dupe to his friends, and generally kept an elegant house where he maintain'd almost a set of gentlemen who were of no great consequence in themselves nor credit, and by this means, 'twas said, hurt his fortune considerably. About 1773, he sold his borough of Weymouth to Mr. Luttrell who, it was said, got a considerable sum by the bargain. This borough was so much in Lord Waltham's interest, the inhabitants thereof living in his estates, he was always secure in his election, but on his disposal of it, his seat in Parliament for that borough became vacant to him in 1774. He thought himself secure for Maldon but was disappointed.

April. Mr. Palmer of the Bull Inn, West Chapell, was a kind of banker, many people leaving money in his hands and drawing on him for it when they were in the country. My Father and his predecessor Mr. Strutt always used it as a banking house for many years. They owed my Father £450 for which he received about 2d. in the pound. This was a matter which caus'd as much surprize and noise as anything of the kind I ever heard of, for Palmer had been (apparently) in a most successful way for 20 years and upwards and always honoured every bill with great exactness. Mrs. Palmer is a genteel, indefatigable woman and did all the money and accounts business. . . At this time money became scarce and everybody drew their money out of their hands and they soon stopp'd payment. My Father was thought very ill-treated, being a friend to the house so many years and holding Mrs. Palmer's family in high esteem; and he wanted the money exceeding too, at that time, and I must say I never saw my Father's spirits so injur'd. . .

June. Spain declar'd war against England.

Mr. Hance of Maldon died; a merchant taylor in the Town, who by his industry and closeness of living, being of a parsimonious disposition, saved a very handsome fortune for 2 sons and 2 daughters. He retired from business 8 or 10 years before he died, and built a very handsome house in which he prayed without ceasing and did some few alms, by way of expiating the crime, I imagine, of getting money too fast. Mr. Raven, his nephew, succeded him.

July. Went to the British Museum in which there's something of all kinds...

Daniel Beale, a capital flour factor of London, fail'd, owed Mr. Barnard of Hoe Mills[17] fifteen hundred pounds, I believe; he paid two shillings in the pound. Mr. Barnard upon this gave me half his flour commission.

Sept. 18 and 19. Mr. Hudden and Weedon went with me in my whisky to see Warley Camp. We din'd at the Cock and Bell in Romford; afternoon went to camp. Bad weather, so we see but little of it. Got wet to the skin in coming back to Romford; dryed outselves, borrow'd small-clothes.

Got some supper and merry we were. Got up very early Sunday morning, went to camp again. Came back to breakfast; after which dress'd ourselves very smart. The evening being rainy, there were some mud heaps gather'd up in the town. Tom Hudden, having on a black stock and looking tremendously fierce, thought himself most proper for charioteer.

About 5 minutes after he had the reins, a post chaise coming briskly along, fearing it should run over him, and there was room enough, to be sure, for 2 coaches and six, he steering too much to the left ran on to the causeway and foul of a post; and over we went into a mud heap, I with my head quite in, and they with their knees. Our beast, not being of the most spirited sort, stood still, whilst a good Samaritan came out of his house, set his shoulder to the wheel, and soon set the whisky right. We all in this pretty trim went back to our inn, got mopp'd and dry'd, and finding no bones broke, set sail again.

Went to Earl Tilney's,[19] see the gardens, grotto, etc., which are extensive and handsome; after went to the Bush, an inn near there, and got our dinners; mounted our carriage and drove up to Woodford, a beautiful village 10 miles from London.

September. I left Mr. Love's and went to Mr. Cole's, Tower Hill; took lodgings there at 20 guineas per annum, found bed and everything, board besides. Mr., Mrs., Master and Miss Cole are as good a family as ever lived and behaved in so genteel, civil and so kind a manner that I shall ever respect them.

A sloop belonging to Mr. Edwick of Maldon taken by the French in her passage to Sunderland with 100 sacks of Mr. Robert Barnard's flour of Hey-bridge. She was ransom'd for £300 (May).

Inscription on a medal found at Maldon many years ago: Nero and his mother Aggripina; his queen drawn by 4 elephants in a triumphant car; it's of gold and in the possession of Mr. Jonas Malden, surgeon.

October. Went on board "The Favorite", a very handsome merchant ship belonging to Messrs. Collins and Co., Jewry Street. Mr. Cole's family, Mr. Collins's, the Capt., mate, etc. and other friends. We drank tea, supp'd and pass'd a few hours as agreeably as ever I did in my life. I happen'd of a little catastrophe; being about half seas over, and having a large bowl of punch in my hands, offering some to a lady who was sitting, either the ship or I gave a reel and fill'd her lap pretty near full. But it being of fine spirit and pretty rich in flavour, nothing got damage.

John Wilkes, esq., made Chamberlain of London in November.

1780.

Capt. Strutt, son of John Strutt, esq., of Terling Place, died at Lisbon, brought to England and buried in the family vault.

The ever-memorable Capt. Cook was kill'd by the natives on a new discover'd island; he was in search of the north passage to the East Indies.

Narrative of a little tour to Brightemstone to see a friend who was there for
his health: May 25. Went from London on Thursday morning; the road from
hence is very pleasant, having often views of London and it's environs, particularly Clapham Common about 6 miles from Town; being ornamented with
country villas out of number, added to a variety of prospects, no description
can scarcely do justice to. . . About 5 miles further is Dorking; nothing particular
in it. . . Dorking to Horsham, 14 miles; very hilly and rather stoney, being
repair'd by flakes of stone dug out of the earth and beat to pieces by hammers
and strewd over the road, which being ground to pieces by the carriages makes
a very good cement and becomes an excellent road. Thus they are mended in
general for many miles.

Soon after leaving Horsham the hills in Sussex begin to discover themselves,
and I must confess I was never more pleasingly suprized in my life. . . The next
town is Steyning; din'd there; nothing of consequence there. . . From hence to
Brightemstone is 10 miles. You descend from the last town into a vale which is
rich and cultivated with wheat, oats and barley. . . From hence you keep
ascending the downs or hills . . . which are very steep, but the ascent is contriv'd
to be very easy, being made on the most accessible side, and becomes soon very
entertaining. You soon get on the top of the downs which are cover'd with
sweetest verdure imaginable, on which feed a vast many sheep making the
finest mutton in England. You soon get a view of the sea flowing on the Sussex
coast, a fine sound gravelly beach.

The town . . . lies on the shore. I imagine formerly inhabited only by fishermen, being now plentifully supplied with fish of various kinds (particularly
mackrill) which are generally sent from hence to London by land. The waters
being found very fine for bathing and the country so beneficial in recovering
people in a weak and languid state, a vast number of people of all ranks have
resorted thither in the summer season; some, the major part, for pleasure, others
for benefit, that from time to time the town is entirely rebuilt and the houses in
general let for lodgings. There are some tolerable houses, two very noble inns,
the streets very narrow but clean. At the back of the town there is a green
platform, call'd the Steine or parade, commanding a view of the sea and some
hills us'd by the company to walk up in public. There is an orchestra in which
there's a band of music playing, kept up by subscription. Likewise a library and
another shop or two.

On Friday morning we took a ride over the downs, which are high, commanding prospects by sea and land. We rode till we came to what they call the
Devil's Dyke, a prodigious deep vale; went down it. . . At the bottom of the
Dyke there is a river and trees, and on one side of the hill there is one of the
most natural and pleasing flower gardens I ever saw, being compos'd of all the
flowers blooming together that are wild in the fields, appearing as if they there
had socially assembl'd to relate the tales and customs of their several provinces.
You then begin ascend the downs again, and when you compass about $\frac{1}{2}$ the
hill you have an extensive view of 20 miles hill and vale, as luxurious and
beautiful as ever I beheld.

We return'd to Mrs. Diner's to dinner, an agreeable family where my friend
lodg'd; passed the rest of the day there and about the town. We spent the

evening at the Castle. Saturday morning set off for London. . . Arrived in Town the same evening.

July 24.   Went to London by water on board Edwick's vessel; had a very pleasant voyage.

Bought a ticket in the Irish lottery for £5.4.0. Came up a ten pound prize, which according to the price of stock . . . sold for £7.7.0.

Mrs. Fisher of Woodhamwalter died in Sept. A person of very industrious, hospitable disposition; and her respect for the matrimonial line was strongly exemplified by taking to herself four husbands, to all of whom she discharg'd the strictest conjugal duty.

In the same month died Mrs. Malden, widow of the late Dr. Malden, physician in Maldon; noted for his sense and skill in his profession and fam'd likewise for his Epicurian abilities.

Sept. died Sir John Fielding, a magistrate whose name will ever stand recorded for his excellence, agility and perseverance in his office.

December.   My horse fell down with me near Stratford windmill; came on me a postchaise coming by exactly at the same time, one of the wheels of which struck my head and cut me to the skull, but did not fracture it. A surgeon came and dress'd my wound. The horse tumbling over me hurt my foot so excessively that the pain, tho' nothing broke, was past description; but what's remarkable that I never felt the least inconvenience from the wheel's cutting my head, nor even to it's getting quite well. I speak it to the disgrace of two Ladies who were in the chaise (tho' they see my head streaming with blood) had not even the humanity to stop.

1781.

Sister Eulalia Crosier married to Mr. William Reynolds of Ingatestone.

Rev. Henry Bate[20] convicted at Court and a libel on the duke of Richmond prov'd against him, for which he suffer'd one year's imprisonment in the King's Bench.

August. . . Tour to Margate with Mr. Robert Hewetson. . . Went to Michiner's inn; put up our horse, engaged two sleeping rooms. Went into the sea from the shore behind a distant cliff, but this was uncomfortable. Came to our rooms, dress'd ourselves; went to the public breakfast at Dandelion, so call'd from the name of the farm. You enter for one shilling and sixpence; have tea and coffee; a good band of music under a canopy, two people singing duets, and a very pretty dance on the bowling green of about 14 couples 'till 2 o'clock. After this pleasant entertainment we return'd to Michiner's and din'd. In the afternoon walk'd about the town which is a close, narrow, disagreeable place. The environs are very engaging, a vast number of elegant and handsome buildings; a very excellent Hotel adjoining [in] which there are card rooms, a very large assembly room, and everything convenient and handsome.

Drank tea with some friends and pass'd on the whole a very pleasant day.

Next morning went into the sea in a machine. These are in number great, and kept on purpose for Company's bathing. It's like a caravan cover'd with canvas; the hind part, when you are in the sea, falls down and forms a bath. It's drawn by one horse, the sand being hard and even admits of your going out a considerable distance. There are guides to drive; and I must confess it's one of the greatest luxuries I ever experienc'd, to bathe in salt water from one of these machines.

We then took our morning ride, went to St. Peter's, a little village to see a friend; then to Kingsgate, a seat of the late Lord Holland's. It's built on the cliff fronting the sea; it's a noble house and about it are a variety of buildings in imitation of old ruined castles, churches, etc. . . Amongst the ruins there are several places made for Company to drink tea in, and a great many resort thither to regale themselves; and I must do it that justice to say it's one of the most delightful spots I ever saw.

We then went to Ramsgate, another capital bathing place. . . Din'd there; came back and went with friends to the assembly; had a most agreeable, genteel company as could be.

The next morning went into the sea again; then for a morning's ride; took two Ladies to see friends at Ramsgate, returned and spent the day with them; went to the play at night.

The next day carried two other friends a morning's ride; returned and spent the day with them; walk'd on the sands in the evening, which is agreeable enough, being cool.

Left Margate on Sunday and got to London on the Monday after a very pleasant and entertaining journey.

1782

March. Thursday. Mr. Dean of Langford Mill[12] came to ask my father how he did; about 4 o'clock they sat down to a game of all fours; they kept at it till 2 in the morning; retir'd and the next morning began again after breakfast; played all day Friday and till night. Next day played 'till 12 o'clock; then betook themselves to Maldon market after a very social set to. I recite this only as a novelty with my father, who never did any such thing in the course of his life, being a man of very opposite cast.

July. Mr. Fox resign'd. . . Mr. Pitt in.

August. A whale caught and brought up at Tollesbury; 35 feet long.

September. Went to Dover with Robert Hewetson. . . The sea is so rough and the beach so stony that they have only one machine for bathing, and they go into the sea here in a public manner. There are guides, men and women, so the Ladies in a morning when they intend to bathe, put on a long flannel gown under their other clothes; walk down to the beach; undress themselves to the flannel; then they walk in as deep as they please and lay hold of the guides' hands, three or four together sometimes. They then dop over head 20 times perhaps. Then they come on to the shore where there are women that attend with towels, cloaks, chairs, etc. The flannel is stripp'd off, wip'd dry, etc. Women hold cloaks round them. They dress themselves and go home. The men go in at some distance.

From the town with a glass you may see the people working in the fields in France, 21 miles over.

November. A Mrs. Siddons from Bath made her appearance on Drury Lane theatre . . . in the character of Belvidera she far surpass'd any acting I ever beheld.

1783.

As a compliment to the donor I cannot refrain mentioning one of the most agreeable days I ever had in my life. Mr. Cluff of High Street, Mary le Bonne, gave an invitation to Mr. Printer, Mr. Grenville, Miss Depford of the Fondling, Mr. Pepys of the Poultry, and myself.

We din'd with him at $\frac{1}{2}$ past three o'clock; the party were Mr. Cluff, four Ladies, one gentleman and ourselves. He gave us a plain hospitable dinner, wine and punch of the best sort; after dinner the company standing sung "non nobis Domine" by way of grace. Drank a toast, sung a fine glee of "Inspire us all, ye Muses"; a toast again, then 4 or 5 glees, then tea.

Some fresh company came, a Lady and gentleman, of which sung some pretty duets, catches, etc. Then by desire "non nobis" was sung again. Then a Mrs. and Miss Mitts left us to go to Lord Abingdon's concerts.

Then was sung a number of choice glees; a great deal of the tea company left us and we became as at first, and just as we were set down to supper, in came Mrs. and Miss Mitts who bought with them Mr. Charles Westley, a young man whose talents in the musical line stand unrivall'd, and it's thought an acquisition to hear him play.

After supper "non nobis Domine"; then Mr. Westley played and Miss Mitts sung an Italian song; Mr. Printer and Miss Mitts play'd a double lesson on the Piano Forte. The Toast and Glees. Mr. Printer sung "Mab" in which he excels; Mr. Westley play'd an extempore piece and made all the company in rapture; sung another glee; Mr. Westley play'd another extempore piece and finish'd with his own and his brother's march; and no description can give (at least that I can relate) even an idea of his excellence. He left us and then we had a single song, and finish'd with a few more glees.

We then left Mr. Cluff after enjoying a day and evening in the most generous, genteel, harmonious manner imaginable, and so said all. All the glees were sung without instrumental music, and I must say, I never heard 'em executed with such taste and precision.

On every Easter Monday, for the diversion of a number of people from London and the adjacent country, a stag is turn'd off on Epping Forest; and the number of people of all denominations that attend on this occasion caused the most diversified and entertaining sight I ever beheld of that kind.

Rev. Mr. Bates,[20] who erected a very handsome house at Bradwell, gave a cup of ten pounds value, to be sail'd for by 10 Fishing Smacks. Hawkins of Burnham got it. It was a very fine day. The Company in hoys, pleasure boats, with music, etc., made a very pretty appearance. June.

July. Mr. Shuttleworth made a new cut thro' the Abbey grounds to save the falling in of the Abbey lands; cost him three or four hundred pounds, and upon the whole can answer very little purpose, being done in a very precipitate manner. The consequences will be bad to Beeley mills; caused the tide to remain longer there by considerable, and shoals continually in the cut which was an impediment to the Lighters getting down. Mr. Glynn survey'd it at my father's expence and found many things wrong.

Prince of Wales came of age, Aug. 6, when his household was form'd in a very splendid manner. I cant say much as to his abilities, prudence or conduct; therefore I will cease description.

A little tour to Uxbridge, etc.: The road from London there is pleasant, fertile in the country and adorn'd by the Thames. . . It is one of the largest corn markets in England. The sacks are all pitched in the Town which is pretty and agreeable.

Din'd there; afterwards went to the Dutchess of Portland's where there is in the Park the handsomest variety of hill and vale I ever saw, and the greatest

C

number of Deer. She is a charitable, excellent Lady. Return'd to Uxbridge; spent the evening at Mr. Hull's, a miller of great property, a quaker, in a very agreeable manner.

Next morning went to Windsor. The King lives here in the stile of a Country gentleman, and the queen and family reside here in the summer in a plain genteel house on a beautiful lawn. Here I was even charmed for some hours; the elegance of the Castle, paintings therein, terrace, park, no description can do justice to. The prospects of a beautiful country fill'd with towns, villages, etc., afford a most wonderful sight, and from the round tower in the Castle you may discern twelve different Counties. On the terrace the Royal Family walk in public, and Company are allow'd to walk there too, which is generally much throng'd.

After being very much delighted return'd to London the same day.

New Store room built at Beeley in 1782.

A young lady in our neighbourhood, who, by some part of her family connexions dying without legitimate issue, when of age came to a very pretty fortune very early in life. She receiv'd a very liberal education, moved in a very genteel sphere of life at the place where she had went to school.

Her family friends dying her affairs were put into the hands of the Lord Chancellor who appointed a family in Maldon as her personal guardians, but however they were so, she then came to Maldon and boarded at the mother's of her guardians, a widow lady who had two sons, the one a young widower holding a farm not an hundred miles from Woodhamwalter. This young lady and him soon form'd an attachment; the consequence of this was they frequently walk'd to the farm where, I imagine, they *tended their flock* and admired the innocence of the skipping lambs and *gently drove those that were with young*, and nothing more likely to inspire love. . . No wonder then at so much affection between our young farmer and his fair attendant.

Being the fashion of the year to form coalitions they did so too, and a son was produced in July, at the farmer's own house. This being a matter of general conversation all over the country, she was pitied by every body, knowing her to be left without real friends, and being deceiv'd by those on whom she most probably rely'd. He was thought very reprehensible.

These are always the conclusions on these subjects; as a batchelor I give no opinion as I cannot tell what feeding of flocks, rolling on haycocks, making love on a bank by a purling rill, might inspire me to; but joking apart, it was a sad piece of business and as badly manag'd.

After all this and the boy was put out to nurse, every effort was made to bring it to a matrimony job. They were ask'd in the church, thinking that would obviate every inconvenience. Whether the state of the case was represented to the chancellor or not I cannot tell. I imagine her being under age was one great obstacle; but however they could not accomplish their design.

After being well she went and boarded at Mr. Hance's at the Wick. However, after many Changes and Chances, the Lady became of age; they were married, and no couple conducted themselves with more propriety nor were more respected than Mr. and Mrs. Hance; and bless'd with a charming family.

July. Wheat at £15.10.0 a load. In August fell to £13.10.0. The Corn factors at Bear Key endeavour'd to raise their commission by having 3d. in pound insurance. They settled this privately and all their employers were wrote to that they should charge so-and-so; never consulted their friends about the matter but made it a matter of force.

On this account they call'd a general meeting, and the greatest number of farmers met on this occasion that I ever see. Rev. Mr. Bate was chairman. Messrs. Scott and Stonard were there and they unanimously agreed, if they did not rescind their resolution, they would immediately take away their commissions and employ others to do their business.

They gave 'em some time to consider the matter, and appointed a committee who were to meet the factors at Maldon soon after; they did so, and their resolutions were they would not think of doing the business, only at the insurance of 10s. per quarter, and 20s. on oats, etc. They totally denied their demand and immediately employed two firms, the one Dixon and Co., the other Chessell and Co., and likewise others commenc'd. The old factors laugh'd at this piece of business; the young ones got stands upon the market and soon got capital, and appear'd to go on well. The pride of the old ones seem'd very much stung, and such cowards were they that even before the young ones had a trial of doing well or ill, they gave it up in October, I may say, to the disgrace of the whole set.

For a wise set of men, as they certainly are, to be guilty of such a piece of folly, is rather strange. They had a noble trade, and if they ask'd in a proper manner for 2d. or 3d. a quarter more for selling, there seems not a great doubt but they might have obtained their wishes; but suppos'd they could not accomplish their design, they had better have submitted, than let nearly a dozen young men upon the market, who will consequently have a great share of trade, which they never can hinder.

The gentlemen of Maldon keep a very genteel yatch for their pleasure and give their friends a many pleasant voyages.

November.   Mr. Chipperfield died; in the office of Church clerk conducted himself with great propriety, and behav'd in a very civilised manner to everybody. Was taken off with a violent fever in a week.

December.   Went into partnership with my father in the milling trade.

1784

Dined at Mr. Strutt's, Terling Place, 1st. January. This is his usual day for his tenants paying their rents; he gives 'em an elegant dinner, plenty of wine, punch; we dined in a fine, large room, 50 in number. Mrs. Strutt and one son at one table; Mr. Strutt and the other son, at another table. A sight pleas'd me much; we spent a very cheerful day.

January.   Went to see Gosfield Hall, the seat of Earl Nugent; an old house, nothing very remarkable in it; the Park, Lake, etc. are very extensive and handsome.

Feb. and March.   Mr. Smart, attorney in Maldon, died; a man noted for his integrity in his profession, an indulgent parent and a social friend.

The Parliament dissolv'd.[1] Mr. Strutt was rechose, and Lord Waltham in the room of Mr. Harvey; Coalitions being the rage of the times they join'd parties, were chair'd together and afterwards themselves with their friends, Churchman and Presbyterian indiscrimately, met at the Inns and din'd, where all the economy with sufficient Liberality was observ'd; and one gentleman attended at every house and conducted the Tables, etc., and discharg'd their friendly offices with great propriety.

Some old friends of Mr. Strutt rather found themselves hurt at this joint business, remembering they had taken for himself and party to support it for years with spirit and certainly with indefatigable attention. To join a party they before would have spurn'd at, gave these election veterans some disgust, and their day of mirth was rather of the lukewarm sort. Mr. Strutt no doubt had a policy in this scheme that was to answer an end for his own convenience and the good of his constituents, and it must be concluded that no gentleman ever consider'd the welfare of the people in the borough of Maldon both individually and publicly more than Mr. Strutt.

C. Afflick, a gentleman who had done a great deal in the naval line for the service of his Country, was chosen for Colchester, and a Mr. Potter against Sir Robert Smith. 'Twas the astonishment of the Country that any people could chuse such a man who had neither principle nor property, who had once compounded with his creditors, and nothing but a fine person with an unexampl'd effrontery could carry him thro' the piece. The people seem'd to have a great antipathy to Sir Robert, for an oppression of his Tenants.

Mr. Bramstone and Colonel Bullock were chosen for the County, and perhaps there never was a more unanimous and joyous day pass'd in the Town of Chelmsford.

April. Went to Newmarket with Mr. Ray and Mr. Wakom of Bocking[21] . . . I din'd at Mr. Ray's, where I took care to cloathe my internal part with Salmon and Lobster Sauce which were kept down by Mutton, etc., and after dinner some red. Off we set for Bocking parsonage, near the renown'd city of Nineveh (commonly call'd Church street, where upon a very minute enquiry you will find Bishop Blazes, grandmother's Tom cat, was kitten'd).

We soon muster'd, but on my getting down at the Rev. Doctor's gate to girt my horse, Harry's nag being very full of joy thinking of what he and his master were going to see, he kick'd out at me and luckily only just brush'd my new leather breeches on the knee. That catastrophe being reconcil'd, we all mounted in style, it must be said, three as different horses and characters as ever you see.

Before we got 4 miles the Salmon began to be very rumbustical in our Stomachs, on which account were oblig'd, in fact, to call at the first alehouse and there I took medically a dram apiece. This in some degree quieted the fish; set off afresh, rode about 8 or 9 miles further; came to anchor, and gave our beasts some oats. Refresh'd our weary selves with bread and cheese, etc., and afterwards were nearly poison'd with brandy and water, being all true British spirit. After being recover'd from this dramatic indisposition we made the best of our way to Thurlow Cock inn where we put our *equses* into a good stable for the night.

Stuff'd ourselves into the Bar, call'd for punch, ale, and the cribbage board. At it we went. Our parson soon espied in the street a brother of the black order; he hail'd him and entreated him to sup with himself and 2 friends at the aforesaid Cock inn; but the before-mentioned little parson (one of the oddest characters I ever beheld) being engag'd at home with some friends, we reluctantly gave up our man of pious memory.

We got our supper and were jolly enough, but on our calling for bed, a dreadful Catastrophe ensu'd; the bay maker pulling his new boot off (made at Coxall) his heel popp'd through. The names we call'd (being in a rage) this

Coxall man, are too tedious to mention. We sent post-haste for Crispin of
Thurlow, who being warm in bed, called out lustily that he would wait on the
gem'man by 5 o'clock next morning. My door being next the stair, I heard him
knock. I told him to walk in and go to the next bed-chamber and shew the boot
to the gem'man on the right hand side, and desir'd him to talk Piano. But the
joyfull news of "Sar! Shall I mend yar bute?" should frighten the Bay-maker
into Hystericks. He being a man of slight texture in make and of a nervous
constitution, could never stand an attack.

After Crispani and his master had reconoiter'd the breach in the boot 'twas
agreed a staunch piece should be patch'd on to stop the slit from going any
further; and after the learned Cobler left us, we took a gentle slumber and rose
by ½ past 6. View'd the nags, wash'd our Phizzs. etc., order'd out the cold leg of
pork, ale, and the cribbage board. Sir Harry Shuffle beat me enough to pay the
boot mending. All this time our young Doctor was offering up an ejaculation
for a fine day and good race with good accommodation at Newmarket. We
now began to be very impatient for the Cobler, and just as Sir Harry was going
to wish him at old Scratch in he came, and relieved us from our state of suspense.
We soon mounted and called on our little friend in black, where we finish'd
our breakfast. . .

We all mounted afresh and had a delightful ride to Newmarket town, where
we got our elevens; and rode on to the Heath, where we see fine races. The
ground is the largest and most commodious in the Kingdom. The Prince of
Wales was there, attended only by one little footboy. He is a very fine young
man, but certainly has a vacancy of countenance. The Duke of Charters was
there, and a fine tall athletic Frenchman he is, and various other Noblemen.

After dining with several friends in the Town we went to see the horses
exercise, which is on the contrary side of Newmarket, and a noble sight it is.
The horses are all cloath'd and the jockey boys with the liveries of the gentlemen
they belong to.

Mr. Ray in riding thro' two posts, by not having so much smell in that
science as he has taste in many others, he unfortunately run against one of them
and hurt himself much; he recover'd a little and rode to Bury. On the road he
was taken worse and meeting with a mail cart he was so imported into Bury.
A surgeon was sent for and Sir Harry put to bed, and his leg poltest'd and he had
a very good night of it.

I left him the next day and went to see Mr. Hawes of Cavendish. I pass'd that
evening with him; set off next morning to carry this pretty news to Bocking,
which was unpleasant enough for me; soon after Sir Harry came home in the
Coach and his family, believing my story too favourable of the accident, were
glad to see him arrive in a whole skin.

I got home on the Saturday night about 10 o'clock, after a comical, agreeable,
unfortunate kind of an exhibition.

May 2.   Died Mr. Heatherley, apothecary in Witham, a man respected for
his abilities in his profession, likewise for his mirthful and social turn of mind;
but was of too liberal a cast to save much money.

May.   Daniel Beal of Goodman's Field, factor, fail'd the second time, and I
believe paid 5sh. in the pound; the first time he paid 2sh. in the £; at which
time he ow'd Mr. Richard Barnard of Hoe Mill[17] £1,500.

In May and June made a voyage to Rotterdam and return'd with a cargo of fine Zealand wheat, which was certainly very dear. Sail'd from Maldon on board Capt. Ward's sloop, with himself and wife on board, whose hospitability with very fine weather render'd a tedious voyage comfortable. . . At the time of loading our vessel I went to see Mr. Pillans at his country house within three miles of the Hague. I travell'd in a scoote, which is pleasant enough in fine weather, and landed in his garden in which stands his dwelling house, surrounded by various beautiful trees cut in different diverting forms. . . I din'd and stay'd with Mr. Pillans till the next morning. He has a spacious summer house, on the brink of the canal by which pass vast numbers of scootes and barges, in which we drank tea and pass'd the evening.

The following morning Mrs. Pillans took me in her carriage to Delf. From thence we took the scoote, which she politely paid for, to Rotterdam; there was a Hackney coach ready to take us away. I was set down at the Exchange. . . I then see to our ship and went to my English hotel where I liv'd, and Mr. Crabb, who kept it, and his family were very good and reasonable. Every day at 2 o'clock there was a very excellent ordinary of fish, meat and pudding at 1s. a head. London porter reasonable enough, claret about 10d. a bottle, very good indeed. All kinds of people and nations almost, dining at this ordinary, made it, tho' odd, agreeable enough. . .

We went down on the Saturday evening to the Brill, weigh'd again Sunday, and were at Maldon on Monday night.

August. Races, Ball, and public breakfasts at Maldon; and altho' a popular man in the town whose ideas are always *Bright* did this thro' a party matter, carried thro' with great spirit; but 'twas thought his pocket rather suffer'd, but that he did not mind; and in order that nothing should be lost in declaring the good conduct and elegance of this business, I give from the newspaper the following extract. . .

Maldon. All this week has been devoted to mirth and amusement. Our races began on Wednesday when the plate was won by Mr. Brewster's bay mare Rose, though the bets were four to one against her. The give and take plate was won the next day by Capt. Winches' horse Little John. Everything smiled upon the meeting. There was the greatest concourse of people ever known upon such an occasion. The first Ball, which was given by Lord Waltham, who is adored by his constituents, was exceedingly brilliant.

The public breakfastings were crowded with people of the first distinction. Some excellent fireworks were play'd off every evening, under the worthy master of Felix Hall. The assemblage of beauties is not to be described; upwards of fifty couples danced at the last Ball. . .

August. Rev. Bate Dudley[20] gave a cup to be sail'd for off the Bradwell shore under particular sailing orders. The river is very broad there, and a fine day with numbers of boats of various descriptions, with music, etc. Company afforded a day highly agreeable and entertaining.

September. Mrs. Draper, organist of Witham church, had a concert of instrumental and vocal music at the George inn. For having a small company it prov'd a loss to her. She is esteem'd a very rapid player and with great execution, particularly in quick music, but has so indifferent a voice that in my opinion should never be articulated.

A tour to Cavendish in Suffolk with my friend Mr. Peck of Chelmsford, who married the daughter of . . . Hawes, apothecary in that village. This excellent family is himself, his wife, 3 sons, a daughter and Mrs. Peck. . . This sweet village, I'm sure, would inspire a poet to write a volume on it's several peculiar beauties. A nice green, the Doctor's house white, his garden and all about it as clean as possible, a noble church, a snug alehouse where you may quaff a pot of good nut-brown ale; a little distance is an inn for the genteeler sort, and fine shop that sells everything of the best sort, another smaller one in the chandlery way, a good honest parson that makes all his flock feed in pastures green and meadows gay. To complete the scene there's a gentleman of property, a great woolstapler; has built a fine house, high brick walls, etc. And that this place should hear how the world goes, and have everything they want, there is a capital carrier, by name Lorkin, who goes to and from London once a week, and by his assiduity and care has got together a pretty fortune.

With this worthy son of Esculapius and his excellent neighbours we carous'd in all the good things of this life for some days, and with regret, I will say, we left this excellent man and family. With Mr. and Mrs. Peck and child, Miss Godfrey who was visiting there, went to Mr. Godfrey's at Sudbury, at whose house we pass'd a very merry evening. Set sail the next morning after breakfast, myself, Mrs. Peck and child in my chaise, Mr. Peck per coach. All reach'd Chelmsford by tea time, and I arriv'd the same evening at Beely after as pleasant an excursion as ever I wish for.

October.   Got a bad fever which nearly kill'd me; left me in a weak languid state for a long time.

Nov.   Chose a member of the Upper Bull club in Maldon, a very social meeting of neighbours.

In January, 1784, my uncle White of Aldenham died. He kept the Brewers Company's school there. A man of a good classical knowledge. . .

In February, 1784, Mr. Carne of Danbury fail'd. He was a loyalist in South Carolina where 'tis supposed he lost his property and could get no redress.

December.   Maldon assembly. 65 present. J.C. junr. and Js. Quilter stewards.

1785.

January.   A tide coming sooner by 2 or 3 hours than usual, Mr. John Bygrave lost above a hundred sheep that were feeding on the saltings. A hare, being in distress, sav'd itself by mounting on one of the sheep's backs where it remain'd.

February.   Died the Rev. Mr. Shaw, a very sensible shrewd man; his powers in the pulpit perswasive, and his discourses excellent; but unhappily subjected himself to drinking drams which impair'd his faculties, which caus'd him to lose all consequence and in the end kill'd him. He left a widow but no family, a woman whose hard lot it was to have two drunken husbands.

March.   A Justices' sitting[22] for the first time held at the King's Head inn, Maldon. Present, Reverends Dudley,[20] Petwin and Bridges.

An assembly at Maldon. 89 present.

April.   Died Mr. A. Bullen, miller of Moulsham mill, a man who by the prosperity of his trade, his own industry and living very closely, amass'd a good deal of wealth. . .

In 1783 the mode of hanging alter'd; before Newgate a platform (a temporary one) was fixed so that the culprits came onto it, and after being tyed, the gallows stood and the part on which they stood dropp'd in a moment. After this they soon adopted the same mode at Chelmsford, 1785.

May.   Mr. Blanchard alighted on Laindon Hills with his balloon; pack it up in a post chase and went to London.

Tour to Bergholt with Miss Ray, whom I carried in the chaise, and Mr. Ray on horseback. Set off from Bocking in the morning and got to Mr. Heard's, a worthy family at Bergholt East. Of the presbyterian perswasion, Mr. Heard, a widower with 2 sons, one at home, the other living at Brantham near Manningtree; two daughters, one at home, the other married to a Mr. Allen, a considerable shop keeper in the street.

After dinner the first day we took a walk over the fields to Dedham, which are declining and beautiful to the town, being laid out by gentlemen, who own them, in the paddock style. In ranging these verdant meads we soon found out that we all lov'd harmony and music; and the young men understanding that science, we had a song and chorus wherever we went or at any place we stopp'd. One day we pass'd a very pleasant day at Mr. Heard's at his farm house, and in the evening went to a Catch Club in his village where I was vastly pleas'd; return'd to Bergholt at night. In a day or two after Mr. Ray and self went to Harwich. Saw the man-of-war Castor launch'd. This being a day of mirth and festivity the town was all alive. Return'd to Bergholt at night.

This before-mentioned village is esteem'd one of the handsomest in England; it stands exceedingly high, insomuch that you may see over the chimneys in Dedham; most inhabited by gentry.

There's a very neat church, but the steeple being partly thrown down many years ago was never rebuilt, and the bells hang in a cage, and are chimed there. They tell a ridiculous story of the parish's building it in the day time and the devil pull'd it down in the night. But this story, I believe, is true enough, that a gentleman in the village did offer to find all materials to rebuild it if the parish would find workmanship, and his offer was rejected.

This place has by no means been resorted to as it us'd to be, since the death of Mr. Hankey who unfortunately shot himself; no cause was ever assign'd but an unhappy fit of insanity; a man of fortune, generous and noble spirited, a genteel wife and large family.

A Mr. Constable, a man of fortune and a miller has a very elegant house in the street[23] and lives in the style of a country squire.

There's a schoolmaster of very odd appearance; his character I know nothing of, but I could not help remarking the comicality of his dress, and in particular his breeches, which were leather dyed of a purple colour. There's a very genteel family in the street who are so particular in absenting themselves from their windows when anyone passes that they're always call'd the Shies.

After making our observations and taking leave of our family of Mr. Heard's, we arrived at Bocking on the Sunday evening after a very amusing and delightful little tour.

Maldon post, which used to be 3 times a week only, by the interest of Mr. Strutt came every day. After that was alter'd to come every day and Sundays, and Mondays wholly excluded; by which means the Saturday night letters were at Maldon on Sunday mornings; but must likewise be answer'd on the Sunday. This I imagine was to serve the purpose of some individuals and the people seem'd in general very contented with the scheme.

June.   A large balloon descended in a field near Farmbridge Ferry[24] with a Major Money and another gentleman, heavy men. They came down there about three o'clock in the afternoon, pack'd it up and convey'd it to Maldon in a cart. The car, in the form of a boat, was superb. They carried it to London on the carriages of post chaise.

1785. June. Went to the Commemoration of Handel at Westminster Abbey. . .

Went with Bocking gentlemen to Passick[25] green where they, with neighbours, have erected a temporary tent for the purpose of playing the game of trap-ball for an afternoon's amusement; and about 9 o'clock they go to the alehouse and partake of a cold collation and smoke their pipes, drink a few glasses, and go home. There are provided by the subscribers a number of bay jackets of various colours for themselves and friends.

July. Mr. Fisher of Woodhamwalter, whose hospitality being larger than his house, under his canopy in the garden (which was contriv'd by throwing a sailcloth over the drying posts) where he entertain'd in a very friendly and genteel manner 27 persons.

All Saints steeple set fire to by a serpent being lodg'd in the shingle on gunpowder treason night; but by vigilance was soon extinguish'd.

December. A great number of gentlemen met at Woodhamwalter Bell to spend a jovial day; the harmony was broke up by a Mr. Ward giving an illiberal toast concerning a young Lady in Maldon, for which he was reprobated by all the company and hooted off the green.

Dec. Maldon assembly; 90 present.

Dec. 24. The darkest night ever remember'd. On a Saturday as I was riding homewards, myself and horse lost our way – they generally can find it – but I dismounted and he would not stir. But luckily I got hold of the gate at the top of the lane and so steer'd my course home. My brother lost his way in the hilly field and ran over a plough. Carriages of many sorts were oblig'd to be lighted along the road.

Samuel Bulley of Maldon, who had suffer'd a great deal with the Stone, went up to Bartholemew's hospital where he was cut. He surviv'd it some days but soon died; was brought down and buried at Woodham Mortimer.

Frost began about Xmas and lasted very severe for a few days. The most wild ducks caught ever known.

1785. The Rev. Mr. Petwin of Burnham, a Justice of the Peace, fail'd.

1786.

January. Mr. Harry Pattison and myself were coming from London together. I wish'd to stop at Romford to dinner but he being very pressing for Ingatestone, I consented, where we reach'd about 3 or 4 o'clock. Order'd some steaks for dinner, after dinner the glass went briskly round and staying late I began to wish to go; therefore we paid our bill and I rode off.

As liquor has different effects upon people, it's intrusion on Mr. Harry's feelings were the captious and the consequential; a Quaker gentleman came in after dinner and drank with us, and when we came to pay he thought so-and-so would be his part; but our settler of the reckoning said "Sir, you shall pay so-and-so". Our neighbour bore everything very patiently, often giving him a home reply, but seem'd determin'd not to be put out of temper. I got half a mile, I believe, before Pattison came up. I said something I don't recollect but perhaps ridiculous; and he replied that I was drunk and foolish and know'd no better. I was not very sober, nor he either; so I believe I told him 'twas a lye, and he called me a scoundrel.

I immediately hit him with my whip, and he me with his stick with a peg to it and gave me a Black Eye. Then on dropping our weapons we went at it with our fists, so every time we rode at one another a passing blow took place, so we kept at it down almost to the Maldon turning to Galley Common;[26] but Mr. Seaman and Finch coming up, held me and my horse and left him to do as he pleas'd, which I did not think very honorable, tho' their intentions were good.

Here the fray ended, but they then left us, and on Galley Common I told him he had behav'd so much like a blackguard, to get down and finish it in the same manner. I pull'd off my cloathes but he would not dismount, so it ended; and we bruised one another in the word way all the road home. Thus ended this ridiculous business.

Jan. 4. In riding home from Bocking I experienc'd the most severe night I ever remember; it snew very small and with the wind cut my eyes which caus'd some tears (which is frequently the case); but on alighting at Witham they were froze to my eyelashes, which the fire dissolv'd immediately.

1786.

Between 80 and 90 at the Maldon assembly.

January. Died John Luther, esq., member for the county of Essex, three parliaments. He spent an immense sum to acquire a seat wherein I dont recollect he ever made himself conspicuous for his oratory or services; but of late years he devoted most of his time to Bacchus who sent him to the other world.

Jan. My father and Mr. James Wright laid a bet about they're being together at a fair. Mr. W. was so positive that they were not that he laid J.C. 15 guineas to 5. Mr. W. being soon convinc'd of his error he honorably paid the 15gs. There being a condition that 3gs. were to be spent, they and their friends met at the Blue Boar in Maldon; din'd and pass'd the afternoon in the highest Bacchanalian Festivity.

1786. March. Died Mr. Smith of Bradwell. This man's character I cannot pass over without giving some description of his notorious life. He originally was a drover, in which line being industrious he saved some money and took a farm; I believe he was married. In a few years his wife died. He soon by his cunning and care got other farms, from the distress of tenants or some rapacious means, insomuch that he got to be a man of property in the course of years, but by means that soon blacken'd his character. And in a quarrel with a man one day he call'd him by some opprobrious name. "Then", says he to Smith, "You shall be call'd the Earl of Hell"; by which name he went by till 'his death. . .

1786. April. Died Edward Codd, esq.; this gentleman in the younger part of his life came from London with a pretty fortune. Liv'd in a gay sociable manner, being a man of fine athletic stature and handsome person, witty and entertaining. Was the admiration of all the country and no company, public or private, without Mr. Codd. At about middle age he married a very amiable young lady, Miss Marston of Witham, by whom he had a very large family, leaving two sons and two daughters.

He then carried on the coal and corn trade which he gave up to Capt. Acklom, and he remov'd to Woodham Mortimer Hall, which farm himself and Mr. Wright took as partners in 1769, where they laid out a large sum of money to get it in order. Mr. Codd repair'd the house and gardens and made them, the house convenient, genteely neat with a very handsome forecourt, and near the house he made the sweetest place of two ponds in a wilderness that I ever saw from such a ruin'd boggy place. In this sweet spot he liv'd in rural gentility, visiting and visited by all the country, till about the year 1784.

His health fail'd him and he fell into a kind of melancholy languor which accompanied him until he died, when everybody lamented him, losing a generous excellent man of plain dealing, who was never known to do a mean action. He was, in the former part of his life, a Captain in the Militia. He left Mrs. Codd with two beautiful daughters and two fine sons who apparently will be an ornament to their noble and excellent father, who left them a pretty fortune.

A queer piece of business happen'd in Maldon in the Gallantry style. The young Lady who boarded at the Wick Farm in 1783; to keep her in the family 'till of age, and the baby being put out to nurse, herself and the family, not quite agreeable in their sentiments, parted, and her intended spouse took a little snug box for her in the town.

At this time there was visiting Capt. Acklom a Mr. Kempthorn, I believe an half-pay officer, a gallant shrewd man, I fancy of trifling circumstances; was acquainted with the young farmer and sometimes call'd on the Lady with him. Soon after he call'd alone; but however by flattery and saying such a person as herself should ride in her coach and should be above being married to a farmer, particularly the destroyer of her innocence and so on, and by saying he could, introduce her, if his wife, into elegant families, and between his fortune and hers they could keep their carriage and move in a genteel sphere of life, fallacious as these arguments were, they had near prov'd effectual to his intended purpose. For she certainly form'd an attachment for him of a very warm nature, and great uneasiness was felt by J. Hance on this account.

And on going one night to the Lady's house caught the Capt. there, and was agoing to play the Devil with him; upon which the furious blade in red drew his sword to escape a drubbing he richly deserv'd and so got off with an whole skin. The friends now began to interfere and inform her of the danger she was throwing herself into. And their arguments prevail'd so as to perswade her to renounce the Capt., tho' with some reluctance.

The some time after she went to the young farmer's house under the escort of her mother-in-law, 'till she was of age; and then Hymen tack'd them together in the honorable bands of matrimony, in which state they now live, happy and independent. Were married in July.

Saw at the Lyceum in the Strand the Learned Pigg. . .

May.   Stood Godfather to Edward Payne, with Thomas and Mary Malden.

Went with a party to Lord Maynard's at Easton Lodge.[27] The house is very ancient, of no form or elegance; the views from it are fine and the gardens and park modern and pretty, except in one part of the garden; there is a large kind of rotunda, first form'd by making a frame of wood, and then planted outside with hardbeam or some such trees which have entirely grown over this model and forms arches within the alcove and altogether is one of the sweetest bowers I ever saw.

I cannot but mention the gentility of the steward and housekeeper who, after shewing us every part of the house, treated us in their own apartment with cake and wine. We return'd to Dunmow and din'd at Mr. Edwards.

May. Mr. Argent of Blue Mills, returning home from Maldon market, was robb'd.

The Exciseman of Danbury was robb'd.

Steam mill to grind corn erected at Blackfriars of a great magnitude. . .

Petitions were sent from all counties and towns, congratulating the King on his miraculous escape from the hands of an incendiary. Mr. Strutt presented the address from Maldon.

August. Went to see Vandyke's pictures of Mr. Great's family and the Roman pavement at Wallis's, Colchester. Both worthy observation.

September. Went to see Sir Ashton Lever's museum which no description can give proper due.

The weather-cock and shingling of the steeple of All Saints, Maldon, being out of repair, several vestries were held concerning the modes, means and methods. The wise men had committees. At length a drawing of a weather cock big enough for Salisbury Steeple was agreeable and fix'd on; and they all with one loud voice said "Yea, verily, 'twill cut a dash upon All Saints'. The other consultations were held about the colour of the steeples; some would have it all stone colour, others white, and others lead colour. But however, as they hoped to please all the gemmen, they would paint it about three quarters up lead colour, and the rest, white; which was the absurdest thing on earth; for the lead colour being the largest colour, at any considerable distance you could not see the top at all; and appeared like a man in the dark with his nightcap on.

Now the grand weather-cock, loaded with a fine tulip, at top a crown and ball, were to be convey'd up. This was a serious business. They then examined the wood at the top; then something must be done there. By way of security for this bright ornament there was a star made of lead which was certainly a great ornament, but they said "Star, thou has shone lone enough", and cast it from the air to earth. Then up went the weather-cock, and down it tumbled, being too ponderous for it's situation. Then a meeting amongst the contrivers being call'd, they agreed Nem. Con. to lop off the crown and other things and Up it went again; and there it stands, the wonder of all the country around.

Sept. Died Mrs. Bayley the widow of the famous Mr. Bright,[28] whose waistcoat held fairly 9 people. She then married Mr. Bayley, a tallow chandler in Maldon. They carried on that with the grocery and drapery, and no one excelled her in economy, attention and vociferation of tongue. Was a good wife and an excellent mother; had two children by Bright which turn'd out well, and two by Bayley that were no ornaments to their parents.

In the summer season the gentlemen of Maldon associated into a Cricket Club, and a regular set played the game in the marsh,[16] and the other members staid at the Ship, smok'd their pipes and play'd a game of cards. And at the finishing of the season they din'd in the Assembly room, 58 in number, when mirth and festivity flourish'd, and Bacchus began his jollity for the Winter season.

September. A strange piece of business happen'd at Dunmow concerning a Pump which stood very inconveniently against the Saracen's Head door; and at a meeting of Justices they agree to move it to a small distance, equally conveniently for the service at the town. But the gentlemen of the Mob Class were determin'd it should not be moved; and at the alteration a great mob got together and a great riot ensu'd. As some dug others fill'd it, and people interfer'd, whose memory will be blacken'd by this infamous piece of inconsistent business. A second attempt was made at this pump, I believe at the time of the Justices' sitting, and then the Mob became violent indeed, abus'd the gentlemen and broke the Inn windows, which endanger'd the lives of those within. The ringleaders were taken up and put into Chelmsford jail.

The Government, considering the number of convicts on hand, devised a place to transport them to; they fixed on Botany Bay, a place found out by Capt. Cooke.

1787.

Aunt White of Panfield died; an excellent friendly woman; had a large family who married well, some of them, and tho' in a small farm, by industry and care bro't them up handsomely and left a son and her daughter something pretty when she died.

Feb.   Lord Waltham, one of the members for Maldon, dying, a place then being vacant, the Presbyterian Party hasten'd to London to invite a candidate and muster'd up a Mr. Curtis of Wapping, an alderman and a man very great in the line of a biscuit baker, and contracted very largely for Government. He was well assur'd by the party of the great probability of success. They had several meetings at taverns and the alderman always behav'd very genteel, they said. (That means, I suppose, he always paid the reckoning.)

He came and canvass'd the town where he found Sir Peter Parker after the same business on the other side the question. The alderman, with a friend or two, was riding about the country for votes, which he found come very slow to hand; at the same time Sir Peter was follow'd by a number of friends, colors flying, music etc., and were near meeting the Alderman on Heybridge Causeway but did not.

Well, Curtis push'd up to London, gave some of the freemen and friends a treat, thank'd the gentlemen for the trouble they had taken on his part, and then begg'd leave to decline it. On the day of election there appear'd a Mr. Church who got 13 votes. Sir Peter return'd, and never was an election night spent with more jollity and mirth. This Mr. Church came thro' a bet he had laid, a considerable wager of £3,000 or £4,000 that he came down to Maldon and without canvassing or asking for a single vote, that he would carry 7. Of course he won.

Taken with a bad fever in London in November '86 and remain'd there till the May following. On this account I was brought into a low nervous state with a pain in my side, and continued so a long time.

May.   My father and self dissolv'd partnership, and he allow'd me £100 per annum and the Grange house to live in.

June.   Mr. Griffiths, attorney in Chelmsford, was unfortunately kill'd by a chaise turning over, going to Lee. The person with him was not hurt. A man of good social abilities but not in high rank in his profession.

Carrington, of the White Horse, Maldon died very young of a consumption.

June 11.   One Mr. Phillips of Shoebury in the Hundreds of Essex, an excellent, cheerful, social worthy man, was fix'd on to preach the Visitation Sermon at Danbury. He there laid open the improprieties, bad examples, and illiberal conduct of the Clergy in general, with admonitions, exhortations, and correcting language. The parsons could scarcely sit it out, and afterwards had at him in the public papers, but he gave them as good, and for a long time a paper war continued; 'till the paper, its readers, and the combatants grew tired. He printed the sermon which I think lashes the tribe very deservedly.

August. A buck cook'd at Danbury Griffin; only 8 met to eat of it; the Rev. Mr. Williams president. This meeting, about 4 or 5 years ago, was held annually and all the respectable people of Maldon, Chelmsford, and the neighbourhood made a point of attending, to the number generally of about 20; but by some expensive and unsocial maxims it dwindell'd to nothing.

August. Mr. William Pillans from Rotterdam here. . . The harvest got in very fine.

The buildings in general at Beely painted in 1787.

Mr. Child of Chelmsford married to Miss Barnard of Woodhamwalter. This was a run away match, but the old folks, after some months remaining rather obdurate, came to a little, and Mrs. C. went on a visit to her Father's, and all things appear to go on smooth; and 'tis in general suppos'd and hoped that the old miller will send a golden grist to the Doctor's mill.

Mr. and Miss Chirtier, Mr. and Mrs. Payne, Miss Malden, Mr. Richards, self and two sisters went a jaunt of pleasure to Mr. Rigby's whose house[10] is elegantly neat, the grounds by nature and art beautifully pleasant. There is a church he has built in imitation of stone, of a superb structure in miniature. The lawn is extensive and of a remarkable handsome verdure; has a fine view of the Manningtree river and port of Harwich. We refresh'd ourselves at Mistley, Thorn Inn, and return'd to Colchester to dinner, and got home in very good time in the evening, after passing a very harmonious, cheerful day.

September. Mr. Mitchell, attorney, died; a man more celebrated for his voluptuous abilities than knowledge of his profession.

Difference of the dulness and briskness of trade by J.C. junr. August sold only 46 sacks of flour in London, and in September sold 260 sacks.

In Mr. Addison's time the Ladies wore so little to cover their necks that he gave them many letters in his daily paper and advis'd them to put on Modesty pieces. In the year 1778 the Ladies, growing tired of such thick coverings, went to an extreme highly improper; for some Ladies at Court appearing in thin gauze set all the looms to work and in a month every woman appear'd with a kind of covering but not in any degree to hide her charms. This caus'd such ogling amongst the men, and some writing appear'd in public, they threw off this thin stuff and put on a large quantity of thick covering; and in order to make the natural protuberance appear round and large, they sew'd withinside the handkerchief pieces of cane curving outwards. This whim had its day. Then they alter'd to a high tucker, then added another which they term'd Fortifications. But these not keeping the ramparts from ocular assaults, they added a third Tier, and this not proving sufficient, they employ'd the bulwark of a thick handkerchief over these. And thus I leave them bountifully defended in the year 1788.

Died Miss Clarke at Mr. Royce's in Woodhamwalter. She, being the companion of his late wife, kept this house after she died. Miss Clarke suffer'd a long and painful consumption.

In October my father built a new stable, ox-house, etc., at the Grange.

The Barn with corn and the Stable of Mr. Hurst of Sutton,[29] burnt in 1787. The same gentleman's buildings were destroy'd by the same means in 1786, suppos'd to be done by some wicked people who were never discover'd. This gentleman was a Justice, and a man who subjected himself to great passions and abuse, and was by no means admir'd, either for filling his office properly or his other conduct. It took an effect upon his spirits; was suppos'd to hasten his end, and he died in February, 1788.

December. Came into Maldon a building on Wheels, wherein a man, his wife and six children, liv'd. By the side there was another large building in the form of a Tea Kettle. This was shewn for a sight. You first was shewn into the house where every thing, tho' useful, was in miniature; thro' which you was usher'd into this Tea Kettle, which form'd a complete little parlor hung with red baize, a fire place, table and complete seats; these being wholly the work and contrivance of this poor man. Great numbers went to see it and gave something, by which means, travelling from place to place, they procur'd a lively hood.

December. Died Mr. John Payne of Fullbridge. This was a piece of ill fortune that caus'd great lamentation in his own family and amongst all his friends. He having about 4 years ago married Miss Elizabeth Malden, by whom he had two sweet boys and left her with child, had establish'd a fine coal and corn trade and a noble wharf, all within his own premises; had rebuilt his house which he made convenient and handsome. . . He left a very handsome fortune . . . and the trade to be carried on for the benefit of the children.

December. Mrs. Codd at the Holiday time, having all her young Folks at home, gave an elegant treat to her friends. We went to tea; there is a hall between two parlors, all of which being lighted up, the gentlemen were in one and the Ladies in the other. Tea, cake, and biscuits being handed and done with, a dance was announc'd by the entrance of the fiddler. Partners being chose at it we went, and danc'd till about 12 o'clock, being frequently refresh'd with cake, wine and negus. We were then usher'd upstairs into a large room where there was tables spread with the greatest number and variety of things I ever see in my life. I dare say there were from 70 to 100 different dishes, and the best display of Fancy I ever see in public or private. After feasting our eyes and partaking bountifully of this sweet repast a large bowl of punch crown'd the board; and after singing several songs and giving a few social toasts, we left our friends after passing one of the most genteel agreeable evenings I ever pass'd in my life. Sat down to supper 27.

1788

January. Woodhamwalter church robb'd, suppos'd by a man who had lived at many places in the neighbourhood, but was never discover'd. Soon after, Mr. Jonson, who lately had taken a shop at Danbury, was robb'd of a great many haberdashery and hosiery goods. Was taken with a great many of the things upon him, but his accomplice was fled. He was taken to Chelmsford, tried and, I think, cast for transportation. Mr. Jonson found some more of the goods by the side of a wood, but upon the whole was a great loss to him.

Queen's Birth Night; gave a little dance to Mrs. Codd and family and about 12 more friends; which evening was pass'd very agreeably.

Friday, Jan. 25. The highest tide I ever remember'd.

January 28. A very genteel ball at Maldon. Sir Peter Parker, Olmeus, Sir Simeon Stewart, and several other people of consequence present.

February. A whale seen in the Wallett but they could not catch him.

February 25, 1788. Died the reverend and learned Mr. Cook of Maldon. In the early part of this gentleman's life he was unfortunately troubled with fits, which caused him to give up doing any Church duty and live a recluse life.

These fits hurt his health and spirits much, and for many years scarcely see any body and gave up all thoughts of matrimony. At length he, by the advice of his friends, he took exercise, see his friends, kept a deal of company and became a cheerful man; went to all the Assemblies and places of diversion, and by these methods he kept clear of his fits and in a perfect state of health.

He was a generous, genteel, clever man, and possess'd a general knowledge of political and social life.

The last 4 or 5 years of his time he had his fits again, with a long fever which brought him into a low declining way, and by art and regimen he was kept alive a long time, but suffer'd a great deal, but with such patience and Philosophy as were highly exemplary. It was said he never could shed tears. He possess'd a very pretty estate which he will'd to Mr. Pillans, his cousin, and left several small legacies, Mr. J. Wright, Collector White, Tanner White, Augustin Finch and Mr. Bugg, £50 each, and I believe to each of the executors the same, Mr. Strutt, Mr. Parker and my father.

In his lifetime he did great service by lending several people money which was the cause of their future prosperity. One person who owed him £40 he forgave him; and some years back he lent a clergyman 7 or 8 hundred pounds, which he borrow'd for him upon the mortgage of one of his estates; in his will he desir'd the bond to be burnt, and the mortgage to be paid from his own property. This action, like many others of his, ought never to be forgot. His house he gave to Mrs. Robert Pattison in Maldon. His age was about 60, and was buried at Burnham, from or near which his family originated.

February. Several houses in Maldon were robb'd, and they attempted Mr. Jo. Pattison's house in 7 or 8 places but could not get in. After this three watchmen were appointed for the security of the town. The people were not taken, but a fellow or two in the town were suspected.

II

This account of "partukler things" by Joseph and John Savill, father and son, together with their other papers which are not reproduced here, remains the only substantial record of an Essex clothmaking family and its business. From being a relatively small part of the Braintree and Bocking cloth industry in 1750, the Savill business became the largest and then the only surviving concern. In 1780 it may have employed nearly a thousand workers, not in a central establishment, but in their own homes, and their total output may have been worth some £15,000 a year. Joseph left John over £14,000, apart from legacies to two other children. As late as 1817 John's receipts for the year from one branch of his business reached £3,000. Only in 1819 did he decide to cease clothmaking and sell Bocking Church Street Mill, where he had spun yarn by water power, to Samuel Courtauld, thus making the physical link between the now ruined woollen industry and the newly established silk industry that was partially to replace it.

The diary records both economic and social matters. The most interesting point to emerge from the entries about their business affairs is the extent to which the Savills show themselves as technically progressive in a locality in which methods of textile production had generally been stationary for centuries. They also emerge as humane and public-spirited people, qualities which were of particular value to their community in the painful transition from woollen to silk textiles.

The whole of the diary is reproduced here, except for the notes on local marriages and burials, weather records and a few other minor items. There are a few gaps in the original, such as that for 1784–8, when hardly any entries appear, perhaps because of the transfer of ownership from father to son which occurred at that time.

The diary is in the Essex Record Office [D/DCd Z7] together with other records of the Savill family and its business [D/DCd, especially A1–3]. There is an account of the business in *Essex At Work*, 1700–1815, 6–10, and a much more detailed one in a typescript work by Mr. J. Rayner, 'An Account of the Textile Industry in Bocking', a copy of which is at the Essex Record Office [T/z 27].

1754. Apl. 20   Bot of my bror., Wm. Savill, hiss field and house in Church Lane and I gave him £180 for itt, his circumstances being bad. I gave him more money than it was worth.

May 8.   Bror. Savill and hiss Bror., Jno. Walford, Saml. Webb and myself mett about Bror. Wm. Savill's affairs and wee found hee was difficent in the hole about £70. . . I proposed to Mr. Jno. Walford, as he stood in the same relation to the family as I did, that if he would give £35 down, I would doe the same. Upon my request he did it, which was better than to have him exposd as to pay composition which I hope this will prevent.

May 20, 1754.   Thos. Garrett's time came out as an aprentice and, being a very good servant, I have him £5. 5s. od. to buy him a Coming suite of cloths.

June 8.   Went into Suffolk and bot. fleece wool, the best at 16sh. p. tod, midlin at 13sh. p. tod, at Sudbury Hall.[1]

1754. May.   Provisions very dear, beef 4d. p. lb., mutton 4½d. p. lb.

1754.   Bot of Bror. Wm. Savill hiss cistern at 4. 15. 0. Very good one.

Octobr. 18.   Laid in 600 tod of fleece wool one with another at 14 shill. p. tod.

Feb. 26.   Mr. Harrinton of Tay was robed of £400 in his own house by five men unknown.

March 14.   Sir Harvey Elviss was robed of £1000 in hiss own house by six men unknown at Stoke by Clare.

1755. March 31.   Sold a long bay, thick down to 6 quarters, dyed blew, to the workhouse at 3 shill. p. yard. 62 yards came to £9. 6. 0. The same day agreed to serve overseer with Mr. Jas. Nottidge, Mr. Jer. Brock, Mr. Jno. Tweed.

Apr. 22   Such was our weather as has not being known in the memory of Man.

June 18, 1755.   Mr. Wm. Shepherd died, aged 46, July 1. Mr. Jno. Wyatt and self apraised the stock.

1755 July 7.   Esq. Honywood was buryed at Marks Hall. Mr. Howard, R. daniell, P. Church, J. Totman, J. Tweed and self where pall bearers, had hatbands, scaffs and rings.

1755. Aug. 14.   Cousin Thos. Lorkin's wife died, aged 24.

1755. Octr. 2.   Such a quantity of hops at Braintree fair that there was not more than half sold, and what where sold where sold for fifty to three pounds per cwt.[2]

Nov. 1, 1755.   There was an earthquake at Lisborn, which with the fire in the buildens entirely destroyed the city and put such a stop to our trade that wee rise from six notts a penney woof to eight in one day and 2d. p. lb warp to 3d. p. lb. Most of our merchants meet with such losses as wee are affraid will ruin them.

Feb. 10, 1756.   I bot. of Aunt Ann Lorkin her farm at Shalford. I paid her £150 and to pay her £30 p. year for life, quarterly.

Feb. 6 was a fastt day and kept very strict.

1757. Feb. 8.   Corn very dear, Wheatt £16 a load by weight, Barley 31 shill. p. quarter, Oats from 18 to 21 p. quarter. Made a gathering for the poor. Collected £39 and gave itt in bread and mony. Put 10 bush. barly to a load of the best wheatt.

May 30.   Wheatt at £17. 10shill. 0 p. load to carry to Malden by weight. Mr. Benjn. Haward's waggon was stoped at Braintree, as itt was agoing to Malden with 7qr. and ½ of wheatt by a mobb of woman, and they took away 7 sacks of itt to their own use, and the same day Mr. Baines' waggon was acomming through Church Street with a load of wheatt and a mobb of woman stopd the waggon and made them unload and sell the wheat in the street at 5shill. p. bushells.

June 27.   Wheat sold from 18 to 19 pound p. load.

1757, Aug. 31.   Mr. Saml. Ruggles barn in Church Lane was sett on fire and burnt down with 20 acrs of corn and 50 pk. wool. About £300 damage done.[3]

Novr. 6, 1758.   The weavers and tradsmen differed about bringing home their wast.[4] The master insisted upon the wast and the weaver would not bring itt home and so they left of weaving and whent to Camp.

1759, Jany. 20.   Had one bay broughtt home by Jno. Haward with the ends and thrum and this is the first.

Surely trade never was worse. I traded from Decr., 1757, to Decr, 1758, without having one bay sold till I had gott by me 726 Long Bays.

1759, Feb. 6.   Came on the election for Corroner at Chelmsford. The candidates where Jas. Lorkin, attorney of Danbury, and Wm. Reynolds, attorney of Chelmsford.

For Reynolds   974
For Lorkin   809

Weavers plaid 14 weeks and then submitted to bring home the waste.

Apr. 16, 1759.   Weighed myself and I weighd 9st. just.

June 12.   Uncle Jno. Savill died, aged 72.

Sept. 4.   Was drawn for a militia man and was forcd to gett a man in my stead. I gott Danl. Tyler to serve and paid him forty seven shills.

Sept. 10.   Bot 2 lottery ticketts at £11. 5s. p. ticket.

Octr. 25, 1760.   Hiss Magesty King George died, 77 years old.

Oct. 31.   Hiss Magesty King George the III was proclaimd at Braintree and Bocking. The Sherriff not giving proper notice, there was very few to attend the Proclamation.

Decr. 15.   Sett my rowing mill to work.[5]

Decr. 24.   Paid for my rowing mill and it came to as under.

	£	s.	d.
Mill wright	25	12	6
Crosby bill	3	3	0
Stebbing Do		16	
	29	11	6
. . .Irons and work came to	26	6	0
	55	17	6

[1761]

Feb. 5. Jno. Walliss time came out. I allowd him 4/13 for a Coming Suite.

Sepr. 7 Queen Charlotte arrivd at Harwich and took a night lodging at Lords Arbycombs at Witham. A great many people whent to see her. Married Sepr. 8, 1761, at nine at night.

1761, Sepr. 22. King George 3 was crownd. The grandest show ever seen. I was at Cambridge.

1762. Jany. 4. War was declard against Spain this day at London.

Jany. 22. Mr. Jno. English died, aged 77 years.

July 26. Aunt Ann Lorkin died, aged 73.

Novr. 2. Uncle Jos. Lorkin died, agd 63.

1763, Jany. 12. Sett my horse wool mill to work. Cost upward of £45.

March 30. Peace proclaimd between Spain, France and Pourtagle and England.

May 14. Mr. Saml. Beckwith died. Left me exctor.

1763. May 5 was kept as a Thanksgiving day upon peace being proclaimd. Kept very well.

1763. Bot this year in Lincoln Shire for my own part 1704 tod: 14 lb. fleece wool from 19 shill. to 20 p. tod.

1767, Jany 9. The deepest snow I ever knowd. Could not send to spinners. It snowd for a week.

Feb. 22. Provisions exceeding dear.

Wheat at £13 p. load	
Barley	20 shill. p. Qr.
Oats	18 Do.
Beef	4d p. lb
Veal	$4\frac{1}{2}$
Mutton	$4\frac{1}{2}$
Pork	$4\frac{1}{2}$

Octr. 1 Mr. Jonas Beckwith died, aged 55. Died at his inn in London very suddingly.

Octr. 31., 1768 – Bot a large new beam and scales. Cost £5. 15s. 0 in London.

1769, Augt 10. Phil. Hance made mee a new wool mill . . . £6. 15. 2½.

1770, Jan. 31. Had 53 yards of a Long Bay stole of the Bay stock in the night time.

May 1. Andw. Fuller was married to Miss Bett. English. Wedding dinner was 2 legg of mutton, 2 pudings.

1771, May 10. Had a new barrill to my mill for rowing, with two barrill.

Mill Right Bill	24.	10.	0
Black Smith Do	19.	5.	0
and my mill cost to build in 1760.	56.	0.	0
	99.	15.	0

1772, Jany 1. Sold Thos. Pasfield the house he now lives in that I bot of Mr. Thos. Ruggles for £200.

Jany 23.   Mess. Tabor, English, and Co began brewing in their Common Brewing Office.

Ap. 10.   The mobb was up[s] in all the towns around us upon acct. of provisions been so very deer. The mobb stopd the waggons with corn and meatt and sold as they pleasd and whent to farm houses and collected money and some places took the corn and made the farmer bring it to town and sell it at there price.

1772 Novr. 5.   My daughter was married to Mr. Sayers Walker and whent to Bristol Wednesday, Novr. 11.

Novr. 16, 1772.   Was lett blood.

Octr. 21, 1774 Son Jos. married to Miss Eliz. Stannard at London.

Jany 16, 1775.   Was lett blood.

March 25, 1775.   The Norwich coach turnd over in Bocking Street over against Saml. Archer's, being over loaded at top with six passengers, as such Mr. Stockdall Clark of Sudbury, attorney at law, by hiss fall broke hiss legg very badd. . . Other passengers much hurt.

1775, Apl. 4.   Planted 6 Turin poplar trees the bottom of my further field, Church Lane.

June 15, 1775.   Mr. Jos. English sett his new rowing mill to work.

Octr. 23   Was lett blood.

1776.   Decr 6. Jno Ruggles, Esq., died, aged 26 years.

Paul bearers

Mr. Thos. Shepherd

J. Gainsborough

Jos. Englis

Thos. Yeldham

S. Clakanthorp

Jno. Savill.

Decr. 19.   Mrs. Thos. Ruggles was brot through Town and carried to Clare to be buryed. She died at Lisborn – whent there for the recovery of her health and died.

Decr. 19.   Son Jos. Savill child and infant died.

1777.   June 27. . . Wm. Dodd, a popular preacher at London, was executed for forgery.

Decr. 4.   My barn, late Jno Ruggles, Esq., was broake open and a full sack of wheat taken of the heap ready drest.

1777. Decr. 20.   Had my new wool mill made. . . £10. 1. 1.

1778, Augt. 6.   Was litt blood.

Feb. 6, 1780.   Was lett blood.

Jany 7.   Took in eight notts per penny woof yarn. Was in hopes I should never have taken eight notts any more. Spinners not half work to do. What with America and Spain and French war with us and a very alarming mobb at London about the Roman Cartholick Bill, I think I never lookd upon our nationall affairs in so glomey a light. I have now unsold more than 1050 bays and no prospect of selling. Wool never cheaper and trade never worse.

1781, Jany 19.   Was lett blood.

1781, May 10.   Weighd myself. Weighd 8.14.

1781, Decr. 24.   Gave as under to Abrm. Medcalf, Robt. Straight and Saml. Skinner, relations of Wd. French, for the loss Wd. French sustaind going to law with Saml. Ruggles, Esq., I think Wd. French was usd very ill and I gave as under, though there was no obligation upon mee to do it.

	£	s	d
Abr. Medcalf	50.	0.	0
Robt. Straitt	10.	0.	0
S. Skinner	40.	0.	0
	100.	0.	0

1782. Octor. 5. Mr. Jos. Green, factor,[7] died aged 59 at the house late Mrs. Reeves. Dropt down in a fitt. Left 9 children. He was buried in Bocking Church.

1783, Decr. 19. Miss Tabor came from Holand. She was gon full 4 months.

1784, June 17. A day of Thanksgiving on account of a general peace. Mr. Davidson engaged in prayer and Mr. Thorogood preached a sermon from Ezra, Ch. 9, verses 13th and 14th. Illuminations at Bocking and Braintree with fireworks.

1788 Novr. 3d. My father died at 68.

1788, Nov. 8. Lord Nugent[8] was brot from Dublin, where he died, through Bocking to be interred at Gosfield. Lay in state one night at the Queen's Head Inn here.

1789, Jan. 6th. I whent with my Bro. to Great Bardfield, the first of his reciving the rents and tyths for Guy's Hospital.[9]

Jan. 23. I bought of the Revd. Thomas Baines two fields (with a barn), containing twelve acres freehold, adjoining to my field called Hall Field at Pebmarsh for £290.

Mch. 10. A very grand illumination in London and the places adjacent upon the recovery of his Majesty after a state of insanity.

Apl. 6. Gosfield Hall lake fished, a great concourse of people, the fish very moderate.

Apl. 13. My first appointment to the office of Overseer at the Easter Meeting.

May 29. I was admitted at Bocking Hall Court to the tenements in Church Street, to the fields and tenements where the new barn is erected Church Lane.

1790, May 14. Mr. Saml. Bright married at Nayland to Miss Smitherman of Braintree, his fifth wife.

May 20. Mr. Jno. Swift of Braintree was found drowned in a pond in one of Mr. James Pear's fields near Gibbons End.

Novr. 12. Docr. Tweed began to inoculate the poor of this parish, No. about 500, for £5.

1792, Augt. 6. Altered my stables.

Novr. 13. Made a drain from Mr. Tabor's ditch to supply my combers' wash house with water.

1793. Jany. Louis the 16th, King of France, beheaded.

Mch. 23. Jno. Turner, my mother's coachman, died.

Apr. A wonderful scarcity of cash in London. Private bankruptcies numerous, and a great failure among the Country Banks. Trade very bad.

Apl. 18.   Five pounds bank notes first issued from the bank.

1793, Octor. 12.   I purchased of Hannah Isborn, Widow, two tenements belonging to her late husband, Charles Isborn, situate near the windmill, Church Street, for 40 £, very much out of repair.

Octor. 16.   The Queen of France beheaded.

1794, Augt. 25.   Henry Ray and myself whent to Weymouth.

1795, Jany 11th.   Collected for the poor of the congregation at the Meeting House £20.

Jany. 12th.   Began a subscription for the poor of this parish to be given away weekly in bread, 2lb to each one in family. Bread very dear. Agreed to give the bakers, viz. Wm. Low, Wm. Tiffen, B. Blake, Jos. Joscelyne, 13d. for 8lb. of bread, which lasted 4 weeks.[10]

1795, Jany 19th.   The French took possession of Holland and called the first Day of Liberty. The Stadholder and family are come to England. Stopped some days at Colchester in their way to Hampton Court.

June 8th.   Messrs. Thos T. English, Joss. Nottidge, Junr., Jos. Savill and myself took the waggon, horses, etc., valued at £128 of Jas. Challiss and undertook the business on our own acct, he not being able to carry it on. Standing indebted to us in a bond of £100.

Sept. 17.   Bot Mathews Farm and Jacobs Hall, late Thomas Beckwith's, for £1120, by auction at the White Hart. Take possession immediately.

Sept. 18.   Mother, sister Walker, Miss Walker and myself whent to New Southend.

1796, Feby. 17th.   Began to pull down my house.

Sepr. 5.   Heny. Ray and self whent to Margate, Ramsgate, Dover, etc.

1798, May 14th.   A contested election for a Coroner for this county between Mr. Wm. Andrews of Chelmsford, Attorney, and Mr. Parker, Junr, Do. A very wett day. Andrews on the second day declined, being upwards of 400 behind.

June 5.   The North Middx. Militia came into the temporary barracks here, abt. 650.

1798, Octr. 13th.   Planted four walnuts I brot from Cambridge last Sterbich Fair.[11] All failed.

1800, Feby 5.   Commenced the manufacture of hemp with Josias Nottidge Junr., for the employment of the poor.

1801. Decr. 7th.   Made a tour into the North with Joss. Nottidge, Junr., to gain what information we could in the mode of their manufacturing by machinery and to procure some for ourselves, which we did.

1802. Mch 1st.   Sett my Rowing Mill to work.

Feby. 20.   Coniah Wood came up from Newark to sett to work my machinery to spin warp and yarn.

Apl. 24.   Bot of Mr. John Tabor the premises, late Josh. Englishes, from my garden down to the High Road, including mansion house, out-houses, and about 7 acres, 4 free and 3 copyhold, of land with four tenements, adjoining the Spread Eagle, Church Lane, for the sum of £700, a good purchase.

June 2nd.   John Jubb, Junr., came from Leeds to put up my carding and spinng machines.

6th.   Stepn. Bumpstead came from Norwich to spin and to attend my machinery.

18th.   Sett my machines to work.

Augt.   This year the Bishop of St. Davids, Lord Geo. Murray, now Dean of Bocking, took the tythes of this parish in kind, which afterwards brot a heavy expence on the parish for measuring, valuation, etc.

Augt. 27.   Bocking and Braintree Volunteer Corps of Infantry accepted by Government.

1804, Mch. 15.   Colours presented by Miss Goodrich.

Septr. 21.   Bot Bullford Mill of Thos. Nottidge, Esqe.

24th.   My wife and self whent to Buxton to bathe.

1805, July 1st.   Sett my fulling stocks to work.

1806, Jany 27th.   The first day of my son going to school to Mr. Hagon.

1807, Novr.   Compt De Lille came over from Russia to Gosfield Hall when he assumed the title of King of France with his nobles about him, was visited by most of the French Noblesse in the Kingdom.

16th.   Paid Lord Chas. Aynsley a morning visit at the Deanery.

1808, May 5th   Lord Charles Aynsley, Dean of Bocking, died aged 37.

19.   Miss, daughter of Ezekiel Wood, was married to Mr. Robert Holmes, Clerk to Braintree Bank.

Octr. 31st.   My son had the meazles very full, did very well in about a week.

1809, May 15.   The Local Militia assembled here for 28 days, 1000 strong.

1810, Apl. 7.   A riot in London, the military sent for from the country, on account of the commitment of Sir Francis Burdett to the Tower for a libel on the House of Commons.

Augt. 2.   Son Saml whent to the Revd. Wm. Carvens, Melbourn, Cambridge.

1812, May 11th.   Mr Percival, the Secretary of State, was shot in the lobby of the House of Commons.

Augt. 28th   My father-in-law, Mr. John Webb, died, aged 69.

Decr. 30th.   Bot of John Hubbutt his water mill and premises at Bocking Church Street for £3450, to pay for it at Lady Day next, he to give me possession on the 31st Jan. next.

1813, Feby.   Sett my spinning machinery to work, Church Street.

Octr. 12.   Sett my rowing barrell to work, Church Street.

Novr. 13.   Sold my Bullford Mill to Richd. Dixon, Wickham.

1814, June 28.   The first meeting of the Hinckford Hundred Branch Bible Society held at Braintree in Mr. Bright's barn, Hyde Farm. A good number of persons attended.

1815, Feb. 20th.   Newman's silk machinery, Bocking End,[12] was entirely consumed by fire early in the morning.

Oct. 7th.   Mrs. Wordsworth died rather suddenly after a lying-in.

1816, May 8th.   My wife and myself whent to Buxton. Returned June the 1st. A very cold wett season.

1817, July 7th, My son and myself whent to Holkham Sheep Shearing.

Decr. 24th, 1817.   I this day bought of the Revd. Jns. Thos. Nottidge all the arable and pasture land, containing about fifty acres . . . together with the mansion house . . . situate in Bradford Street in the parish of Bocking and opposite to my house in Church Lane, to take immediate possession, for the sum of £5000.

March 12th, 1818. Sold to Wm. Harrington and Jno. Boosey the above house . . . for the sum of two thousand, two hundred pounds.

1818, July 6th. My son and I whent to Brighthelmstone. Staid one night at the Prince Regent Hotel. Liked it very well.

1819, Mch. 3. My son when to Mr. Kendle's at Masenham, Norfolk to be instructed in agriculture at £250 pr. ann.

Apr. 20. My wife and I whent to Malvern Hills for change of air, from which I received much benefit and was well pleased with the tour.

Sepr. 4th.[13] Sold to Saml. Courtauld all that my water mill with lands, garden, etc., situate at Bocking Church Street for the sum of £2500, he to take possession at St. Michs. Day next and to give me a mortgage deed for the same with interest at 5 pr. cent.

Sepr. 18. My wife and I whent for her recovery from indisposition to Cheltenham where she remained for six weeks and received great benefit. I returned very unwell.

Novr. 9th. Sold to Wm. Carter the double tenement situate in Church Street, now in the occupation of Charles Isborn and Thos. King, for the sum of £110.

1820, Jany. 8. Sold to Danl. Leader all my copyhold tenements in Bocking Church Street . . . for £200.

Sepr. 26th. Bot at the sale of the late Revd. Thos. Barstow of Copford one set of chariot harness, used but four times, made at Colchester, for twelve guineas. Cost twenty seven pounds, now as good as new.

1821, Octr. 25. My old servant, John Raison, died, aged 76.

1822, March. On Sunday night, the 17th, or early on Sunday morning, the 18th inst., the shutters of my kitchen windows were forced open, an aperture made in the window and entered by one or two persons at least. Several doors opened by forcing the bolts, etc., by a strong hand crow bar which was left behind. . . My loss consisted of 4 common silver spoons, a valuable tea pot stand, a tinder box, part of a roasted leg of pork and a piece of cheese. My plate was saved in the store room, I believe owing to a strong wind at the time blowing a door to very smartly which alarmed the family and the thieves made off about a quarter past 2 o'clock. Mrs. Thorogood's house was enterd and robbed the same morning, her bed room was entered and some rings taken from off her table and other valuables carried away without alarming the family.

1823, May 6th. My wife and I whent to Hastings for the restoration of my health, where I received great benefit. Absent abt. 6 weeks.

1823, July 22nd. My wife and I sett off for Yarmouth. Absent about 7 weeks.

Novr. 25. My wife and I set off for Brighton, Bath, Cheltenham and Malvern, for the benefit of a change of air, etc., etc. I was extreemly unwell at times during our absence, my wife so bad as to require the aid of Docr. Coley and Mr. Wood of Cheltenham. Confined to our lodgings some weeks and were fearful we should not see Bocking again. Did not return home until May the 6th, 1824, after an absence of 23 weeks.

1827, Mch. 1st. Entered on the house late Mrs. Webbs.

III

The author of this memoir was brother of Sir Grey Cooper, Secretary of the Treasury in the North administration. He had attended Trinity College, Cambridge, and later became Archdeacon of York. He arrived at Thaxted, which was probably his first parish, already enjoying connections that entitled him to a place in local polite society, and he obviously made full use of the amenities thus open to him. He was a kindly man, but far less preoccupied with church affairs than was the Reverend D. N. Yonge a century later in the adjacent parish of Broxted.

The memoir is reproduced here almost without omission from a version printed in the *East Anglian*, new series, X, 152–7. The whereabouts of the original manuscript is unknown to me.

JUNE 12. 1759.   I arrived at Thaxted in Essex, where having first in ye most solemn manner implored that God would favour and assist me in ye great charge which I had undertaken, I paid a visit to my Church, to which I was conducted by Mr Bowtell ye Parish Clerk, a very Revd Greyheaded old Man; after having taken a sufficient survey of ye Church (which for ye elegancy of its structure far exceeds any in that part of ye county), I enter'd into a long confabulation with my new acquaintance ye Clerk, who gave me very satisfactory answers relative to ye questions which I put to him. He drew ye characters of Mr Heckford,[1] ye squire of ye place, and many of ye neighbouring gentlemen extremely well, and accurately described them, such as I afterwards found them to be. Some days elapsed before I had an opportunity of being acquainted with anyone; at last I received a very Polite Card from Ld Maynard[2] inviting me to dine with him at Easton Lodge: accordingly I waited upon his Lordship: he received me with great civility, and at parting desired that I might meet him on ye Tuesday following at Dunmow Bowling-Green.[3]

On ye Tuesday following I went to Dunmow, where his Lordship took particular notice of me, and very obligingly introduced me to Sr Wm Maynard, Sr George Beaumont (who afterwards became my very intimate and particular Friend), ye Honble Mr Hervey, and many others; from that day I soon got an almost universal acquaintance, and was in ye space of a few months better known in ye County than many gentlemen who had lived there several years.

As ye several offices and duties of my Parish demanded my strictest care and attention, ye greatest part of my time was taken up in a constant and punctual performance of them; every morning I visited ye sick and ye poor, and, to ye utmost of my Abilities and Power, aided and assisted them both; every afternoon (without some particular business prevented me) I rode out to Easton, Dunmow, Ashdon, or some of ye Neighbouring seats, where I agreably spent my time with those whose Integrity and good Sense might be of Service to me in my further progress through ye World.

Here let me remark that I never, either before or after, have been so perfectly happy as I was during my residence at Thaxted, being conscious to myself that I was doing all ye good that men in my profession ought to do; that I was not (as God knows too often is ye case) avariciously hoarding up ye income or profits of my Cure, but at intervals disposing of it to those whose needs and distresses, as they came under my own eye, more particularly required my help and assistance.

As Ld Maynard was one of my first acquaintances in ye county of Essex, I shall in ye first place draw a short sketch of his Lordship's character, and then describe ye situation of his Lordship's house at Easton, his private Chapple, and his Parish Church, at which ye Revd Mr Forester officiates as Vicar.

His Lordship is far advanced in Life, being now in his 68th year, yet you do not perceive in him any of those infirmities and inconveniences which generally attend men of his age: Exercise and Temperance (for no man can live more temperately than his Lordship) keep him in constant health and spirits. In his duty towards God no man is more punctual: Divine service is performed in his own Chapel morning and evening, at which he causes all his Domesticks, upon pain of his displeasure, regularly to attend.

Fortune has not bless'd his Lordship with a very considerable Income without acquainting him how, and in what manner, he most properly may use it. He has entirely at his own expense, repair'd and beautifyed ye several Churches

of Thaxted, Little-Easton and Much-Easton; yᵉ Poor of which Parishes frequently feel yᵉ good effects of his kindness and benevolence. Hence he is
universally beloved, admired and esteemed.

Easton Lodge is situated in a very large and extensive Park containing
upwards of three hundred head of Deer: from yᵉ diningroom Windows you
have a most noble and delightful prospect: yᵉ romantic Tilty[4] (for so it properly
may be call'd) adds not a little to yᵉ grandure of yᵉ scene. Altho' Easton Lodge
is very judiciously laid out, yet yᵉ chapel, which contains some paintings
wonderfully well executed upon glass, and yᵉ Library, which contains a very
fine collection of books, are best deserving the notice of yᵉ curious.

Little Easton Church, Lᵈ Maynard's Parish Church, is extremely neat in
every respect; there is a small gallery at your entrance into yᵉ Church, which
contains about 40 Pews well made and painted: yᵉ Altar peice is decorated with
4 Colums, in which you read yᵉ Lᵈˢ Prayer, yᵉ 10 Commandments, and yᵉ
Beleif. Yᵉ Monument which his Lordship has erected in this Church to yᵉ
memory of his Relations, and which cost upwards of £1,000 is highly finished,
and well worth seeing.

Having made mention of Lᵈ Maynard's house at Easton, his Chapel, Parish
Church, &c., I must not here forget my Particular friends, yᵉ Revᵈ Mʳ Pinsent,
and yᵉ Revᵈ Mʳ Forester, his Lordships Chaplains. Mʳ Pinsent lives in yᵉ house,
and is a constant Companion to Lᵈ Maynard; he talks little, but eats much; the
fat of his Lordships venison has fed him to a very considerable size. Mʳ Forester
is a very good natur'd well-bred man, not overstock'd with polite literature,
yet serves properly enough for yᵉ office of a Country Rector: his house is
situated in Lᵈ Maynards Park, from whence you have yᵉ same views as from
Easton Lodge. He has in his garden a very pleasant Arbour in which he sometimes reads a peice of Divinity, a sometimes a News-paper; also a fish-pond well
supply'd with Tench, which however he is not remarkably expert in catching.

His House contains six Bedchambers, a Parlour, Drawing-Room, Hall,
Kitchin, and other conveniences.

Here, as I have mention'd some, gratitude will not permit me to pass over
others of my Essex friends with whom I have spent many a chearful and agreable Hour. Particularly Sʳ Wᵐ & Lady Maynard, Sʳ George & Lady Beaumont,
yᵉ Revᵈ Mʳ Mangey, Mʳ Wyatt, Lᵈ Maynards Steward, yᵉ Revᵈ Mʳ Drake,
yᵉ Revᵈ Mʳ Allen, yᵉ Revᵈ Mʳ Crane, yᵉ Honᵇˡᵉ Mʳ Hervey, Mʳ & Mʳˢ
Sparrow, Mʳˢ Burrows of Great Samford, &c., &c., &c., &c.

Sʳ Wᵐ Maynards seat at Ashdon[5] is most beautifully situated; it is 9 miles
distant from Thaxted, and fourteen from Cambridge: from Sʳ Wᵐˢ you
plainly see Lᵈ Godolphins house upon Hogmagog Hills. Yᵉ Walks, yᵉ Partirres,
yᵉ Avenues, are laid out with great taste and judgement; yᵉ whole house is very
elegantly furnished; in it there is one room which cannot fail of attracting yᵉ
Eyes of yᵉ beholders, as yᵉ furniture of it is remarkably splendid, and yᵉ Paper,
yᵉ finest India paper, I ever saw. In this room you see a very good picture of
Lᵈ Maynard, done by Wills, who some years afterwards, being touch'd in his
pericranium, quarrell'd with his Art, and commenced a Parson.

> *Qui fit, Mæcenas, ut nemo, quam sibi sortem*
> *Seu ratio dederit seu fors objecerit, illa*
> *Contentus vivat?*[6]

Here, by way of anecdote, let me observe that if any Person at any time should take it into their heads to say "You play very well upon yᵉ Guittar, Billy," such a person, making such and so very judicious an observation, must immediately be informed "that it is by no manner of means to be wonder'd at, as yᵉ Player had yᵉ honor of receiving his first Instructions necessary to his Improvement on that sweet, delicate Instrument, from yᵉ pretty mouth, and fair hand of Lady Maynard, one of yᵉ Handsomest Women he ever beheld."

Mʳˢ Burrow's house stands opposite to yᵉ great Church in Samford: it is well built and furnished; in yᵉ Parlour there are some good peices of Painting, easpeacially one of a Sea-peice, by Vanderveld, and another of an Arabian Horse by a very eminent Master. From yᵉ walks in Mʳˢ Burrow's gardens you have a view of "Squire Stanton's House": Squire Stanton and Mʳ Mangey are yᵉ two only Musical Folks I met with; Musick is very much neglected in yᵉ County of Essex: Guittars indeed may flourish, but yᵉ more noble Instruments are almost entirely forsaken. Yᵉ Church at Samford does not look like "a house of Prayer," nor its vicar like "a man of God": yᵉ Inhabitants forget to repair yᵉ Church, and yᵉ Vicar forgets to instruct his Parishioners. Yᵉ Vicar's name is Watson: his ill-conduct and dissolute behaviour is universally known, and therefore he, with great justice, is universally Detested. His own Clerks account of him to me was Characteristic: Sir (says yᵉ Clerk) our Vicar makes nothing of missing ten, twelve, sometimes twenty verses at a time when he reads yᵉ Lessons. In yᵉ Chancel of this Church lie interr'd all yᵉ family of yᵉ Burroughs; and in yᵉ Church-Yard lies interrd yᵉ body of a very remarkable Personage – a Colonel Watson: he was originally of a mean extraction, but going into yᵉ Army when very young, he there distinguished himself so much by his un-commɔn bravery, that from a common Soldier, he arose to yᵉ dignity of a Colonel. He died in his passage from Carthagena, but in his last moments requested that his remains might be brought over to England, and deposited near to those of his Poor Parents.

Malo pater Tibi sit Thersites, dummodo Tu sis
Æacidæ similis, Vulcaniaq. arma capessas,
Quam Te Thersitæ similem producat Achilles.[7]

JUV. SAT. 8TH.

JOURNEY FROM THAXTED TO COLCHESTER

I set out from Thaxted on yᵉ Sunday Even. after Prayers, and lay that night at Sʳ George Beaumonts; next morning about 9 Mʳ Forester, Mʳ Mangey and I began out Journey.

Cambden, in his *Britannia*, says that from Dunmow (which formerly had yᵉ appellation of Cæssaromagus) to Colchester there are many Roman remains, which highly merit the Attention of every learned Traveller. Whether our understandings were unequal to yᵉ Task, or whether someone more judicious than ourselves had removed them thence since Cambden's days, I will not pretend to determine: certain however it is, that there were none of them visible to us during our whole peregrination. As we travell'd with great composure, making every observation that there was a possibility of making, we were two hours and twenty-two minutes in going from Dunmow to Braintree, altho' it is but eight miles.

Here M[r] Mangey advised us to put up at y[e] Fleece, but we imprudently slighted his advice by which means we got a bad dish of Coffee at y[e] White Hart. At Braintree y[e] Church is tolerably large: Y[e] Vicar's name is Morgan; y[e] Curate's, Caley: M[r] Caley, says y[e] Sexton, is a charming Preacher, Sir; his voice is so loud, Sir, you may hear him a quarter of a mile out of y[e] Church. What mistaken notions y[e] vulgar entertain concerning y[e] powers of true Eloquence; what mistaken notions y[e] generallity of Mankind entertain concerning them: even of those whose understandings are improved and strengthen'd by y[e] means of a better and more polite Education. They may have riches, they may have honors, Fortune may abundantly have poured her treasures upon them; yet are y[e] odds very considerable whether in this point, or no, she will prove equally indulgent. *Quem vis media erue turba,* pitch upon anyone: cause him to rehearse a speech out of Hamlet, or to read a paragraph in y[e] News Paper, 'tis five hundred to one whether he rehearses y[e] first, or reads y[e] last with any kind of Propriety.

In this part of y[e] country there are three very large Woolen Manufactories, one at Braintree, another at Coggeshall, and a third at Colchester: y[e] two first deal with y[e] Portuguese, y[e] last with Spain.

From Braintree we crept on to Coggeshall, where we dined; Coggeshall is a large Town, and y[e] Market place belonging to it very much resembles that at Tuxford. Before dinner we amused ourselves with reading y[e] Inscriptions upon y[e] Tomb-Stones in y[e] Church-Yard (none of which appeared to be remarkably curious), and in examining y[e] Church, which is large, and contains a monument tolerably well executed, which was erected to y[e] memory of *Colonel Robert Townshend.*

Y[e] Person who travells thro' this part of y[e] country will be amazed to see y[e] large quantities of Onions which grow in almost all y[e] Fields near Coggeshall;[8] he likewise will be amazed to see y[e] Vineyards within y[e] Town (for so they may not improperly be term'd) every house almost being clothed from top to bottom with Vines.[9]

If I was to give my advice to Travellers, no one should pass thro' this place without paying a visit – not to y[e] Vicar, altho' he may, upon occasion for ought I know, be able to produce a very good bottle of Port – but to y[e] Clerk, who is indeed a very sensible, ingenious Fellow: by trade he is a Clockmaker, and at his business universally accounted remarkably expert; unhappily for him however he thinks himself very expert also in making Musical Instruments, in y[e] composition of which he has indeed shew'd very little skill or knowledge. How few people in any situation or condition of life exactly know, *Quid valeant Humeri, quid ferre recusent!*[10]

Our Dinners being wash'd down with a bottle of y[e] best, we mounted our horses, and leaving Coggeshall proceeded on our way to Colchester. In our way thither we pass'd thro' Stanway and Lexden: Lexden is a very pretty Country Town: near this place, in y[e] year —44, there was a great Camp. I cannot say that y[e] road from Coggeshall is by any means pleasant till you come upon y[e] turnpike road, which is about five miles from Colchester; here you have a fine open Country, and see many fine Villas, belonging to y[e] Inhabitants of Colchester.

Markstay, a seat belonging to Lady Beaumont's sister, is very pleasantly situated. In my return home I staid here for a few days, and was agreably entertained. About seven in ye evening we finished our journey; we then proceeded to ye Kings-head, where we were rejected, every room being secured on account of ye Oratorio, which was to be performed ye day following: what could be done? Our next Attempt was to secure a habitation at ye White Hart.[11] Here we succeeded, tho' not exactly to our Wishes. Y^e Innkeeper receiv'd us indeed in a very polite manner: he told us we might have beds &c, however being cross-examin'd he inform'd us (our Horses being conducted into ye Stable) that we possibly could have no more than two: this amazed us a little, however contentment being a virtue which we frequently recommended to others, it would seem strange did we not practice it ourselves, accordingly having bespoke a couple of Fowls for Supper, we with smiling faces enter'd ye Coffee-Room, where we soon espied a Brother of the Cloth, but he being an Author, and in his own Eyes a man of great Consequence, took little or no notice of Us.

Colchester is a large, well-paved Town: its Castle was famous in ye Civil wars; Mr Gray has fitted up several rooms in it – a Gallery in ye taste of ye building, a small Room, and a Library which contains some of Arch-Bishop Harsenett's Books. At ye Chapel in this Castle it is said first Christian service was performed, in ye Empress Helena's time, who was born here.

IV

John Hanson explains his family origins and his progress through life so precisely in the account which follows that no further information is called for here. He has a place in a collection of Essex writings because his sort formed an important part of polite society in the county. From a successful family business in London he moved out to a large Essex country house and then, by service as Sheriff and as steward to important county clubs, achieved the standing that qualified him to be made Justice of the Peace, Deputy-Lieutenant of the County and commander of the local Volunteer Cavalry. Yet he could retire from the Essex scene as easily as he had arrived upon it. In Essex most certainly, upper-class society, because of its proximity to London and its readiness to open its doors to those able and willing to spend their money, did not lapse into exclusiveness and rigidity.

ABOUT 1738 my father left Yorkshire to settle in London.

1755. My father married Alice Keene of Bristol . . . went to reside at their Mile's Lane House in London . . . which premises have been since held by my father and myself till the full expiration of 63 years in 1818, when I moved my counting house to Scott's Yard, Bush Lane.

My father's residence in the country was Knight's Hill [Surrey]. . . This place he left in 1763. . . At the same time my father purchased his house called Filly-brook as a country residence at Leyton in Essex, where he continued till March, 1784.

1768. My first visit to the Continent . . . accompanying my father and mother on a trip of pleasure with a party from Brighton to Dieppe, from thence to Rouen in Normandy, where we passed a week. We . . . returned to occupy lodgings then ready for us at Brighton.

1769. I was placed at Mr. Newcome's school at Hackney.

1777. I left Mr. Newcome's school.

Early this year I was admitted a Fellow Commoner and went to reside at Trinity College, Cambridge.

1784. We went to Langtons . . . a country residence in the parish of South Wick in the County of Essex.

1792. After my father's decease I made up my mind, although not brought up to business myself, to continue the establishment in London . . . during so many years carried on by my father.

1792. . . . purchased Great Bromley Hall and Manor, little anticipating that it was soon to become a centre post of a large garrison and indeed the head-quarters of a great army.

Sept. 3rd. Mrs. Hanson and myself left home on Monday morning in our phaeton for a short excursion into Essex, Suffolk and Norfolk. . . We went to Chelmsford where we went to the play at night, saw the Belle Stratagem and Catherine and Petruchio, and proceeded next morning to Kelvedon, where we went to Felix Hall since purchased by Mr. Weston,[1] and in the evening drove through Colchester to Manningtree and Mistley; the next morning visited the Hall, the beautiful seat of Mr. Rigby; from thence on through Ipswich.

1793. Gave up the house on the Forest and removed to Great Bromley Hall, soon after which Miss Hayford came as governess to my daughters.

1794. My son George born in Mile's Lane.

1795. In January the Statholder and his family came for safety to England and we amongst other of the neighbouring families went from Bromley Hall to greet them as they passed through Colchester.

I served the office of High Sheriff for the County, Dr. Kelly of Ardleigh was my chaplain.

1795. Attended at Carlton House with an address on the Prince's Marriage . . . from the County of Essex.

1796. My son William first went to Mr. Newcome's School.

My son James . . . was taken to Great Bromley and buried in the family vault which I had built there.

This year I was appointed one of His Majesty's Justices and Deputy Lieutenants.

I served for Mr. Batch at steward for the Chelmsford Races.[2]

1796. Our friend Miss Rebow married to Capt. Slater.

E

The neighbourhood of Bromley Hall was no longer a peaceful abode, but everything around gave note of the preparations of War, the garrison at Colchester completely filled with troops ready for the defence against the expected invasion.

In the summer with Mr. Hatch and Mr. Tufnell . . . I served as one of the Stewards of the celebrated Florist Feast, always held on the first commission day of the Summer Assize, when Venison, frequently turtle, fruits and every luxury of good cheer were plentifully supplied to a very numerous party in the County Room and of course attended by no trifling expense to those who had received the compliment of being appointed stewards – it was a highly re-spectable convivial and excellent assemblage of all the principal Gentlemen of the country and a most proper one to be supported. The ancient custom of the institution was . . . to exhibit the choicest flowers which continued in some degree for many years, but got into disuse and at length wholly left off from the waggery of the late well known Bamber Gascoigne, who was noted as a bon vivant and fond of good living, who bought in his carriage an immense cauliflower, observing that of all the flowers he was acquainted with, he did not know any so much to be admired as the one he now produced at the meeting and for which he would beg to put in his claim for the first prize. The joke did not fail to amuse the party and to be long remembered as truly characteristic of old Bamber Gascoigne.

1796.   It was on a fine but very cold day that Mrs. Hanson and myself had set off to pay a wedding visit to Mr. and Mrs. Harris at East Donyland.

1797.   In the summer went with my wife, Charlotte, and William to Aldborough and a short excursion on the Suffolk coast.

October.   A grant Feu de Joie at Colchester in consequence of Admiral Duncan's victory.

1798.   I raised and commanded a troop of Tendring Volunteer Cavalry, Thos. Nunn, Esq., of Little Bromley Hall being my Lieutenant and Fred. Nassau, Esq., of St. Osyth Priory, my cornet, until succeeded by Major, since General, Slater Rebow, of Wivenhoe Park and of the Life Guards. Colonel Villiers of the 1st Light Cavalry Fencible Regiment, then quartered in Col-chester, assisted us by his Sergeant Major in our drills and exercise and, on that Regiment changing quarters, Colonel Lord Hawkesbury, afterwards Earl of Liverpool, and Major Dundas Saunders, now Lord Melville, commanding the Cinque Ports Regt. of Cavalry, which succeeded the 1st Fencible, continued to us the same kind assistance. We might be called the advanced corps of the British Army, as our own particular part of the Essex coast was the threatened point, in which the invading army was expected to attempt a landing but where within a few hours a force of 30.000 men from the garrisons of Colchester, Weeley and Ipswich of the neighbouring camps were ready at once to oppose them.

Aug. 1st.   Great rejoicings at Colchester as well as elsewhere on Lord Nelson's victory of the Nile.

1799 Sept.   Some of the servants being ill of a fever, I removed the nurses and children to the Old Manor House of Little Holland, long since reduced to a farm occupied by worthy people, John Bancroft and his wife, beautifully situated close to the sea on the Essex coast where they remained six weeks.

Nov.   Presentation of the standard to the Tendring Troop by Mrs. Hanson when the whole neighbourhood and great numbers of the military were assembled and a large party entertained at Bromley Hall.

1800 Aug.   Colchester rendered very gay by the military both previous to this time, and in succession, having in their numbers many of the nobility of the first rank with their ladies under the gay auspices of Sir William and Lady Howe, the former being Commander in Chief of the Eastern District with a large portion of those general and distinguished officers who by their skill and bravery during the course of the late War have immortalised their own and their country's fame, not omitting the name of my old and early friend, Sir John Shirbrooke, K.C.B., whose renewal of old acquaintance gave me such satisfaction. . . Lady Howe was the general promoter of gaieties of all descriptions, not excepting the rustic sports and games of footraces, sack races, gingling and grinning matches, etc.

Dec. 20th.   We gave a ball and supper at Bromley Hall to the military and neighbourhood which was numerously attended and a few days after another to the Tendring Troop with the principal respectable yeomanry of the neighbourhood and their families.

1802 Jan.   My son William went to Eton.

1803 Jan.   Great alarm of invasion, the threatened landing of the French being daily expected from the forward state of preparation and readiness for embarkation of their immense force. On our part preparations for defence were made with equal activity and measures taken for removing cattle, provisions and property of every kind that might be useful to the enemy; signal staffs were placed on every church tower and fire beacons of lofty piles of wood erected on all the eminences ready to be lighted to give notice on the first alarm; and having been appointed Lieutenant of the District, the principal charge devolved on me of seeing the several duties assigned to the inhabitants executed. Many females and other inhabitants, who could remove, did so for security till the danger passed over.

1804.   Purchased my house in Russell Square.

Sept. 7th   Took my whole family to Lowestoft for 6 weeks. Whilst there, went to the Assembly at Beccles and made many excursions to Yarmouth, Southwold, Norwich and other points of attraction.

1805.   At Christmas this year my 14 children were all assembled in perfect health.

Of the amusements of Bromley, in addition to the usual enjoyments of society in a very respectable neighbourhood though not thickly planted, we had regular good assemblies at Colchester and Dedham; for 6 weeks in the autumn the Theatre at Colchester was well supported by the Norwich Company, amateur concerts, military entertainments including garrison balls at Weeley by the Scotch Brigade under General Hope, grand reviews, sham fights, etc., and above all frequent picnic parties to the shores of Walton and Little Holland, at the former of which places was discovered at extreme low water of a spring tide, after a violent storm had washed away the sand and shingle, a great collection of antedeluvian remains of animals of immense size and the tusks and teeth of the elephant and rhinocerus, of the horns and heads of deer of extraordinary dimensions embedded in one mass of the lower soil. The difficulty of collecting them was very great not only from the tenacity of the soil and the brittleness of the bones themselves, but from opportunity being so short from the reflowing of the tide, the covering of sand and shingle was quickly restored and the whole mass afterwards concealed under the sea as before. From the activity of a man employed by me, whose station was always upon that beach, I was more fortunate than the other collectors in obtaining a large proportion of these curious specimens; many indeed were washed up at different times. After keeping the collection 25 years, I have lately presented a large proportion of them to the Zoological Society and many are yet retained in my own possession. These bones are mentioned in Parkinson's Antedeluvian Remains and also by Professor Buckland and other Geologists.

Our water parties, to which our situation afforded us the best opportunities, were particularly pleasant, we frequently taking the proper time of tide embarked at Mistley and enjoying the beauties of the River Stour sailed down to Harwich, sometimes visiting Landguard Fort and amusing themselves till the return of the tide suited our sailing up the River Orwell to within a mile of Ipswich, where our carriages met us and our return by land, a distance of 15 miles in fine weather in summer time, compleated our day without fatigue or difficulty. We had also the usual pleasures of the country gentlemen, the fox hunts in the next parish, also good shooting, coursing and fishing. When bad weather prevented the enjoyment of outdoor amusement, the friends in my house had always the resources of a well furnished library or an excellent billiard table.

These days of sunshine and pleasure were not altogether without their shade; my very spacious but well fitted mansion with ever open doors required a large domestic establishment within, the gardens, domain, extensive woods and manor, with their necessary protection and the preservation of game called for an equally extensive establishment without, to be maintained at a very heavy expenditure, when to this might be added the considerable calls on my purse from my troop of Tendring Cavalry and the gratuitous discharge of their public services which the times and my duty required me to fulfill as a friend to my King and Country.

The consideration of this subject would not allow me to be blind to the advantages of an alteration, while my family were young and numerous and concentrated to one point, a large accommodation was not to be complained of, indeed was unavoidable and the situation could not be better adapted to their health or enjoyment while in the nursery or as school boys, but in looking forward to the future the pleasant society in which we then indulged did not appear desirable for my children to [be] in at a later period. The Military, who composed the greatest part of it, did not offer any solid advantage, from being merely birds of passage; they were men of estimable and gentlemanly manners, yet not examples for young men intended for business and the more plodding walks of life, and the natives not more so, or of that description to offer the prospect of forming desirable connexions in after life. My sons, with the exception of my eldest who had already made his choice of the army, I wished to be brought up to the mercantile or other professions, by which they might, by their own exertions, advance themselves in life; therefore it would not be reasonable to continue them to be made country idlers and contract ideas beyond their proper level by a style of living and a course of pleasure to which Bromley Hall would appear wholly devoted. I therefore considered a home that could be made comfortable to them near the seat of their occupation and made up my mind accordingly to leave Bromley the following Spring.

I have omitted to enumerate among the amusements of Bromley the opportunities I had of joining my friends of the Walden Stag hunting meeting, the
distance being little more than that from London, about 43 miles, where I used
to go over on the Friday and return on the following Tuesday. Neither have I
measured the pleasure of a very respectable and old established society of the
King's Head Club at Colchester,[3] of which I was a member, who dined together
every Saturday and, when not prevented by other engagements, I was a pretty
regular attendant. The club consisted of most of the respectable gentlemen of
the neighbourhood and town. Dr. Topping of Colchester was, I believe, the
oldest member and almost unfailing attendant; the other old stagers were
Colonel Bullock of Faulkbourne Hall, one of our county members, Charles
Whaley, Thos. Brand, John Hadley, John Round of Colchester, his eldest
brother James Round of Birch Hall, T. T. Cook of Messing, Major Harrison of
Copford Hall, with many others; and subsequently Colonel Rigby of Mistley
Hall, General Slater Rebow of Wivenhoe Park, George Caswell of Mount
Bures, etc. etc., the whole of whom, with very few exceptions, have since paid
the debt of nature and are in their graves; except Major Harrison and General
Rebow, I hardly recollect any now living and this once pleasant club, since the
death of Dr. Topping about 10 or 12 years ago, has ceased to exist. Among the
rarities, which occasionally appeared at our table, was the annual present of that
scarce bird, the bustard or wild turkey, which the Revd. N. Corsellis, a member
of the Club was in the habit of receiving from his friend, Mr. Pickering, as a
compliment to the club from his very extensive manors in Norfolk, and in which
he seldom disappointed. But that race of birds is believed to be nearly, if not
entirely, destroyed and extinct in that county, as it is said also to be on Salisbury
Plain and other parts of England where it was formerly numerous.

1806. March 26th. We finally left Bromley for Russell Square. Upon
coming to town, I took a house at Kensington for my younger children and
their nurses.

1807. I took a house at Chigwell as a temporary country residence.

My Great Bromley estate, from the additions of numerous farms and woods
surrounding it, had become one of very large extent and value, and reflections
on its future destination had for some time past occupied my mind. That which
would have been a considerable pride and which I had myself once entertained
whilst a father of only three or four children, would be unjustifiable in a father
of fourteen. It is the establishing a family estate, which must either be to the
advantage of an elder son at the expense of younger children or to leave that son
merely nominally a man of fortune by an estate burdened with charges to pay
younger children's portions and a spacious mansion and domain, entailing on
him the necessity of a large establishment to keep it up and an expensive style
of living corresponding with it. I began, as opportunities offered, to part with
detached farms and woods so as to decrease its amount and this course I continued to pursue until I finally compleated the sale of the whole remaining
estate in 1822.

My first tenant who had occupied the Hall was Mr. William Leeson Wall,
who however proved necessitous in his circumstances and plundered my
property; not satisfied with the plentiful supply of game, fish and rabbits which
the estate afforded him, even shot the greater part of the fine stock of pidgeons

from my dovecot towards the maintenance of his family. I was fortunate in getting rid of him at the end of three years at the sacrifice of a considerable amount of arrears in rent and other amounts due to me. He was succeeded by Lieut. Gen. St. Leger, who from absence [for a] great part of his life in India and elsewhere, was totally unacquainted with either domestic or English country concerns. His servants chiefly were Irish and equally undisciplined, except to personal attendance on himself, in the care or preservation of anything around them, but were only as foragers from a bivouac in a strange country, seizing upon whatever they could make use of; they dragged my fishponds, destroyed my game for sale, everything about the place became exposed to injury and dilapidation; even the wires of a harpsichord, not in use and placed in a spare room at Bromley Hall, were taken out to be converted into springs and snares for catching of birds or snaring hares and other animals. The General, though himself an honourable man, was unconsciously, from imbecility and neglect, a miserably bad tenant and I could not but rejoice at my exchange to another general in the person of Sir John Byng, who was an exact man and perhaps even too minute in his petty concerns. He had the command of the Eastern Districts and made his Headquarters at Great Bromley Hall, which he continued to occupy as my tenant for about four years till in the autumn of 1816 he gave it up.

1809.   Purchased the Rookery estate at Woodford, Essex, of George Smith, the banker, and taking possession of it this month occasioned my giving up the house of Chigwell. Among the amusements of this latter place was the great fair annually held under the celebrated Fairlop Oak in the midst of the secluded and beautiful scenery of Hainault Forest the 1st Friday in July; this was the resort for many years of the best company and all the respectable families for many miles round furnishing an extraordinary and enchanting scene and was a day exhibition equal in interest and effect to that of a night one of a Gala Festival at Vauxhall, but of late years from the excess of disreputable people coming from London and annoyances taking place, it has been on the decline and neglected and the old tree itself, partly by fire and wantoness and partly by the axe, is now compleatly destroyed and not a vestige of it remains.

1817.   Woodford Church rebuilt at the expense of £8,000. Mr. Brumester and myself treasurer in the concern, of which I had a considerable share of the trouble.

1818.   Mr. Wellesley's bold attempt was now made to destroy the beauties and enjoyments of the neighbourhood by the entire enclosure of both Epping and Hainault Forests by Act of Parliament. In this however he was fortunately defeated and a piece of plate was deservedly presented to Mr. John Hall for the ability and judgement which distinguished his services as chairman of the Committee appointed to oppose this very unpopular measure.

1820.   Having in February visited Bromley on business, taking with me my daughter Mary for a few days in August went there again with my three daughters. . . Having given up the occupation of the Hall to Capt. H. C. Cooper, we took up our quarters at Rudlands Farm, to be called the New Manor House, where I had fitted up a few rooms for occasional visits either of myself or family and, in seeing our old neighbours and old scenes, remained some days. To Capt. Cooper I had agreed to sell Bromley Hall with a certain portion of land around it, reserving to myself the Manor Woods and several of the farms. He had already possession of the Hall, the property being mortgaged to me for my security, but from the deranged state of his affairs becoming unable to pay for his purchase, it was annulled and the estate restored to me.

1821, June 4th.   I made a short excursion to Southend where our friends, Mr. and Mrs. Hume, were staying. Then directing our course through Baddow, Dunmow, Saffron Walden and the beauties of Lord Braybrooke's at Audley End to Cambridge, we returned and reached home again on the 11th.

Aug. 13th.   I, with my daughters Elizabeth and Harriett, set off on a tour, varying our usual road to Bromley by going through Harlow, Dunmow, Braintree and Coggeshall. After a short stay at Bromley we crossed the highway at Lawford towards Cataway Bridge just as the procession of Queen Caroline's funeral was then travelling to Harwich for embarkation.

1821.   In May and June had three journeys to Bromley with Mary to settle the various concerns on its sale. After having in previous years satisfactorily sold at different times a large portion of my Bromley Hall estate . . . I succeeded now in the sale of the remaining reserved estate of Bromley Hall itself and Manor, the total sum for which the whole sold after a deduction of all charges, expenses and losses in default of payment by my last purchaser was clear £84,000.

1822.   Suffered much from giddiness and could no longer attend either the Assizes or County meetings at Chelmsford, which I had been in the habit of doing regularly for nearly the last 30 years.

V

MARY REBOW, GENTLEWOMAN, OF WIVENHOE PARK, 1771–1779

The first three letters in the selection were written when their author was still Mary Martin. The rest belong to the period after her marriage, when her husband, Isaac Martin Rebow of Wivenhoe Park, was absent, serving in the Militia, first at Warley, in Essex, and later at another camp, possibly the one situated on Tiptree Heath, also in Essex. The Warley camp was visited by John Crosier in September, 1779 (see p. 21).

The whereabouts of the original correspondence is unknown to me and I have therefore been unable to check my transcript against it.

FROM Mary Martin, writing from Warley where she is on a visit, to "My dearest Mr. Rebow":

June 23d, 1771   The reason it seems of our being so suddenly and pressingly invited was to meet Mr. Tringham in order to have some little concerts, and what with Miss Martins playing on the organ and the harpsichord, Messrs. Tringham and Arnold on the German Flute, Mr. Adams on the violin, Mr. Keyder on the violincello, and Mesdames Adams and M. Martin's singing, we have had such concerts as have charmed all our hearers. I was never better in my life, and between Musick, Trap Ball, Haymaking and Walking have spent my time very agreeably.

July 2nd, 1771   . . . Capt. Adams[1] says you are to come to the Assizes (is that spelt right? It don't look so) at Chelmsford, he is to meet you there and you are to return together to Warley, from whence after a few days you are to meet the yatch at Grays, and as Mrs. Adams cannot live unless I favour her with my company . . . they propose that we should make t'other little trip in the Brentwood Machine, stay there as long as we like and then all come up to London in the yatch.

April 20th, 1772   . . . I am very much rejoiced to hear your Mobility continue quiet, for I have been under a thousand apprehensions, as I heard they had again assembled and done a great deal of mischief in several parts of Essex, particularly at Chelmsford, but surely your subscription must put an entire stop to all riots in your part, for if they should prove refractory after such kindness and attention, it must be clear they are not actuated by real want and of course everyone will join in punishing them with the utmost rigour. The Adam's found a great party of them assembled at Great Warley Place when they returned home that day, but they were very peaceable and only came for his worship's[1] advice, which he gave them very freely and assured them he would have the peace kept (which Mrs. Adams says he has done nothing but repeat every day since) but they preferred breaking the peace and so went and attempted to regulate Brentwood Market,[2] for which they got heavily punished by the townspeople and his Worship's warrants have gone forth.

The Park, July 17th, 1778.   It was a smoking hot day again yesterday, and of course delightful pleasant at Alresford, Miss Whaley and her brother went with us and they were all prodigiously pleased and charmed with the place. . . Mary and Emma were in high spirits and drank syllabub at such a rate that the latter was quite lillyvated. . . Someone has been from Ld. Rochford[3] to beg a boar pig.

The Park, July 19th, 1778   . . . Mrs. Corsellis and Miss Dyer, a very agreeable, plain girl, sister to the Colonel, drank tea with me. Miss D. is come to bathe and tried hard to persuade me to let her teach me; she says they have lately dug a reservoir; that I may have a fresh bath at any time. If so, a great part of my objection to the Wivenhoe Bath[4] will be removed and I will go in there at any time. Best part of the peas were got in o' Friday, two good jagg and a small one, of such peas as the farmer is sure will not be matched in this county this year. . . The corn all comes on apace and looks very fine. . . It is church going Sunday and as it is to fine, I intend to venture.

The Park, July 22nd, 1778.   Daye killed a buck on Monday morning, and a prodigious fine one it is, he says the oldest in the Park, one of his first marking, and the finest he ever shot. . . Fan and I dined at Capt. Harvey's[5] yesterday, there was the Corsellises, Mrs. Goodall, Frank Smythies and his wife, a Mrs. Bliss and a Mr. Finch who has a tender at Wivenhoe and seems to be the true honest Jack Tar, for he calls the French every odd name and says he is certain they will never invade us . . . for they know they would be so sea sick that they would not be able to stir hand and foot when they were landed.

The Park, July 24th, 1778. . . . The turnips are all sowed and the farmer has brewed ale and small beer this week.

The Park, July 26th, 1778. . . . I am very pleased there is no time for the bottle, for, as you know my opinion of some of your party, it relieves some of my fears. . . Mr Woods went away o' Friday evening and told me he had put everything in such a train that he should not have occasion to come down any more until October, when he should just beautify and put the finishing touches to one of the most pleasing pictures in England.

The Park, July 29th, 1778. . . . The rye is began today and the wheat is in such fine order that the farmer thinks he shall go straight on to that. The remainder of the peas were got in very well, are a fine sample and there is a pretty piece of hay brought home from the Falcon field and there will be some fine rowens in a short time. The farmer let the harvest to the men, before these rains set in, at 5s. 6d. or 5s., I don't know which, the wheat; and 1s. 6d. the barley and oats, an acre. He says you and he settled to put the rye on a cock, but thinks that the two chambers and the cart lodge will hold it very well and will be more handy, therefore begs you will send him word if you approve of his putting it there.

The Park, July 31st. . . . We dined yesterday with Mr. Ennew, who is quite recovered and proposes to set out next Wednesday on a tour of pleasure and thinks he shall see you in camp.

August 2nd, 1778. Capt. Harvey seems very well in health, but very low and dejected and I don't find he has the least prospect yet of getting back either his men or his vessel[5] . . . P.S. I have inclosed some toothpicks.

The Park, Aug. 9th, 1778. I am sorry to find, my Dearest love, that I must give up all expectation of hearing from you oftener than once a week, for it seems such a tedious long time, that I know not what to do. However, they say that what cannot be cured, must be endured, and as I am thoroughly satisfied you would not let it be so if you could otherwise help it, I will not perplex you with my complaints, but will go on to tell you of what I think will be more agreeable to you, (viz.) that we are all keeping well. The coachman has had no more returns of his fever, and so yesterday morning I ventured to Colchester for the first time since you have gone, except for that day when I dined with Mr. Ennew. Going up East Hill I met Mr. Corsellis just returned from Warley Camp, who says he never saw a place so improved as it is since he was there last. Yet at the same time he never saw any people so heart sick at any thing as they one and all are of a camp life; even W—n, who made such a fuss at first, is tir'd to death and impatient to be at liberty again. I told him that I was quite shocked to hear it, for I had been informed by several that had been with them, that in point of business, their's was only play to your's, and that they had such liberty allowed them that, upon an average, not a quarter of the officers ever layed in camp. He said that it was very true but they were all heartily tired for all that. He goes to Chelmsford Races tomorrow, and from thence talks of making your camp a visit.

I fancy from the various messages I have brought and sent me you have a vast many visitors. I heard yesterday Mr. Whaley and Tom Younge came to you on Friday, and that Mr. W. intends to try to get lodgings to bring all his family next week. They are all to drink tea here this afternoon. Captain Blatch, I find, came home last night very ill. Pray, is there any truth in his wanting to resign?

Do you know, to my great astonishment, I received another letter from Mrs. B. yesterday, to say that for fear I should go to Maidstone sooner than I thought of, as she was got quite well again, she would be with me by tea-time to-day, and should make her visit longer than she had first mentioned, provided that I treated her *sans ceremonie*, and then by way of post-script says that, as she is an invalid, begs I will permit her to bring her Abigail, which last piece of business I should have been very glad to have been excused, but it is not in my power to tell her so, if I would, and so she must come, and I must do the best I can with them, without any ceremony I can tell her; I wonder whether *he* knows anything about this move? She writes that she proposes to dine at the Bell, at Thorpe, tomorrow, in order to look for lodgings, which happens rather lucky, for Fan. and I have promised to dine with Mrs. Corsellis, and I should have been distressed to have carried her too, because it is to be quite in the family way.

The man has this morning brought home the colt, and he assures me that it rides better than ever he had a colt in such a short time or that he had any notion of at first, is very gentle, and will have very easy paces, but he has had a very bad cold and running at the nose, which disorder is very much among horses at present. He was vastly sorry you was not at home, for he could have wished to have had him rode continually, but as I could say nothing to that till I had heard from you, he advised that I should turn him out, for fear of his learning any tricks, and when you returned home, he would fetch him again for a little while. He took the other home with him, and as he said nothing about money, I did not offer him any ...

I was a little premature in regard to carting the wheat, for though the farmer set out to do it, yet the oats and barley ripen so exceedingly fast this fine weather that they are obliged to cut them as fast as possible, and so have left the wheat on the shock; is that a right term?

The carpenters and painters go on apace with the railing of the bridge, now they have all got to work one side is fitted and the other begun. It is set up by the saw pit, and you can't think what delight Mary takes in carrying every body to see what she calls her prospect. Lupton has not done a stroke of work these two Saturdays. I sent Beven yesterday to know the reason, and the excuse is that he has gone to Colchester for change and is writing out his accounts; should it be so or would you have me speak to him about it?

The boy came some time ago, therefore Accept our love and believe me ever,
My Dearest Life,
Yours most affectionately
Mary Rebow

P.S. I hope you will receive the venison, and on Wednesday, for I spoke to Reynolds myself yesterday to give proper orders to the coachman about it. Remember to look for the seal on the locks.

The Park, Augst. 14, 1778. I told you Fan. and I were to dine with Mrs. Corsellis o' Monday, but behold he [Mr. Corsellis] put himself into a most violent passion o' Sunday night, turned a new French butler out of livery he had got out of doors and gave almost every other servant warning, all of which frightened Mrs. C. and Miss D. out of their wits. As he had taken the only servant that could wait with him to Chelmsford Races, she walked over to beg I would excuse her receiving me.

The Park, Augst. 14, 1778. . . . You expressed a wish some time ago that I would let Miss Dyer prevail upon me to try the Wivenhoe Bath, which I would have complied with immediately, but certain reasons rendered it impracticable till now. On Mr. Corsellis asking some questions the other day, Munnings[4] chose to come up this morning and desired to speak with me, when he informed me he had heard I had some thoughts of bathing and if I would do him the honour of coming to his Bath, he would not value disobliging anybody to let me have a fresh bath from the reservoir at any hour I chose; but if it would suit me to come down about ten o'clock on any or every morning, I might depend upon having one without any kind of difficulty. So I intend to consult Mr. Sterling and, if he approves of it, will try two or three morning next week to see how I like it. What they call the bathing season lasts till the latter end of October or the beginning of November.

The Park, Augst. 16, 1778. . . . Price no doubt told you of my consulting Sterling about Bathing, who very much approved of it, only desir'd I would go in every day instead of every other day, and wish'd I would intice the children in with me, for as they are so delicate, it would be of infinite service to them and strengthen them greatly. Accordingly I bought myself a petticoat for decency's sake, before I went home. I determined to go in tomorrow morning, but I believe there is a spell set upon my determinations in respect to bathings, for I was taken very ill about five o'clock. . . I must not attempt to bathe till my bowels are quite settled. . . Nurse has got a return of her old complaint, which they say bathing could do her more good for than anything and I dare say they would go in with her as well as with me. As I am really afraid that if something is not done for her, the woman will go into a consumption very fast, if you have no objection, she shall go in with them while I am away. The terms are a guinea for the season or a shilling a morning.

The Park, Augst 19, 1778. . . I have fixed everything to take a dip in the Wivenhoe Bath tomorrow, but have come to a determination not to let the children go in till I return. . .

Aug. 21st, 1778. We are all vastly well and I have the pleasure to tell you that I tumbled into the Wivenhoe Bath both yesterday and this morning with the greatest success imaginable, find it has every good effect upon me and like it prodigiously. The bath I think very much improved since I saw it last, or I saw with different eyes then. For it is very light, there is a pretty little room to dress in, the water is perfectly clear and very salt, and the people are civil and obliging to a degree; I intend to go in every morning till I come to you. . .

Augst. 23rd. The bathing, added to the delightful prospect of seeing you soon, puts me in such spirits that Mrs. Harvey, who drank tea and supped with me last night, declares that I don't seem like the same person. I sent for Mr. Sterling to Mr. Ennew's. . . He only hopes I will continue the bath as long as I possibly can when I return.

Augst. 23rd. I have taken the liberty of altering the plan of our horses bringing me to Kelvedon, for on recollection there would be four horses, with Mannings' saddle horse, for the boy to bring back and as our horses are not used to lead like post horses, I thought they might get a kick perhaps or the post boy might not take proper care of them. Therefore have ordered a pair of horses and a saddle horse from Mannings.

Augst. 3rd, 1779. Fanny Corsellis came to me o' Saturday. I drove her in the Whiskey to Alresford and back again with great success not touching one gate post or having a single puzzle.

The Park, Augst. 11th, 1779. I am doing as you desired in regard to making visits, for I was at Mrs. Keelings (a rout of 36) o' Monday, am to be at Mrs. Gray's tonight, at Mrs. Powell's next Monday and intend to send to Mesdames Hills and Mayhew for Friday and Saturday. Capt. Harvey is to return on Friday with his new cutter with Mr. Gascoign.[6] Corsellis is at home and quite crazy about these harriers, a huntsman was advertised for o' Saturday. . . The farmer has put the cows into the Falcon field.

The Park, Saturday night. . . I was mistaken about the cutter, for it is the old one there has been all the fuss about, and she is expected down today with the Admiralty colors flying on board. The business, it seems, is for Mr. Gascoign[6] and some others to go in her the beginning of the week to fix small cutters at all the principal buoys on the coast, which are to take them up and destroy them as soon as any of the French Fleet appear in sight, and after that she is to go as a privateer.

VI

CHARLES HICKS, FARMER OF GREAT HOLLAND, 1778–1865

The memoirs of Charles Hicks of Great Holland Hall are a straightforward account of those incidents and developments in or near his village that engaged his interest, together with comments on agricultural matters and national affairs. They contain much of local interest for those living in the vicinity of Great Holland, but for those unfamiliar with the topography of the district their value lies in the representative nature of the views which Hicks expresses and of the changes in rural life which he describes. He dislikes the 1832 Reform Act and the Speenhamland System, while thoroughly commending the New Poor Law of 1834. He accepts uncritically the current gossip about the idleness of working people under the Old Poor Law and shows little understanding of the miseries which caused local farm labourers to join the Swing riots of 1830, though he himself provides some of the information which helps to explain those events. Nor does he show compunction about the intimidation of those workers who led the attempt to secure for themselves and their fellows a somewhat less wretched living.

Many of the developments that changed rural Essex in 1815–65 are mentioned in the memoirs. The agricultural slump of the 1820s gradually gave place to better times in the 1850s, with wages rising just enough to mitigate the bitter discontent of earlier years, but the New Poor Law was firmly imposed at Government insistence and with enthusiastic support from local ratepayers. Parish help to emigrants, the enclosure of the few remaining pieces of waste, the building of a steam flour-mill, the penetration of the railway into rural areas, such commonplaces of village development in this period of slow but sustained change find a place in these pages. Most characteristic of all, perhaps, is the arrival of the evangelical Rector, who struggles to maintain an evening class for young workers, successfully opens an Anglican day school and rebuilds the parish church, all in the brief space of a few years.

The manuscript is in private hands, but there is a copy of it in Essex Record Office [T/B 243].

Annals of the Parish of Great Holland
by an Old Stager

GREAT HOLLAND from its proximity to the sea was formerly a notorious place for smuggling. When a boat came ashore, the labourers assisted in working the goods, consequently they became much addicted to drinking.

In 1778, Mr. Peter Baines, when about 18 years old, lived with his mother, a widow, at the Lower Farm on the Green at Gt. Holland. From information I had from him, he and a man used to see after and work the horses. They often kept gin in the stable. As soon as they had given the first bait to the horses in the morning, they used to drink some gin from a small tin mug kept for that purpose. He also told me there was a gang of smugglers came regularly from London on horseback with from ten to fifteen horses. They generally traded in gin, sometimes in dry goods. They arrived at Holland about five or six o'clock of a winter's night, would go down to the Lower Barn at the Hall and let the horses feed round the corn stacks, Mr. Fisher receiving compensation by a constant supply of gin, of which he was very fond. When out of stock, the old gent. would call after some of his men, when leaving work at night, to have the Lane gate "locked" – it was well understood what it ment – and the next morning there was sure to be a tub of gin under the horse-block.

The lane called Whitton Wood Lane at Frinton, there is no doubt, communicated some years ago with the Dead Lane at Kirby. Mr. Baines said there used to be gates from the end of Dead Lane through fields then occupied by Mrs. Baines, by the Brook Ditch at the back of Holland Hall Wood to the Bull Hills and Breakneck Bridge, through which the smugglers used to go and return from the beach.

There was not a resident Rector, or a school, in the parish for many years of the latter part of the last century. The labouring classes had a bad example then, it was no wonder in 1800 they were found to be an uneducated, ignorant and rather an outlawed race of men.

1800. Michaelmas J. T. Hicks came to Gt. Holland Hall the population of the parish being small. Most of the labourers employed on the Hall the first few years came from the neighbouring parishes. Horsemen boarded and lodged in the house. Very few cottages in the parish. Several single men from Langham followed J. T. Hicks to work for him and settled themselves on the parish. Cottages were soon erected and better accommodation provided.

1801. White peas in the Spring sold at a guinea per bushel. On the 25th of March wheat sold at 177s. per quarter. The average for the year was 119s. 6d. per quarter. Flour at one time in the year 7s. per peck.

1802. Frost and snow from the 13th to the 18th of May.

1803. When Buonaparte had his flat-bottomed boats made and threatened to invade England, it was thought probable he might attempt a landing on the Essex coast. It created considerable alarm in this neighbourhood. Orders were received in the parishes along the coast to appoint persons to take charge of the live stock and have it removed, if necessary, to the upper part of the County on the borders of Cambridgeshire.

Mr. Joseph King and Robert Draper daily expected to be called into active service for this parish, being appointed for that office. The Revd. Shaw King, residing at Commarques at Thorp, had all his plate and valuables packed ready for starting. It was said several families in Colchester made similar preparations.

1805. Before the barracks were built at Weeley and ready for the troops, between two and three thousand infantry were encamped on the cliffs at Little Holland, and a small hut was built on the grass piece at Gt. Holland near the lane leading to the Lower Barn, at the South end there was a room for an officer, in the middle a room for thirty soldiers, and at the North end a stable for eight horses.

1806. A fire occurred by accident at Great Holland, the old Mill House and premises were all burnt; nothing escaped but the windmill occupied by Mr. James West.

1809. In July, Government purchased 4 acres of the Horsemarsh on Gt. Holland Hall near the Old Haven, on which a Martello Tower was built in 1809; and 1810 at the same time one was built at Frinton and one at Lt. Holland.

1811. Mr. Butcher of Orford in Suffolk undertook and by contract made a new sea wall from Great Holland Gap to Frinton Battery.

As Essex has always been said to be celebrated for calves, in truth it might be said Great Holland about this time was noted for donkeys; as many as twenty might be seen on the Green when riding over it. The music from them was heard all over the parish. Many of the labourers used to ride to and from work daily, mounted on donkeys, with their victuals in bags flung across the pannell; what should we think now in 1865 to meet half a dozen of them so mounted? The masters had the trouble and expense of keeping them during the day, of which they grew tired, and when the rates increased, relief was refused a man who kept a donkey.

1812. There was a very high tide in July. It occurred in the middle of the day. It ran over the old wall from Holland Gap to Sand Point. It was a still day, the sun shone bright, and the sea as smooth as glass. The water gradually rose and kept running over till the tide turned, just as if the water had been poured into the middle of a bason and caused it to run over. The marshes were soon covered; some sheep on the marsh near the wall got on to a quantity of faggot wood. They were taken off one at a time without loss.

1813. Some alterations were made in the church at Great Holland to afford more sittings and accommodation. The Gallery was brought forward and enlarged and the stairs placed in the Tower. The whole expense amounted to £122. 14. 10. Two old bells had been lying in the Belfry many years unhung, were sold for £40. 1. 5. and the proceeds went towards the repairs of the church.

1814. Frost set in on Christmas Eve and lasted 14 weeks. The Thames was frozen over and a bullock roasted on the ice. Wild fowl so numerous along shore they were frequently heard up at the Hall, the noise much like a pack of hounds at a distance.

1815. In the Spring a vessel, laden with oats from Boston, was driven on the Gunfleet sand in the middle of the day just before the flood of the tide. The crew abandoned her, took the boat and went to Brightlingsea. The wind was blowing strong directly on shore. The men, before leaving, left her sails set, thinking she might drift off; she did so and came right ahead ashore, bang against the wall, about half way between Holland Gap and Sand Point. I went down immediately and never saw so rough a sea before. When the waves broke against the vessell, they sprayed nearly to the top of the mast. There was a dog alive under the hatches. The crew came alongshore and claimed her and cargo.

The oats, damaged by the water, were taken out and sold for what they would fetch and the vessel got off.

1820. The Martello Towers at Frinton, Gt. Holland and Lt. Holland, belonging to Government, were sold by auctions and taken down this and the following year.

1822. It was unanimously agreed to build at the expense of the parish a range of five cottages, with bake-office in the centre, on part of the Green. A grant of a piece of land was obtained of the Lord of the Manor, on which they were erected and completed in 1823 at the cost of £193. 4. 11. The bricks and other material used, formed part of the Martello Tower, taken down on the Tower Marsh at the Hall Farm.

1824. There was during the last two years great depreciation in the value of all farming stock and produce.

In 1822 the price of wheat for the average of the year was only 44s. 4d. per qr; it had not been so low since 1792. Many farmers that commenced business with war prices and borrowed capital were ruined. Those that did continue their holdings experienced great difficulties, for want of money were obliged to have less labour performed. The land was not so well cultivated, numbers of hands were thrown out of employment, had to receive relief weekly from the parish, causing the Poor Rates to be considerably increased. Farms that were re-let, the landlords had to take less rental.

The harvest of 1824 was principally a wet one, the barleys were badly got up. I sold some at Manningtree of bad colour and out of condition at 47s. per qr in Nov. . . This price would not have been obtained but for the existing Corn Laws.

From this time, and for many years after except during the harvest month, there was not employment for all the labourers in the parish and during the winter months in particular numbers were out of work and had parish relief.

The Magistrates, having continual applications from paupers, had at last a scale drawn up, and printed on a card, to regulate payments to paupers from the Poor Rate. Day wages were calculated according to the price of flour. If a man lost a day or two in a week from bad weather or insufficiency of earnings to support his family, the deficiency was made up according to the number of the family by the card, and paid by the Overseer from the Poor Rates.

The Magistrates about this time used to "lord" it over the farmers and others more than they dare have done in after years. If a man with a family was destitute, whether from improvidence, laziness, drunkenness, or whatever cause, [and] applied to a Magistrate, he would give the man an order, addressed to the Overseer, to relieve him to whatever amount was therein named.

I knew a man, a drunkard, that worked with his boys at Gt. Holland Hall. He had a barn and made good earning by thrashing many weeks during the winter. His wages were paid on the Saturday night. On his way home he has sometimes gone to the Ship Inn and stayed two or three days without going home; his wife has joined him there. He would not go to work again until his money was spent. When destitute, he would go to a Magistrate and the Overseer had an order to provide for the family the rest of the week.

This system of relief proved a great evil, it worked bad for both employer and employed. The labourer would not work or earn money if he had a chance; his pay was the same, whether he worked or not.

F

1829. Chas. Hicks succeeded his father at Gt. Holland Hall, Sept. 29th.

1830. Richard Brett, a labourer belonging to Gt. Holland, was at work with others on the sea-wall. The day before Christmas they assisted some smugglers in getting a freight on shore. Having indulged too freely drinking gin, at night they were most of them drunk and could scarcely walk. Brett, in crossing the plank over the river[1] from Lt. Holland Battery to Gt. Holland Marshes, fell into the river. His companions with difficulty got him out on the sea side, laid him by the side of a hay stack near the Wall, covered him up and left him. The night was clear and a sharp frost; he was dead when they went to him the next morning. He left a widow and six children chargeable to the parish. A few years after, a fine young man about twenty, named Martin Lott, of Lt. Holland, who had been assisting the smugglers, died from the effect of having taken too much raw spirit.

1830. The new Rectory House was built in Gt. Holland and the Revd. Henry Rice came to reside. He succeeded the Revd. Jeremiah Ives in 1812. There had not been a resident Rector in the parish for 50 years. Mr. Ives always lived and died in Norfolk.

The population of the parish having increased so that there was five able-bodied working men to 100 acres of land, besides boys, from not having constant employ and other causes, the labourers became discontented, disaffected and ripe for anything. In the Autumn firing of stacks, etc., commenced in several agricultural counties; and the labourers in this neighbourhood began rioting and breaking thrashing machines. In Essex the labourers were paid better than in any other Eastern county; particularly all round by the coast one shilling per week was generally paid more than 10 miles inland. Where best paid, the men behaved the worst. In Suffolk the men remained quiet, with two shillings per week less wages. The men had been some days forming their plans. Kirby, Gt. Holland and Gt. Clacton took the lead and with other parishes agreed to strike simultaneously on a fixed day. When the day arrived, some men, well disposed, went to their places of work as usual. Others assembled with large numbers, some with bludgeons, and went round to the different farms, intimidating the farmers, demanding employment for all and 2s. 3d. per day wages. They forced the men who had commenced work to leave and accompany them round the parish. When the force was complete, they went about noon to "Jenkins Farm" on the Green and broke a thrashing machine to pieces. There was no work done that day. The whole neighbourhood was in great consternation and alarm.

Immediate steps were taken by the Chief Constables to quell the riot. The following morning the Magistrates met at Thorpe and before night hundreds of Special Constables sworn in. The Yeomanry mustered immediately in a large body on horseback and apprehended several before night, some at Gt. Holland. At Kirby there were several desperate fellows, who, as they had not been called upon during the day, imagining themselves secure, retired to their beds. In the middle of the night the Specials surprised them, broke into their dwellings, took several out of their beds and sent them under a strong guard to Thorpe. The Magistrates, as they came in, sent them off immediately to Chelmsford. A Special Commission was ordered to be held at Chelmsford to try the prisoners. Before a week some of them were sentenced to transportation for life and sent off immediately.

Three of the convicts belonged to Gt. Holland. Two of them had la ͜ families, the other, a man about 32, wife and no children. He ought to have been well off, he had all the best work at the Hall for some years and was then earning 15s. per week and beer.

One man in Great Holland, who well knew that he deserved the same fate as the others, was afraid to go home to his wife and family, spent some days and nights (not the happiest in his life) in Holland Hall Wood. This man has proved of late years by his conduct to be quite an altered man and respectable for his situation in life.

The prompt measures taken to suppress the disturbance frightened the labourers alarmingly.

Average of flour for the year 3s. per peck. Wages 11s. per week and beer.

On the night of Sunday, the 13th of March, a fire broke out at the Lower Farm in this parish. . . The corn was nearly all thrashed and sold, the barn, sheds and fences round the yards were consumed, the house and stable saved.

This Spring Wm. Smith and family, a wheelwright, John Green and family, Isaac Duffield, Wm. Morris, labourers, and James Scarfe from the Red Lion Inn left Gt. Holland and embarked for Canada. Having so many out of work, it was thought advisable to assist such as were disposed to emigrate. The passage out of Green, Duffield and Morris was paid out of the Poor Rates.

From Michaelmas, 1831, to the 25th of March following Chas. Hicks was Overseer of this Parish. . . It was the custom for some of the parishioners to meet the Overseer at the Church on Fridays to pay the poor. The first week in January, 1832, eleven ablebodied men had no work, besides two or three ill. On Feb. 6th the relief paid by Chas. Hicks to paupers entered in the Book for the week was 55, $\frac{1}{8}$ of the population of the parish. This number included old and infirm sick, widows, widows with children (children not included in the 55), unemployed and some in work whose earnings were not sufficient to maintain themselves and families. The sum paid weekly was over £10.

1832. The Whig Ministry could not carry the Reform Bill they introduced to the House of Commons; so Parliament was dissolved. The elections took place in a most disgraceful manner. . . Intimidation, violence and disorder prevailed in several boroughs; numbers were taken out of the way and not allowed to record their votes. Alarming riots took place and were encouraged and no steps taken to suppress them. . . From this time the destiny of England was given up to the power and control of the Working Classes.

1836. The Whig Government introduced the "Act for the better admini-stration of the Laws relating to the Poor". . . . Much credit was due to the Ministers for it, as it saved the country from anarchy and confusion. Indeed, something good they were expected to do for the mischief they did the Landed interest by the Reform Bill in 1832.

1835. Guardians were appointed under the New Poor Law Act. Chas. Hicks was elected for the parish of Gt. Holland and served the office 28 years and the two following years for Frinton, making altogether thirty years.

Mr. Leake of Thorpe Hall, a Magistrate and Chairman of the Quarter Sessions, was Chairman of the Board [of Guardians]. Brought up as a barrister, with legal acquirements and abilities, to him we were much indebted for his able assistance in carrying out the Act. We met weekly on Wednesdays at the Maid's Head Inn, Thorpe, before the Union House was built. We also held

District Meetings to revise the pauper lists at some convenient place for the paupers of four or five parishes to attend. About twelve of us went to Harwich, which caused quite a consternation, as the inhabitants were so averse to the New Poor Law. Thursday was the day fixed for the Relieving Officer to attend at Great Holland to pay the Poor, which was done part in money and part in bread. The contractor for the District usually sent weekly what number of loaves were required to a house where they met on the Green. As we had at this time a good many out of work, you may suppose this new arrangement did not please the paupers, and the Relieving Officer had not a very enviable time of it. One day when the cart arrived with the bread and it was placed in the house, some of the male paupers assembled, proved riotous, bid defiance to the officer, rushed into the house and carried off the bread. William Duffield, Solomon Draper and two or three others, the most active, were committed to prison for six months for the offence.

1836. Saturday, the 24th of Dec., the ground was covered with snow in the morning, the wind blew strong from the N.E. and kept increasing until it blew a perfect hurricane such as few men could remember. It continued the same up to Tuesday night with falls of snow, which drifted so much that many roads were blocked up from 7 to 18 ft. deep of snow. The mails could not get out of London for two or three days or arrive from the country; in a few instances the bags were taken to Town on horseback and with much difficulty. Trees were blown down, tiles were taken off houses and chimneys blown down, farming buildings unroofed and stacks more or less robbed of their thatch. There was much damage done to the shipping along the coast. On the Tuesday morning eighteen vessels were ashore within five miles of Harwich, five or six on Walton Hall.

The same morning a Russian ship of 300 tons, laden with deals, was driven on shore at Little Holland within a few rods of the new Haven. A barge from Harwich came round with the intention of taking in part of her cargo [and] was, as the weather was boisterous, knocked to pieces on the beach. The barge was broken up and Mr. Beckwith bought it and with it made a fence round his garden at Gt. Holland Mill. The Russian ship, after part of her cargo was taken out, was got afloat and towed into Harwich, after being thirteen days on the beach. Christmas day, being on the Sunday, passed without the usual comers and goers, and those were lucky who arrived to see their friends before the storm set in. If not the dullest Christmas ever remembered, it was certainly from the inclemency of the weather a most alarming one. No snipes over, but influenza everywhere.

1837. Violent colds and influenza generally prevailed throughout the Kingdom during January. Nearly half the inhabitants of London from illness could not attend to business. Many mercantile houses experienced great inconvenience in consequence of the non-attendance of principals and assistants. . . . One hundred and thirty clerks at the Bank of England absent one day. On the 20th of January ten men and two boys were absent from their work at Gt. Holland Hall from influenza. March the 25th was the coldest day experienced this winter. Very cold weather from the 3rd to the 9th of April. On the 4th the frost was so severe the pumps were frozen up. The ground was covered with snow on the morning of the 6th, 9th and 12th of April. Great demand for all kinds of food for cattle and sheep from the backwardness of the season. The bark would not run and timber could not be felled in the Hall Wood before the first of June. The wheat ears just began to show themselves on the first of July.

This year the Tithe Commutation Act passed. A Commissioner came down to Holland in December and the agreement for the rent charge in lieu of tithes was executed for the parish of Great Holland at the sum of £777. 16. 0. per annum. In 1770 the Great and Small Tithes collected in Gt. Holland amounted to £139. 3. 6. This Act was decidedly in favour of the tithe owner, but generally approved by both parties. It put an end to all those unpleasant party feelings which often prevailed in parishes and frequently led to litigation. Previous to the passing of the Tithe Act the farmer was entirely at the mercy of the Tithe owner, in many instances exorbitant tithes were demanded and, if not agreed to, were taken in kind. Since then the farmer has been in a manner independent. The Tithe owner is now in a much better position. Formerly he looked to the tenant or occupier for his tithes, sometimes losses occurred. The Rent Charge now charged on the estate, if not obtained of the tenant, can by the Act be recovered of the proprietor.

The Poor Law Act after a few years trial corrected many abuses. It compelled the able-bodied and others either to work or go to the workhouse. In a very few years the Poor Rates in Gt. Holland were reduced to about half. . .

Hundred Heath in the parish of Tendring containing four acres was with the consent of the copyholders and Mr. Cardinall, Lord of the Manor, given to the parish. It was enclosed and cultivated some years for the benefit of the poor. This spot was selected and bought of the parish by the Board of Guardians on which to build the Union House.

1838.   During this year the Union House was built.[2] The Guardians for some time objected to having one built – thought they could do with their then District Houses and avoid the expense. When compulsory orders came from the Poor Law Board, a Guardian, a banker at Manningtree who kept a pack of foxhounds and had great influence over the West-end farmers, moved a resolution to the Board, which was carried, that the Union House, if erected, should not cost more than £5,000. The same gentleman was afterwards one of the Building Committee. The House, when completed, cost £11,239. 1. 10 and has since had thousands more expended upon it.

This year there was a capital crop of every description.

1839.   In May half the roof was taken off Gt. Holland Hall and the front wall taken down and rebuilt, stuccoed and slated.

The Guardians received a communication from the Poor Law Board, ordering all parish property, not under the control of the Charity Commissioners, to be sold. The Holland property was sold in July; the range of cottages built on the Green in 1822 were sold by auction to Chas. Hicks for £186. The gardens enclosed when this house was built and now forming part of the property, were awarded when the Green was enclosed in 1850.

This year Mr. Beckwith took the old windmill down at Gt. Holland and commenced building a Tower Mill in its place.

1840, 15th Oct., it rained in torrents all night and continued without intermission up to Saturday night. . . On the Sunday morning there was never known so large a flood. The top of the posts and backs of gates were seen just above the water. A man named Ferris living at the cottage at Lt. Holland used to attend Gt. Holland Church. On Sunday morning he took a boat, came in a straight line over the marshes and landed near the upper end of the meadow belonging to Gt. Holland Hall. There was previous to this flood ninety acres of the best and heaviest grass ever seen on Gt. Holland Hall at that season of the year, which was spoiled, and some beasts, bought at Woolpit a month before, had to be sold.

1850. With the consent of the Lord of the Manor and the Copyholders, Gt. Holland Green and Common were enclosed in February and awarded to the various copyholders in equal proportions. A portion of the Green and a small piece of the Common was granted by the Lord of the Manor to the parish. The Churchwardens were admitted and the Churchwardens hereafter stand tenants on the Court Rolls, paying annually a quit rent of 6d.

1860. An unusual quantity of rain fell, both winter and summer. The land was so wet even in summer the horses could not be got on the land to plough or cart sometimes for days. The corn grown was never known of so bad a quality, it told seriously on all heavy lands. The quantity per acre and the price both bad; some farmers were entirely ruined and others so bent they never got straight again.

The following year was nearly as bad, the quality better. The heavy land farmers had cause to remember the years 1860 and 1861.

1861. The College presented the living to the Revd. Richard Joynes, "the right man in the right place" and no mistake.

1862. After Mr. Joynes had been at Holland a short time, I have no doubt but that he was disappointed in the opinion he had formed of the parishioners, especially as progress was the order of the day. Men of certain age had no education, many of them did not know their letters, of gratitude and good manners they were lamentably deficient. Nearly one half of the labourers were dissenters and several of them good living men; unfortunately they did the same as those who frequented the Church, let their children run riot on the Sundays and go where they liked instead of taking them to Church and Chapel. I have always calculated that one-third of the population of Great Holland never attended a place of worship.

Except the few years Mr. Rice resided (and under whose reign the morals of the place did not improve), we had no resident Rector, but a poor curate with about £100 per year. Of course he did not possess that influence nor was looked up to as a clergyman ought to be in a parish. In 1815 there was no regular curate, a stranger would come down on the Sunday morning, take the duty for the day and off. The Churchwarden has gone to the church gate and requested to see his authority before being admitted into the church. About this time we had 17 different clergymen within twelve months.

Mr. Joynes soon found he had undertaken a difficult and arduous task to put the parish right. However disheartening things appeared, he was determined to do his duty and manifested a disposition to do good in every possible way. He could scarcely entertain even a hope that he could do much with men of confirmed habits from 30 to 50 years of age, uneducated. He turned his attention to the rising generation, the young, was instrumental in establishing a good school on a permanent footing that the children should have a sound religious education. May he live long to see that his labours were not in vain.

1862. The new school room at Gt. Holland was erected on a part of the glebe.

The following winter Mr. Joynes proposed having an evening school to instruct lads and young men up to 30 years of age. They met Mondays and Fridays, the young farmers of the parish assisting. Nearly fifty at one time attended and Mr. Joynes gave them a treat at Christmas, and all went on well the following quarter. After assembling again the next winter, Mr. Joynes, when giving a lecture, alluded to their congregating in the street of an evening and during Sundays, behaving badly and using language not fit to be uttered, they took offence, did not attend often, but gradually getting less in number, it was given up, to their endless disgrace.

1863.   On the 30th of October Mr. Beckwith's mill was again sadly dismantled. The wind, after blowing strong for some hours, became alarmingly high, it quickly shifted to a contrary direction and, it is supposed, got behind the sails before the mill could shift into the wind. The consequence was, it took the whole crown of the mill and the sails off in an instant. Mr. Henry Beckwith and his man were on the mill, endeavouring to get her into the wind, which they could not accomplish. They both had a very narrow escape. Mr. Beckwith immediately applied steam power and the mill was at work again in six weeks.

At Michaelmas Chas. Hicks, having occupied the Hall Farm in Gt. Holland thirty four years, was succeeded by his son, Chas. Thompson Hicks.

1864.   The construction of the Tendring Hundred Extension Railway from Wivenhoe to Walton was began in 1864. The Mistley and Thorpe Railway also commenced at this time. These, combined with the Reclamation Company carrying out their works at Horsley Island, caused a demand in the labour market. The weather also continued fine and dry up to Christmas, there was no loss of time and every man and boy found employment. The average price of wheat for all England being only 40s. per quarter and having an immense quantity of foreign flour in was a good thing for the consumers, but most things the labourer had to buy were dear, the price of butter 15d., cheese 10d. and meat very dear. Yet the labourer was much better off than of late years, receiving for day work 10s. per week and beer, when at token work, horsemen 12s. I never knew the price of two bushels of wheat to be given for a day's work before. After supplying the house with flour, the labourer had a much larger surplus than in past years to provide other things.

1865.   The approval of the Bishop of the Diocese, the patrons of the living and all others concerned having been first obtained, sanction was given to the Revd. Richard Joynes to take down and rebuild the church at Great Holland. . . . Mr. Grimes, builder of Colchester, undertook and contracted to complete the works within a given time. Divine service was performed for the last time in the old church on Sunday, the 11th of June; on the following day Mr. Grimes began to take the church down. Arrangements having been made for affording accommodation, it was decided that from and after this time Divine Service should be performed in the School Room untill the new church was completed. On Friday, the 4th of August, the Dedication Stone was laid at the end of the chancel by the Revd. R. Joynes, the Rector, in the presence of most of the neighbouring clergy and a huge portion of the parishioners and their friends.

VII

ISAAC BOGGIS, COLCHESTER BAYMAKER, 1790-91

Isaac Boggis took over the cloth-making business of his brother at the latter's death in 1790 and, with the help of his brother's manager, conducted it from his own house on East Hill. His system of production was of necessity a complicated one, since both the raw material and the final purchasers were situated many miles away, while the various processes of production, so far from being in any way centralised, took place in the homes of hundreds of dispersed combers, spinners and weavers. This complexity necessitates some further explanation, if the letters, which are reproduced here, are to be fully understood.

Boggis had first to ensure a regular supply of wool, and wool of good quality. This he mostly ordered well in advance from growers whom he met at the annual Stourbridge Fair at Cambridge. These usually delivered it to London, where it was collected by the two carriers employed by him and then taken to his store-rooms at Colchester. Thence it was sent to his "spinning houses", situated in several villages lying near one another in N.W. Essex and S.E. Cambridgeshire, there to be spun by the wives and daughters of farm workers in their own homes. The yarn was then collected by his employees and deposited in his Colchester store rooms until needed by his weavers, who worked in their own homes in or near Colchester. The fulling and finishing were also carried out in the town or its vicinity. The total number of workers involved is not exactly known, but his average weekly output of 33 pieces in 1790-91 would have occupied some 50 weavers and at least another 350 spinners, combers and other workers, so that he was one of the town's largest employers.

Boggis made several kinds of baize and was proud of their quality. He sent his cloth by carrier to his London factors in response to orders received by them from Spain and Portugal, though he also left some stocks in their hands to meet unexpected demand. His factors despatched the cloth to Lisbon and received payment on his behalf. Such of the money as he needed they sent to him by carrier, but he left some of it with them to be drawn on for the payment of his wool suppliers.

One matter referred to in these letters particularly needs elucidation. Boggis' spinners were situated up to 40 miles away and his transport costs were therefore considerable. He could certainly have found labour nearer Colchester, especially as the industry's recent contraction had caused much unemployment. His reason for continuing to employ the more distant labour seems to have been the earlier connection between the firm and the villages concerned, but he compensated himself by deducting 4d. from every 1s. earned by the spinners or else by exacting a comparable subsidy from their parish vestries, which were ready to comply in order to avoid the even heavier burden of maintaining unemployed spinners from the poor rate. However, when in 1791 a minor recovery of trade took place, clothiers in Colchester, Bocking and other textile towns had to compete for additional spinning labour, so that Boggis was obliged to forego the subsidy in order to retain his spinners. The same favourable conditions also encouraged his Colchester weavers to strike for an increase in their miserable rates of pay.

The selection has been made with a view to illustrating the working of a typical Essex clothmaking business. If the letters are pedestrian, they are, next to the Savill papers, the most illuminating original source of our knowledge about this important Essex occupation. Though the year 1791 was a brief interlude of moderate activity, the industry was in general decline, and this the letters help to elucidate. Boggis' preoccupation with the threatening international situation is significant, since a major cause of decline was the industry's complete dependence on markets especially vulnerable to the kind of wars fought by Britain in this century.

The extracts, which follow, are from a book, in which are recorded copies of Isaac Boggis' business correspondence. One letter is from J. Browne, probably the supervisor of the firm's domestic spinners, and another is from Peter Devall, Boggis' partner or manager or both, who is referred to as 'D' or 'P' in other letters. The rest are by the firm's manager or chief clerk, who may have been Devall himself.

The letter-book is in the custody of Colchester and Essex Museum and there is a microfilm of it at Essex Record Office [T/A 460]. There is valuable information about the Boggis family in John Bensusan Butt's 'Notes on Thomas Boggis and the History of the Minories' (2nd edn., 1970, duplicated typescript).

Messrs. Green and Walford[1]   Colchester, Sept. 14th, 1790

Sirs, Your favor of the 9th, 10th and 13th inst. came duly to hand and recd. per Etherton[2] £51. 1. 0., as you mention (Mr. Boggis and self opend the cash and told it together) as I never brake the bag open without a witness with me – it was my late master's particular rule.

Have sent you this week 10 No. 5 Narrow, 10 No. 6 do, 10 No. 2 Common and 4 No. 3 milld to 63 inches for Mr. Field as per order. Please to send this week pr. Etherton £50. No. 6 whitened returned by Mr. Field, as mentioned in your of the 5th of Augt. last. Please to send down by Etherton next week.

N.B. D. has not sent any bays this week.

P.S. You have not brot to acct. the 20 No. 6 and 20 No. 2 Narrow and Short for Mr. Dubois; please to mention them this week. Hope Mr. Kuhff will let you bring his bays to acct. this week – it will look the better against the Fair.[3] I have made 20 very nice and good No. 5 supers. Your advice respecting the times will be very acceptable to me, as Mr. Boggis seems very willing to be ruled by me in the buying of wools.

Mr. Thos. Woolston   Colchester, Sept., 21, 1790

Sir, I wrote you the 14th inst. wishing you to fix the day for Mr. Boggis and your self to meet at the Fair.[3] In answer to yours of the 12th (since which I have recd. no ansr), please to observe, if I do not here from you, I shall be at Sturbitch on Friday afternoon or on Saturday. Hope to have the pleasure of seeing you, your son and Mr. Flawn,

I am, etc, etc.

Mr. Steph. Pettitt   Colchester, Octo. 14, 1790

Sir, Your favor of the 6th inst. came duly to hand with the offer of about 8 or 10 packs of wool at £8. 12. 6, the last price. Have to say your wool was very badly managed; the lamb wool especially had a great quantity of — in it and was very scuddy — was obliged to have it sorted and cleaned — the worst parcel of wool I ever saw of yours. It was not worth the money by 5s. a pack as times are. But to convince you Mr. Boggis means to continue dealing with you, hoping this wool will be managed better, and all your wool in future — will give you £8. 10. 0. for the quantity of wool you mention, delivered at the Bull Inn[4] at London, to come by Etherton, the carrier that took the late Mr. Stradling's waggon. . .

Mr. John Seymour   Colchester, Octr. 14, 1790

Sr. . . I am very much obliged to you for the offer of a load of wool. Had some conversation with your son (or kinsman) at the Fair[3]. . . The symtoms of warr gaining ground every day, Mr. Boggis begs me to inform you he cannot except of any wool at present. I am, etc.

Mr. Thos. Higgins   Colchester, Octor 14, 1790

Sr. . . Observe what you say respecting your wool. Mr. Boggis begs me to inform you he cannot accept of it; the symtoms of a warr seems to get ground more and more. If it should take place, have as much wool as can be traded out for 2 or 3 year. Will take care about the gloves and let you know how they please. I am, etc.

Messrs. Green and Walford   Colchester, Octr. 19, 1790

Srs, Your favor of the 14th inst. came duly to hand and recd p. Etherton £50. Observe what you say respecting Mr. Kuhff. . . Have not sent any bays this week – had not any narrow ones ready worth sending. Hope to send you some next week. Have drawn on you as under. Saturday week the 13th inst. is the day Mr. Boggis friend calls on him for the money, as mentioned before. You will please to send, if agreeable to yourselves this week £300 and next week the same sum. (£50 will do for this week if it best suits you). Wish you to send this cash in £100 or large bank notes, cut into halfs, by the post, the other halfs by waggon.

Messrs. Green and Walford   Colchester, Nov. 9, 1790

Srs. . . Have sent you this week 13 No. 6 Narrow Golds and drawn on you as under. Observe you will pay Messrs. Griffith bill and the quit rents, likewise you have credtd Mr. Isaac Boggis acct £291. 13. 4 recd for him at the bank, which is well. As Peace with Spain seems quite settled, hope you will be able to send us some better news of trade soon.

Nov. 6 Mr. John Bloomfield at 5 weeks No. 56   £85.   0.   0.
6 Mr. Thos Woolston at 1 mo. No. 57   £60.   0.   0.

Mr. Richard White[5]   Colchester, Dec. 2, 1790

Sir, This only serves to beg you will send this week the pack cloths. If you cannot send them any other way, please to send them by the newsman. I am quite distressed for them. Have not a cloth for any use and am in wants of 4 or 5 between this and Monday.

Messrs. Greens and Walford   Colchester, Decr. 7, 1790

Srs, Your favor of the 2d. inst. came duly to hand and recd. pr. Etherton £50. 0. Have sent you this week pr. Etherton

10   No. 5 Common
6   No. 5 ⎫
and 9   No. 6 ⎬ Narrow
and 9   No. 4 Golds

. . . You mention after Xmas you hope to be able to say what is best to be done in respect to raising the price of bays. Have to say, for your government as well as our own, except the price can be advanced, we cannot maintain the command in sp[innin]g which we have done. Within this 4 or 5 weeks have had 5 or 6 of our best Spinning Houses spoiled by other makers bringing wool. Have tryed to make new houses but find it impossible without paying more for the spinning. Your best advice in respect to this matter as soon as you can will much oblige me. Should not like to follow these people; I have for some time gone before.

Mr. Freshfield   Colchester, Dec. 21, 1790

Sir, This day I find the trade very ill used at the last meeting, particular Mr. Boggis, in respect to sending wool to the Long Houses.[6] Find wool is sent to two Houses, I believe more, without the parish being applyd to for the carriage, as such, agreeable to the resolution of the meeting. I beg a meeting of the trade may be called tomorrow evening.

Messrs. Greens and Walford   Colchester, Dec. 28, 1790

Recd. pr. Etherton £100 0. 0. Observe what you say respecting Mr. Kuhff. Please to let him know I mean to serve him on honourable terms and for a president he shall have all the No. 5 Narrow and No. 6 Do. I can get ready to send on the 18th inst, the time he fixes the ship can stay, at the old price. . . . You will receive 2 barrels of oysters by the way of Mersea which Mr. Boggis begs your acceptance of.

Mr. Pirkis   Colchester, Jany 7, 1791

Please to carry the wool to Hinkson[7] and tell Mr. Moore to put it out and for he to tell the spinners that I shall be there on the 27th. inst. about 2 o'clock and that he must put it out at 4d. in the shilling. And that of Ashdon, please to carry to Mr. Youngs at the Crown[8] and enquire for Mary Lowts to assist in the weighing it out and tell the spinners I shall be there on the 28th inst. about 2 o'clock. I am, etc., J. Browne.[9]

Gentlemen, W. Belchamp [10]   Colchester, Jan 18, 1791

I am given to understand by Mr. John Brown, the bearer of this, you seem to be dissatisfied respecting fetching Mr. Boggis' wool from Sudbury and paying part of the carriage which you agreed to some time since. . . Have recd no such treatment from any other parish. Wish you to recollect how Mr. Boggis has treated your town, finding them of work when other places were without and likewise leaving 2 or 3 places, which was very hurtfull to him, on purpose to accommodate your poor. Beg the gentlemen will take it into consideration and remember their engagement before they alter such a plan as has been complied on Mr. Boggis part without wavering and think at least you should give a ¼ of a year notice of such an alteration. Hope trade will never be in such a situation as to have it in my power to revenge your ingratitude on the poor. When you have considered this matter, shall be glad in your answer. Till then shall count you bound to your agreement.

Mr. Saml. Turner[11]   Colchester, Jany. 24, 1791

Sir, your favor of the 16th inst. came duly to hand with £11. 0. 6, which was right, and agreeable to your request have sent you as above, which I hope will come safe to hand, and please, pray return the cloth.

Wish you could make it convenient to remit the cash some other way. The coachman chargd 2/9 for the £11. 0. 6 and porters 2d (so they have two or three times), which makes 2/11 to have £11. 0. 6 brot from Norwich. . . We never used to pay but 1/– carriage and porters 2d. . . I am, etc.

Messrs. Green and Walford   Colchester, Feby. 1st, 1791

. . . Have sent you this week, agreeable to Mr. Kuhff's request 15 No. 6 Narrow in double cloths, which I hope will come up quite clean and give satisfaction; also 6 No. 4 Golds. Have enquired of Etherton the reason the bays were wett and dirty the week before last. He says it raind very hand and some one or two was wett, but the porters are very neglecting and they put them into their wett and dirty cart and trode on them with their dirty shoes. Beg in future you will speak to the porters yourself; Etherton says they do not mind him. They were deliverd here very clean and dry. Pray, is there any occasion to have any of them down? If there be, please to send them down this week.

Gentlemen, Helen Bumpstead.[10]   Colchester, Feby. 1st, 1791

I have your favor before me and observe what you say respecting the parish paying the carriage. For ansr., Mr. Olley has not mentiond it to me to my knowledge. I always intended to take it of, when the trade would admit of it; at present it does not. If you will not pay the carriage any longer, I must take it of spinners, which I hope you will not force me to do. I take 4d. in the shilling at those places where the parish does not pay the carriage and I have never taken more than 3d. of your poor at any time. Wish you for to continue paying the carriage till Lady Day next and then if the trade will admit of it, will take it of and not lay it on the spinner. Your ansr next week to Mr. Brown when he comes to take in the yarn will much oblige me, as I shall give him orders to take in accordingly.

Mrs. Debonaire[12]   Colchester, Feby. 7th, 1791

This serves to say last week I gave Messrs. Greens and Walford an order to pay you £9. 6. 8, what I recd of Mr. John Manning for a year's rent of Cambrell Meadow and inclosed you have last year's Land Tax receipts, likewise this year's do. with receipts for the tax of the New Shire Hall,[13] which your part came to 2/- and make no doubt you will find to be right. Mr. Boggis recd a very fine forequarter of lamb, for which please to accept his thanks, and by Etherton he has sent you this week a barrel of oys[te]rs, which he begs your acceptance. Mr, Boggis, Mrs. Boggis, and family join in respectfull compts. to you.

Mr. Thos. Woolston   Colchester, Feby. 8th, 1791

Sir, Your favor of the 5th inst. came to hand this day and, agreeable to your request, inclosed you have three bills dated this day on Messrs. Greens and Walford, two at one month, value £49. 10. each, and one at two months, value £49. 10., which please to put the same to Mr. Boggis accot and advice of the receipt; and when you want more bills, please to write and as under you have an accot of the wine etc., paid for you. Respecting our trade, it is not worse than it has been for some time past, but cannot get any advance for goods at present. Mr. Boggis and self join in best respects to you and your family. I am, etc.

6 bottles of old port at 7s.	£2.	2.	
26 bottles and hamper		9.	
	£2.	11.	Wine
2 gallons of rumm at 9s.	0.	18.	
2 Do. of brandy at 12s.	1.	4.	
	£2.	2.	Rumm, etc.
Oysters Mr. Flawne left the accot.	£4.	2.	Oysters.

Messrs. Wm. Browning and Son.   Colchester, Feby. 22d, 1791

... Am much obliged to you for your kind offer of some Kentish head wool.

For answer I do not use any of that sort. I use only the very best Northampton-shire and Buckinghamshire head wool.

Mr. James Hill.   Colchester, March 22d., 1791

Sir, I recd your favor of the 11th inst. advising me of a load of wool being on the road for Mr. Boggis, containing 209 todds. For answer, I have recd none nor cannot hear of such a load of wool coming. If you have not sent it forward, please to advice me pr return of post. If you have sent it, pray enquire the reason the waggoner does not bring it – it might have been at our town on Tuesday according to your advice – Hope there is no unfair meaning by the wool been kept back. If it is the waggoner's fault by keeping in on the road, he does not ought to have carriage. Am expecting the wool every day.

Mr. James Hill.   Colchester, March 26, 1791

Sir, Yesterday I recd a load of wool from you, as you advised the 11 inst. Am sorry to have the occasion to inform you that the wool is in no ways agreeable to your agreement with me. It is the worst load of wool that I ever see come on these premises, will not accept it on any terms. Have weighed it and sett it up in the cloths for your accot. Your paying the expence which may arise for keeping this wool—you may order it away. Expected to have had a prime good load of wool as by your agreement, as I have seen good wool from you and I consented to give you your full price on those terms. Let me here from you p. return of post.

                              I am, etc.

P.S. Think you never see this wool your self. Cannot believe, if you had, that you would have sent it.

Messrs. Greens and Walford   Colchester, March 29th, 1791

Sirs, Have wrote you this day by the trunk to which I refer you. This only serves to say Mr. Kuhff may have the 100 No. 2 at £4. 17. 6. Have sent you 50 of that sort this week and you have on hand 54. . .
P.S. Should not have wrote you by the post, but expected Mr. Kuhff would wish to know before the bays came up.

Messrs. Greens and Walford   Colchester, April 12th, 1791

Sirs, . . . You say your friend's order is countermanded. Amagine it was some chap that only tryed to get the price and then suited himself with other makers' goods, which shuffling was very much unlike a tradesman. Please to inform me in your next if Mr. Kuhff had made up his order for 100 before you received the 79 pieces last week and if you have got those last in the Hall, as I sent them up. Wish they had been at home, except you meet with a chapp for them soon, as they would have been cleaner and better with us. . .

Mr. John Lomas   Colchester, May 5th, 1791

Sir, Your favor of the 29 past came duly to hand and the wool as you mentiond this day. Have not examined it yet. Observe what you say in yours and, to oblige you, Mr. Boggis has sent you inclosed a bill dated this day at two months on Messrs. Greens, value £100, and hopes for such indulgence you will be always carefull to use him well. Please to advise of the receipt; and by bearer you will receive 2 gallons of brandy, 2 gallons of Hollands Geneva and 2 gallons of rumm, which I hope will meet your approbation. Could not get any white brandy in the town — tryed every merchant — and enclosed is the bill and, when you return the casks, may order the same to be paid or I will pay it and place the same to your accot. They always charge the casks till they are returnd.

I am, etc.

P.S. Never send more than 16 or 18 todds in a cloth. Will cut those largest to pieces if they come again. Our combers cannot handle them.

Mr. Thos. Higgens   Colchester, May 16, 1791
    Sir, Your favor of the 2d. and 9th inst. came duly to hand and the wool as you mentioned last Saturday. Am sorry to have the occasion to inform you it does not hold out weight by full 2lb. a cloth. The wool was no ways taken out. The cloths were well sown and whole. Shall expect you make better weight in future and make up the difficiency of this recd, which is 18lb. Have sent your cloths this day, directed to you to be left at the Bell, Smithfield, to go by Ward's waggon. . . I am, etc.

Gentlemen of Abington[14]   Colchester, May 17, 1791
    This serves to inform you Mr. Boggis does not expect you to pay the carriage any longer. Have the pleasure to tell you our trade is somewhat amended and the very great quantity of goods on hand are decreased. Am in hopes we shall be able to do better than we have done sometime. The merchant still refuses to pay the price for goods they ought to fetch, so very dear as wool is. Have taken the first opportunity in my power to take the carriage off and, as you was so kind as to pay the carriage in the behalf of your poor, I return you thanks and hope the spinners will be grateful and not take new masters and, if there should be a scarcity of wool again as is very likely, on your application will do my utmost to employ your poor.

Mr. Thos. Higgens.   Colchester, May 23, 1791
    . . . These 8 cloths recd last Saturday wanted full 5lb. each in the weight. The wool appeared as if it had been wetted before it was packed and believe on your enquiry respecting that matter you will find it to be true (by your order, or done by your men without) as the middle of the cloths all proves to be wett. . .

Mr. Richd. White[5]   Colchester, May 26, 1791
    . . . Observe the meeting at Kelvedon[15] is put of a week longer than the time fixt, that is to say the Monday after Whitsuntide. Will take care to inform the gentlemen here. . .

Messrs. Greens and Walford   Colchester, May 31, 1791
    . . . Respecting Mr. Fields having 20 No. 5 Narrow, am fearful it may do much hurt, as Mr. Kuhff has been the only man they have been sold to and were first made by his instructions.
    Our militia are embodied for a month at this time and we shall not have narrow bays brot. home but slowly till they get to work again – say about 5 or

6 No. 5 a week. So you must do the best you can for Mr. Field and not affront
Mr. Kuhff on any terms.

Hope and expect from the conduct of our neighbours we shall be able to
obtain a better price for goods than we have had lately; they say they have
made 7/6 a piece more than they made a few months since. Wishing that orders
may come in to your hands so that we may advance the price in proportion to
them, I am, etc.

Mr. Saml. Turner   Colchester, June 6th, 1791
    Bot. of Isaac Boggis
in one cloth, 1 Pk., 3sco., olb. of waste at £4. 15. £5. 18. 9.

Sir, As above have sent you this day. . . Respecting the price, Mr. Boggis has
accepted £4.10. for the last, but he could have had more if he had choosed to
sell them from you; and several gentlemen from your place calld here and at
other makers and bought all they could get at a higher price than you allowed
for his. He has charged them £4. 15. and Mr. Tabor will not take less than that
price for his.

Mr. B. Smith

Sir, It was our agreement to make no alteration in making new Houses[6] in the
long reel spinning and I have hitherto complyd with the resolution. If it is
departed from, I shall hold myself at liberty to do as I please.

I am, etc.,

June, 7, 1791   P. Devall

Messrs. Greens and Walford   Colchester, June 7th, 1791
    . . . Respecting the price of bays, No. 3, No. 4, No. 2 cannot be afforded at
the price they now fetch. I assure you that some people go on at random and
talk so much about the goodness of trade that there is at least 10/– more expence
in makeing them than there was last Summer. (If the demand continues), after
Midsummer shall be oblig'd to put 5/– on every sort or they will not pay for
the manufactoring of them. . .

Messrs. Greens and Walford   Colchester, June 14th, 1791
    . . . Observe you say Mr. Kuhff cannot goe higher for Narrow No. 5 and
No. 6. Please to mention in your next if he would have me keep on making
them. It will be very few I can make. Our workmen will not weave them, now
they can get plenty of work in other sorts, and to keep the quality up, I must
pay them better. Will settle that matter another time. If Mr. Kuhff continues to
take them and gives no orders of that kind away from me, I shall be the better
able to doe them, and I wish not to have more than a fair price for them. . . I am
confident he will not get better bays of no one, nor yet so cheap at this time. . .

Messrs. Greens and Walford   Colchester, June 21st, 1791
    . . . our weavers talk of making a stand for more wages, which you will
hear more about in two or three days. . .

Greens and Walford   Colchester, June 28th, 1791
    . . . Have not had it in my power to send any bays up since my last. Our
workmen have not been at work since last Saturday . . . nor when they will I

do not know. Their request to be better paid – the manufacturer cannot afford it as the price of goods have fetched, and wool keeps advancing very much. If the merchants want goods, they must pay dearer for them or they cannot be made. Have not sent any bays this week... If the merchants want the goods and will pay a tolerable price for them, Mr. Boggis will be happy to pay his workmen better.

Greens and Walford   Colchester, July 5th, 1791
   ... Will send the other 2 No. 2 as soon as I possibly can. Our weavers have got to work and I hope bays will come in regular after this week...

G

VIII

JOSEPH PAGE, FARMER OF FINGRINGHOE, 1799–1803

Joseph Page occupied West House Farm in Fingringhoe, a village south the River Colne, situated opposite Wivenhoe and some four miles distant from Colchester. He farmed during the Napoleonic Wars when high prices brought great prosperity to Essex agriculture, causing Page to seek to increase the size of his 30-acre farm. The diary gives evidence of the commercial opportunities open to an enterprising farmer in the local and London markets, yet it also shows that Page rarely refused any of his numerous opportunities for sport and other entertainment at any time of the day or evening. These modest pleasures cost him little, enjoyed as they were on his own or his friends' farms, and, even when he had to pay for them, his income, estimated by Income Tax officials at £80 a year, seems to have furnished him with the necessary means; from the same income he supported a wife and three children and employed domestic servants. He rarely went far for his relaxations, since south of the river there were heaths convenient for cricket, Colchester's extensive amenities lay within easy reach and he had only to cross the Colne to Wivenhoe to attend his club or ride on to his friends in Ardleigh and Elmstead. Though he despatched meat to London, he seems himself to have visited the capital rarely or not at all. Such time as he spared for public affairs he spent within his own parish and on its vestry's business.

Though the War affected him mainly in sending up the prices he received for his produce, especially when he could sell it to the quartermasters of troops stationed in N.E. Essex, he did witness dramatic events attendant upon the 1799 expedition of the Duke of York and Abercromby to Northern Europe. Also, prosperous though North Essex farming had become, there are in the diary some faint indications of the incipient class conflict, which was being indirectly set in motion by the War and was to divide village society for many years to come. Generally, however, life in Fingringhoe was placid and uneventful.

The extracts which follow are less than half of the material contained in the diary, most of which consists of day-to-day records of farming activities of an inevitably routine nature. Enough of the latter have been included to illustrate Page's working life, while few of his references to his social activities have been omitted.

The original volume is at Essex Record Office [D/DU 251/89], where there is also available an informative essay on the diary and on the Page family by Jennifer Wright, entitled "A Village Diary of the 19th Century", [T/Z 13/68]. There is also an article by J. C. Shenstone on the subject-matter of the diary in *Essex Review*, XVI (1907), 78–89.

1799

Sept. 16th   The first Regt. of Dragoons began to pass through Colchester in divisions in their route to be embarked for Holland to join Abercrombie.

The 11th Regt. marched through this place to shoot at targets on Mr. Cooper's Marsh.

Sept. 19.   Lent Lord Hawkesbury's steward my cart to go to Harwich to take a survey of the house of John Robinson, M.P. for that borough, Lord and Lady Hawkesbury being going to reside there during the month of October for the benefit of the hot bath;[1] and after that Lord Hawkesbury and family to return to town for the convenience of attending Parliament.

Sept. 21st.   Went to Colchester to sign a lease with John Cooper and Richard Stone to John Pertwee of the Church Land for the sum of £20 per year . . . for the term of twelve years.

Sept. 25th.   Received as a present from the Right Honorable Lord Hawkesbury one dozen of bottled porter with hamper and bottles.

October 2nd.   Mr. Neal and myself went a shooting at Peldon and dined at the Rose and supped at the Lion, Abberton; myself shot 3 brace of birds and a hare.

October 4th.   Shot with Mr. Wm. Simson of Ardleigh and dined with him. Mr. Fenn shot with us.

October 7th.   Mr. Sach of Layer took my colt to break for the sum of one guinea.

From the 24th October to the 31st, The wounded men began to arrive at Colchester Barracks. The first that came landed at Mistley Thorne, some landed at Wivenhoe and the remainder at the Hythe. They consisted of upwards of 1200, the greatest number of which were wounded in the battle of the 19, the rest were ill of ague.

Nov. 1st.   Up to this day I killed fifty two brace of birds and 2½ brace of hares and for which I had shot 176 times.

Nov. 4th.   Shot for Mr. Corsellis[2] and dined with him; and walked round by Colchester on account of the ferryman being in bed.

Nov. 7th.   Shot with Mr. Fenn of Ardleigh.

9th Nov.   This day and for several days preceding different Regiments came to Colchester on their march to their different winter quarters, which troops had been on the Continent with the Duke of York. . . The remains of the different regiments which arrived at Colchester were in a deplorable state, some without shoes, stockings and almost every necessity that is wanting to equip a Soldier.

Nov. 25th.   Went a ferreting with Mr. Jo. Simson.

Mr. Sach of Layer's hounds hunted here this day.

Nov. 28th.   Mr. Jo. Ashwell came here with his drill machine to drill nine acres of wheat.

Nov. 30th.   Finished drilling and put in fourteen bushels on the nine acres. Went to the play at Colchester to see Othrello and Midas.

Dec. 5th.   Bought a coal range of Friend Cross for the sum of two pounds, two shillings, but he asked two pounds, six shillings.

Dec. 7th.   This day at Colchester Market . . . Malting barley was worth three pounds per quarter . . . but wheats were dull sale at £23 a load.

Dec. 11th.   The Revd. Love rode with me in my cart to dine at Langenhoe Hall to pay tythe to Mr. Cooper.

Dec. 13th.   Called Mr. Love and went with him to pay a visit and spend the evening with Mr. Garritt for the first time.

Dec. 14th.   Bought 8 beasts at Colchester. . . Welsh runts for the sum of thirty two pounds and gave a man one shilling and sixpence to drive them to Fingringhoe. Mr. Heffill of Wivenhoe selected them out, for which I treated him with two shillings worth of punch at the Waggon and Horses.

Dec. 19th.   Mr. Garritt and myself went shooting on Fingringhoe Wick marsh.

March 29, 1800.   Inman drew turnips for bullocks.

Mrch 31st.   About 2 o'clock this day the barn of Mr. Richard Stone at his late dwelling house on South Green was discovered to be on fire and not the smallest doubt can be entertained of its being wilfully set on fire.

April 1st.   Bought at the Custom House, Colchester, one lb and ½ of chocolate at 3s. 5d. a lb, and 6 pair of shoes at 1s. 9d. per pair, sold 4 pair for 9s.

April. 11.   A very large tide this day which flowed the banks of the meadow nearly to Manwood Bridge[3] and inundated the Great and Little Marsh very considerably.

April 12th.   Went to Mr. Garritt's for a waggon load of turnips and for which I am to keep his sheep in return. . . John Lee began to set potatoes in the Pidgeon House, one acre of which he is to have, he to find seed and workmanship and I to find land and ploughing, and to equally divide the produce.

April 13th.   Paid . . . for a quarter of a peck of best Pyefleet oysters, £0. 1. 0.

April 14th.   Dined at the Whalebone[4] at the Easter Meeting. . . This day Mr. and Mrs. Simson dined and Mr. and Mrs. Balley and John Ward and children drank tea with Mr. Page, Sen., and Mr. Garritt and wife drank tea with Mr. Page jun. Paid Mr. Thos. Jaggard the Poor's rate at six shillings in the pound, £9.

April 15th.   Mr. Daniel Dyer of Stanway lost one of his sons, the younger, a lad about fifteen years old; he spent the evening with his father at the Waggon and Horses, Colchester, went from there at eight in the evening to walk home but has not since been heard of, though the most diligent search has been made and rewards offered. . . Note. Mr. Dyer's was found in a state of profligacy . . . or more properly speaking, he returned home in that state.

Spent at the Whalebone, 1s. Children for fairing, oranges, etc. 6d.

April 18th.   Court held this day at Fingringhoe Hall and dined at the Hall.

April 20th.   Went and dined W. Simson's, Ardleigh. Could not get the colt into the ferry boat, was obliged to swim it through and left it at Mr. Simson's as I came back.

April 22nd.   Wade's man, King, came and put two drawers under my writing desk.

April 24th.   Mr. W. Simson came this morning to sow carrots, but did not, but advised me to plough the land afresh, which I did. We attempted to fish, but did not, the water being high. Mr. W. Simson and Joe Simson dined with me, stopped till past twelve at night and got mellow.

April 26th.   Paid Vincent for a week's work 11s.

April 28th.   Inman carted muck for a cucumber bed.

April 30th.   Self and Vincent went to Mr. Bawtree's[5] with twenty five coombs of barley and brought a quarter of a chaldron of coals back from Mr. Blyth's.

Mr. Garritt and self went to Colchester yesterday and bought a chaff engine of Mr. Walliss and for which we agreed to pay jointly.

May 1st.   Mr. Westney, Mrs. Cheek, Mr. and Miss Sadler of Mersey drank tea with Mrs. Page, jun.

May 2nd.   Bought a cow of Master Hollis for the sum of ten guineas. The cow is said to be within a fortnight of her calving.

May 3rd.   Spent at Wivenhoe for cyder   1s.
    Paid Mr. Miller a bill for clothes   £5 11s. 0
    Paid Mr. Bowland a bill for rum and brandy   £2 19. 0
    Received of Mr. John Bawtree for 12½ qrs of barley
    at 63s. per quarter   £39. 7. 6.

May 4th.   Gave Vincent for ploughing the Dovehouse field well,   1s.
May 8th   Ben Sebborn, jun., for 4 young rabbits,   2s.
May 9th   Paid Mr. Wm. Simson, Sen., for twelve pounds of
    carrotseed   £1. 10. 0.

May 11th.   Went to Church and then went, self and wife, and drank tea with Mr. Garritt.

May 12th.   In the evening Garritt and self went a-shooting sea swallows but had bad sport.

May 14th.   Brought home from Colchester a grate to be put behind the fire in the kitchen.

May 15th.   Day, the bricklayer, came and put a grate up behind the kitchen coal range.

May 16th.   Perkings hoed wheat ½ day in Nine Acres, then made holiday because of the rain. . . Day, the bricklayer, finished whitening the own and maid servants' sleeping rooms.

May 17th.   Paid Day, the bricklayer, for 3 days work 7s.

May 18th.   Edward Wade's man, King, came yesterday and new leathered the pump . . . and put a new bucket on, which did not throw water right owing to his putting the leather on too deep.

May 21st.   With Mr. Garritt to Layer for the cricket playing between L. de Lay-hay and its vicinity and the players of Stanway and Fordham jointly. The match being put off for some days, Mr. Garritt and self paid a visit to Mr. Sam. Garritt of Messing. Drank tea and smoked pipes.

May 26th.   Mr. Garritt came and pumped water as my men washed his sheep with mine. Then Vincent and Lines got water to brew and ground malt. Self went to Rowhedge to meet Mr. Simson to go and look at some grass of Mr. Corsellis' by the Old Hythe Marsh, that was to sell. . . Mr. Simson and myself agreed to hire them together.

May 27th.   Vincent brewed.

May 28th.   Vincent . . . assisted to tun the beer.
    Expenses at the Club,[6] Wivenhoe, and for sundries, 4s.

May 29th.   Heffil, the butcher of Wivenhoe, came and took 3 lambs part of eight that he bought of me yesterday for the sum of twenty five shillings per head. Self went Captain Baker's sale, Wivenhoe, then came home and dined. Then self, wife and 2 children went and drank tea with Mr. Jas. Mansfield, Colchester.

May 30th.   Thorp, the collarmaker, and his man came and repaired the harness. . . My 25 sheep sheared only 40lbs. of wool.

June 1st.   Yesterday in the evening Mr. Garritt and self, Lines and Vincent went fishing in the river, took several good eels and roach and other fish and one bream.

June 3rd.   Self at twelve o'clock went and dined at Wm. Simson's, Ardleigh, and fished his ponds.

June 5th.   Mr. Joe Simson for two gallons of gin, 17s.

June 6th.   Edward Simson returned from the East Indias, having been gone about 26 months in Lord Duncan Indiaman. Gave Mrs. Simson's nurse girl for finding a guinea that I lost on the bed . . . out of my pocket when sleeping at her house . . . 2s.

June 9th.   Two Workhouse boys Saturday and today, weeding. Perkings came in the morning and took beer for the day but did no work.

June 10th.   The Club dinner at the Rose and Crown, Wivenhoe.
Sunday expenses, and at the club, gave ferryman for sitting up, 6s. 6d.

June 11th.   At noon wife, self and two children went and dined at Mr. Dunnage's, Colchester.

June 13th.   Went to Joe Simson's. I was there to ferret and shoot rats. We killed about 50.

June 15th.   Went to Church. Did not go in, being so late.

June 16th.   Vincent and Lines and old Morris began to cut Rye grass and trefoil . . . two Workhouse boys picking twitch.

June 20th.   Lee and self bent some boughs and trees to make an arbour at the N.E. corner of the back garden and bent a fir tree in the serpentine walk going to the coffee house to make the shade more perfect.

June 22nd.   Settled with George Rayner for the Workhouse boys for twelve days, but 1s. 6d. too much, paid him 6d. per day each, 12s.

June 25th.   Mr. Josselyn and his housekeeper and two daughters came and dined. . . They left a post chaise at Wivenhoe and had it over in the evening at low water.

June 26th.   Expenses at Abberton fair, 1s. 6d.

June 27th.   Went and fetched Mrs. Dunnage and Miss Terry to dine with Mrs. Page and carried them home in the evening.

July 2nd.   Wife went in a post chaise to Dovercourt with Mrs. Dunnage and Miss Terry. Self rode on a horse. Expenses going to Harwich 13s. 3d.

July 8th.   A lb of tea, 4s. 4d.

July 10th.   Received of Norman, the butcher, for two sheep and two lambs, £5. 10. 0.

July 12th.   Paid Ralton for a post chaise a day, £1. 12. 10.

July 13th.   Expenses at Colchester with a design to have Henry Baker re-examined (respecting the settlement of his wife and family) before he took his trial this day for robbing the barn of Mr. John Bloomfield of Beerchurch, for which offence he was transported for the term of seven years.

July 23rd.   Bought a cricket bat for Abberton Club, 3s.

July 29th.   Played cricket on Abberton Green with ten others against eleven of Maldon, but got beat. The first innings there was but three runs difference in favour of Maldon, the second innings they got with great ease.

August 2nd.   Vincent and Lines both left me to go to harvest, Lines with L. Stone, the other with R. Stone.

August 23rd.   Settled with John Morris before a bench of Justices before whom he summoned me, but had to pay the expenses himself and I compelled him to pay ¾ of a year's rent.

Aug. 4th.   Morris mowed 2 acres of oats in street field.

     5th.   Morris began to reap wheat in barn field. . . Old Inman helped ½ day.

     6th.   Ann Smyth raked. Self, Inman, Hoy carted, but Inman, being ill, left off and in his stead set Thompson the blacksmith on, who worked ½ day. Morris rept as yesterday; Leonard Felgate ½ day carting instead of self, as Mr. Merchant and his daughter and Mrs. Garritt and Mr. Love came and dined with me.

Aug. 7th.   Felgate and Hoy and old Morris finished carting oats out of Orchard field. A stranger came at 10 o'clock. . . Ann Smyth raked. Self went with Winstree Hundred Club and played cricket with the Maldon Club, which beat the Winstree Club and 57 runs over. Self got home about 10 in the evening.

Aug. 8th.   Felgate and stranger began to reap in Nine Acres. Morris reaped in barn field. Hoy and self fetched two loads of wheat out of Street field, then travd. sheaves.

Aug. 9th.   Felgate and Hoy fetched oats out of Street field and began to stack them, then fetched three loads out of Hall field. Morris mowed barley. Stranger repd in Nine Acres. Ann Smyth raked. Finished Street field, then began the Hall field.

    Felgate for 2½ days carting, 7s. 6d.

    Stranger   Do   7s.

    Felgate and stranger for reaping 9 acres of wheat at 8s.   £3. 12. 0.

Aug. 12th.   Sold to Mr. John Balls, sen., two bullocks for the sum of 23 pounds.

Aug. 13th.   Boy dew-raking Hall field and gathering the dew-rakings. Self jobbed. Miss Terry and Mr. Mansfield came and dined with us this day. Morris reaping and Felgate and other reaping. Day, the bricklayer, here, jobbing.

Aug. 15th.   N.W. Wind and very hot and remarkable dusty. Self went to Chelmsford to have Baker sworn to his settlement. Felgate and his partner reaped. Morris part of the day but went into the river to grubbing of eels, as did James Cole and Tom Jennings. Frank, the miller, and Hollis assisted them on the outside, as did Tom Jenning's man — knowing I was not at home. Boy reaped in river field.

Note: There was five men executed at Chelmsford this day, three for house-breaking and the other two for killing and stealing a calf. They were penitent.

Aug. 24th.   A very wet day. Went to Church but did not go in, being so late.

Aug. 26th.   Men with John Jennings turned barley, viz. Felgate, John Jennings, Self and boy carted. Suffolk with Ann Smyth gathered till about four clock and then left off carting owing to showers . . . that frequently came over all day and prevented the corn drying.

Aug. 30th.   Felgate and stranger went and tied up the beans and peas in

Street field. Then settled with them for their harvest. The stranger went home.

Felgate and stranger for harvesting   £6. 9. 9.
Ann Smyth for raking   10s.
Boy Hoy for harvesting 5 days   6s.

Sept. 2nd.   Mr. Sam Bawtree and his friend came and shot with me, and Sam Bawtree gave me an invitation to dine with him, but did not.

Sept. 4th.   Mr. John Bawtree and Mr. Wm. Mason, jun., and John Mason came and shot with me. Mr. Bawtree shot one bird, the other gents not any. They left off between one and two o'clock, took some refreshment and then went home much pleased with 2½ brace of birds and hare which I gave them.

Sept. 6th.   Paid three soldiers for threshing wheat, 7s.

Sept. 9th.   Vincent came and began with the boy to plough in the Hall field. ennings came and finished the thatching on the Oat Stack.

Sept. 10th.   Vincent . . . helped boy and self gather apples.

Sept. 11th.   Self and boy picked apples.

Sept. 12th.   Vincent carting beans for R. Stone, where he harvested.

Sept. 13th.   Self went to Colchester, being summoned by the Commissioners to give an account of my income, which they set at £80 a year.

Sept. 14th.   Sunday, Drank tea at T. Simson's, Elmstead.

Sept. 15th.   Pleasant, but a fog in the morning. Self went with E. Simson in Martin Sadler's vessel to see a sailing match from a boat in the River Colne round a boat about 8 miles distance for a silver cup and sundries.

Sept. 16th.   E. Simson came and shot with me, as did Mr. John Mason. The Mr. Simsons dined and slept here.

Received of Pitcher, the butcher, for 6 sheep, £6. 12. 0.

Sept. 17th.   The Mr. Simsons shot as yesterday, stopped and dined and drank tea and then went home.

Sept. 18th.   Boy carried partidges to Mr. T. Cooper and Mrs. Cannings for E. Simson and Capt. Beaumonts. . . Vincent brewed. A deaf and dumb man came a half day and threshed.

Sept. 23rd.   Vincent began to plough in Nine Acres for tares. Self rang pigs and jobbed. Then went shooting. Self went to sale at the Customs House and bought 9 gallons of gin for Mr. Garritt, self and mother. Man threshed.

Expenses at Colchester for gin, £1. 2. 0.

Sept. 24th.   Paid the remainder for gin at 7s. 10½d. per gallon. Self and men carted coal, 1½ chaldron for self and 3 Do for Mr. Love.

Sept. 25th.   Drank tea with Mr. Garritt and played cricket with some Wivenhoe gentlemen on Hornet Heath in the morning.

Sept. 26th.   Went shooting, killed 2 brace of birds and hare and landrail.

Oct. 3rd.   Vincent and boy went to Verlander's mill with 15 coombs of wheat, sold at £26 per load. . . Self with Mr. John Mason shooting, Dumb man threshed barley.

Oct. 4th.   Recd. of Verlander for 1½ loads of wheat, £39.

Boy Hoy and Chamberlain picked apples, pears and plums.

Oct. 6th.   Shooting for Mr. Corsellis.

Oct. 8th.   Went over to Wivenhoe for some horse flesh.

Oct. 9th.   Dumb threshed barley for pigs, then wheat for seeds. Paid for an old horse to kill for dogs. 18s.

Oct. 10th.   Paid Henry Morris my part of the rent of two marshes containing five acres which Mr. John Garritt and myself hired of him, from May, 1800, up to Michaelmas last, £4.

Oct. 13th.   Self hunted, men ploughed.

Oct. 14th.   Self and wife went to Colchester. Self killed a snipe this day, first I had seen this season.

Oct. 15th.   Self played cricket on Hornet Heath, the best of 20 bowls against Mr. Charles Hitchcock, who went in first and got with his twenty bowls ten runs, but was out the 20th ball. Then I went in and with eighteen balls got eleven runs. Mr. Richard Stone bowled for both parties. At the same time there was cricket playing between Doctor Smyth and Mr. Simson, and a foot race. Also playing by Mr. Ben Stacey and Mr. James Kensale.

Oct. 17th.   Mr. Love . . . left his residence to go and reside in London.

Oct. 18th.   Settled and paid the dumb man, Thos Petley

Qrs	Bushels		£	s.	d.
for 9	2	of wheat at 4s.	1	17.	
Do. 3		of barley at 2s.		6	
Do. 3		of oats at 2s.		6	
Do. 1	1	of beans at 1s. 4d.		1.	6
				___	
	Work all came to		2	10.	6
	Paid in part		2.		6
				___	
	Paid the balance			10.	
	and sixpence towards next dressing			10.	6

Oct. 19th.   Mr. Gennings preached today for the first time as curate for Mr. Love. Self did not go to church being indisposed.

Oct. 20th.   Colchester fair day. Settled with E. Cooper of Oakley for 26 sheep at 18 shillings per head. £23. 8. 0.

Oct. 22nd.   Chamberlain carried barley and wheat, one sack each to grind at the mill. Then self and him carried four pigs to Mr. Sage's at Wivenhoe to be killed and packed for London. Could not get through owing to the water not ebbing out, and so ferried them over in the boat. The Brewer for 4 bushels of grains 15s. John Ladbrook for 6 lambs at 19s. each, £5. 14. 0.

Oct. 28th.   Vincent went to Colchester for a new plough. Self and Mr. Garritt went shooting. Then self went to the Angel Lodge,[7] Colchester. Dumb dressed.

Oct. 31st.   Mr. Edward Cooper of Oakley came and dined and slept at my house and went in the afternoon to look at Mr. L. Stone's turnips and bid him £110 for 18 acres which he refused.

Nov. 2nd.   Recd. of Mr. Taylor for a bushel of apples, 8s.

Nov. 4th.   Went to Hornet Heath to see a bunch of harriers that belongs to the regiment of foot guards stationed at Colchester barracks.

Nov. 5th.   Doctor Smyth came and inoculated my wife and 2 children, Sarah Brig, maidservant, and Sarah Everitt, nursegirl, for the cowpox as a substitute and preventive to the smallpox.

Nov. 10th.   Vincent . . . fetched home from the brick-kiln lime and tiles to repair damages that was done yesterday.

Nov. 12th.   Mr. Sach's hounds hunted a big fox past my house. I mounted my horse and joined them against Donyland church, where they were at a check. Then they hit him off again below Donyland Heath and had slow hunting all the way to the back of the Barracks and into the gardens behind Mr. Tabor's house where he leapt over a very high boarded fence into a yard and from thence on to a building belonging to Mr. Tabor, where I climbed up and found him in a lead gutter . . . from whence he ran on to a house fronting nearly the Custom House. I then got from off the house where I first found him. I then got upon a lean-to that adjoined the house, from which I climbed up on to the house where he was and ran him along the gable part of the roof fronting the street, where he looked down to the no small amusement of some hundreds of spectators. He then turned along downwards towards the river where I followed him across the roof of several houses until a man met him on the roof. He then ran and jumped from building to building to the ground in sight of the whole bunch of hounds, who killed him after running about one hundred yards.

Nov. 13th.   Vincent not coming in the morning till past 6 o'clock and this not being the first time of his neglect, I discharged him.

Nov. 14th. Went about ½ past eleven to Mr. Jo Simson's to meet Mr. Fenn and Wm. Simson to shoot rabbits.

Nov. 15th.   Went to town and in the evening went . . . to Astley's Equestrian Riding School in a temporary building of wood in the Castle yard.

Nov. 24th.   Isaac Bunton, who came last night to live with me for a fortnight for 16s. 6d., stopped gaps in Cockcoombs. Went with Mr. Edward Sage to dine with Mr. Sam. Simonds of Brightlandsea Hall where I made an agreement with him, Sam. Simonds, to cultivate a field containing seventeen acres and sow with carrots. . . Mr. Simonds finds the field and ploughs and harrows it and to cart the produce; and I to find seed, sowing, hoeing and takeing up the produce; and the crop to be equally divided, unless Mr. Simonds take the whole and pays me the half of what the whole crop may be worth according to a fair market price.

Nov. 25th.   Chamberlain carried 24 bushels of carrots to Dr. Smyth's Wivenhoe.

Nov. 27th.   Self went to Langenhoe Hall to pay Mr. Thos. Cooper the tythe.

Nov. 30th.   Mr. Mason, sen., came to Fingringhoe Hall to receive the rents, where I paid for the fields.

Dec. 4th.   Went to Colchester to Mas. Griggs with 21 bushels of potatoes at 2s. 6d. per bushel and seven quarters of oats to the Marquis of Granby, which I sold to a quarter-master of the name of Woodhouse in the 3rd Regiment of Dragoons at 46s. per qr.

Dec. 13th.   This day at Colchester Market wheat fetched the astonishing price of 40 guineas per load, but £40 currently.

Dec. 14th.   This day in the morning service Mr. Gennings, the Curate, read a proclamation from the King recommending in a very forcible manner to the masters of all families to lessen as much as possible the consumption of bread, as the average crop of the last harvest, 1800, falls short of a fair average crop full one fourth . . . and also to restrict as much as possible the consumption of oats by pleasure horses.

Dec. 16th.   Went shooting, killed a hare, woodcock and snipe.

Dec. 19th.   In the forenoon General Egerton and Col. Fitzroy called me to go and shoot with them, as I did about 2 hours, but not liking their company and having left my powder horn at home or lost it, I returned home. Fitzroy shot several times but killed nought the time I was with them. In the evening went and smoked with Mr. Garritt.

Dec. 23rd.   Chamberlain and Denny went to Wivenhoe . . . and brought home a barrel of porter from Mr. Bawtree and a dozen of wine and a gallon of rum and bottle of brandy from Mr. Stacey's, Wivenhoe. Went and dined with Mr. John Fenn, Ardleigh.

Dec. 24th.   Chamberlain went to Mr. John Dunnage's, Colchester, with 12 coombs of wheat, sold on Saturday at £42 per load. Mr. John Garritt and self caught eels in the afternoon.

Dec. 25th.   Chamberlain fetched Miss Terry to dine with Mrs. Page and stay a few days.

Dec. 26th   Gardener here. Chamberlain and Denny carted halm. Petley threshed a little but not much. Gave workmen and servants and tenants their dinners. Mr. and Mrs. Garritt drank tea with us in the evening.

Dec. 27th.   Self went to Colchester to dine with the Masons of the Angel Lodge, but was disappointed, it being put off till Tuesday.

Dec. 30th.   Went to Colchester in the afternoon and bought a saddle of Hellen for a guinea, but, he saying that he sold it too cheap, gave him sixpence more.

1801

Jan. 2nd.   A large flood. Self with Henry Stammers rowed a boat over the walls of the different marshes up to John Cooper's.

Jan. 3rd.   Went to Colchester in the cart and carried Miss Terry home.

Jan. 6th.   Went shooting.

Jan. 8th.   Went shooting at Mr. Pearson's, Layer.

Jan. 12th.   Sold to Hubbard of Peldon the 5 acres of turnips before the house for 21 guineas.

Jan. 13th.   Went, the cow leech, went to Oakley for a gun that I had lent to John Josselyn 2 years since and which he promised to send home but did not. Gave Went 2s. 6d. for fetching it.

Jan. 14th.   Went hunting with Sach's hounds.

Jan. 20th.   John Dancy carried 10 coombs of barley to Mr. Bawtree's and brought home a barrel of porter.

Jan. 22nd.   Went to Manwood to meet Mr. Pearson to shoot. Then he came and dined with me, as did Mr. Sam. Simonds of Brightlingsea.

Jan. 24th.   Pd. Mr. Bawtree for 2 barrels of porter £4 16. 0.

Feb. 2nd.   Paid at a parish meeting 6d.

Feb. 4th.   Paid at the Club 6s.

Feb. 7th.   John Jennings, a week's work, 12s.

Feb. 9th.   Petley. . . Paid him off, not being satisfied with his wages.

Feb. 10th.   Went to Custom House, Colchester, and bought 8 gallons of gin at 8s. 10½d. and 10 gallons for Mr. Jo Simson.

Feb. 13th.   Paid Mr. Stacey a bill for wine, £2. 14. 5.
          Paid Mr. Tod of Wivenhoe for a boat, etc., £3. 4. 6.

Feb. 16th.   Bradley, the carpenter, fitting up the knees for the cart lodge. Went with Doctor Went to shoot fowl; there was a great many. I killed a pair, lost one.

Feb. 19th.   Went in the morning to Major Rebow's[3] to make application for Elmstead fen, and in the afternoon Jennings and self tunned beer.

Feb. 28th.   The girl Hart for 2½ days work, 1s. 10½d.

March 2nd.   Bradley making a tray to pickle meat in. At the Plough and parish meeting, Fingringhoe, 2s. 6d.

March 3rd.   Mr. Agniss for fruit trees, etc. 17s. 6d.

March 18th.   Bought a sixteenth share of a lottery ticket £1. 6. 0.

March 23rd.   Went hunting . . . and stopped at Mr. Hunt's Colchester. Dined with him and went to see him and others play at billiards.

March 24th.   Went to Abberton Lion, being subpoenaed on an inquisition taken on the body of Moses Tracey, who was found dead in a field.

March 31st.   Mr. Hedge for 2 pistols £2.

April 3rd.   Went to Church, being Good Friday.

April 5th.   Paid the ferrymen for putting a cart over and horse three times, 3s.

April 10th.   Self dined at Fingringhoe Hall, being Court Day.

April 13th.   Green, Loyd and Medstone came and began to get ready to lay a sluice on the Great Marsh.

April 17th.   Self very ill, kept the bed.

April 21st.   Wife for sundries, £4. 15. 0.

April 23rd.   Recd. of Mr. Edward Sage for seven pigs, sent to London, £7. 12. 0.

May 4th.   Sold a barometer to Talesmenzi 10s. 6d.
              Bought a Do. of him, £2 12. 6.

May 13th.   Day, the bricklayer, came . . . whiting the house.

May 14th.   Self, wife and two children went and dined with Hugh Josselyn of Mount Bures; returned home at night.

May 20th.   Self dined at Rose and Crown, Wivenhoe, being the expiration of the annual club kept there.

May 23rd.   John Cole, a bill for mending shoes and schooling for daughter, Mary, 11s. Went, the horse doctor, a bill, 18s.

May 24th.   I had four sheep died without any visible cause and another the butcher killed, being ill; the remaining 29 Went the doctor bled, as I did 2 of the others that died. Several others were ill, but did not die. We examined the stomach of them that died, but could not discover anything that we supposed to be the reason.

May 31st.   Got ready for brewing. . . A man came from Mr. Francis's of Tolleshunt Darcy with a stallion. . . A parish meeting.

June 3rd.   Bought a looking glass of Galli, an Italian 4s. 6d.

June 7th.   Went to see Mr. R. Westney, he being very ill.

June 11th.   Old man went to carting gravel in the highways.

June 14th.   After tea self and wife and Joe and Mary rode as far as Capt. Beaumond's and carried home his gun that I have had ever since the last partridge shooting season commenced.

June 15th.   Paid Sue Bloomfield for spun yarn, 12s.

June 21st.   A great concourse of people assembled at Fingringhoe Church this day to hear psalm singing, there being upwards of twenty vocal and instrumental performers. The Church was completely crowded; the aisles as well as the chancel and porch were completely filled. Edward Firmin, many years fore man at Fingringhoe Mill, was interred in the church yard this afternoon.

June 22nd.   Self in the afternoon after tea played cricket.

June 23rd.   Paid the first instalment of the Income Tax, 3s.

June 24th.   After tea, wife and self and children went to Abberton Fair, see a hobby race.

June 25th.   Self went to Abberton Fair and played cricket, the Winstree Hundred Club against the Gentlemen of Mersea Island, where we beat and 36 runs over.

July 4th.   Geo. Chamberlain, a week's work, 12s.
            Poll Hart for 5½ days, 4s. 7d.
            Old Levitt, a week's work, 9s. 6d.

July 14th.   Wife and self went to Harwich.

July 15th.   Rained nearly all day — Note St. Swithin. Returned from Harwich, stopped at John Josselyn's at Oakley to dinner, got wet coming home.

July 16th.   Fenning, Robinson, Bailey and Bartle began to clear the side of the river round the Little Marsh.

July 17th.   Wm. Simson of Ardleigh came, and he and I went to grubbing eels out of the river.

July 20th.   For some little time our steeple of the church has been repairing and this afternoon the weather-cock was re-put up and fresh guilt by Sanford of Wivenhoe.

July 22nd.   Paid two soldiers for mowing 3¼ acres of tares, 10s.

July 28th.   Wife, self and children went down to Wivenhoe to see a ship launched, then went over to Mr. Simsons to tea with Mr. Harvey who married Mr. T. Osborne's daughter of London who piloted a ship to Harwich and returned to London by land and in his way stopped two days with Mr. Simson of Elmstead.

July 29th.   Wife and self went to Colchester and in the afternoon came Mr. and Mrs. Tracy and Mr. Stone, Mr. Garritt, Mr. Bloomfield of Beerchurch and several others, and after tea played cricket.

August 1st.   Paid Shepherd Stammers for 2½ chaldron of best Newcastle coals, £4. 10. 0.

Aug. 6th.   This day old Levitt began his month at 16s. per week.

Aug. 10th.   This day about 2 o'clock Mr. Benjamin Page, my brother-in-Law, put a period to his existence by drowning himself below Wivenhoe Wood in the River Colne.

Sept. 4th.   Expenses at Wivenhoe Fair, 4s.

Sept. 12th.   Mr. George Wishart of Dedham for 2 gallons of rum £1. 11. 0.

Sept. 17th.   Mr. Samuel Tracy for 2 gallons of brandy   £1. 5. 0.

Oct. 14th.   This day much rejoicing took place here on account of a peace being made between Great Britain and the French Republic. The morning was ushered in by ringing of bells and firing of cannon and the tops of houses and other conspicuous places was decorated with flags of various devices. Two large booths were erected on the Green and, to add to the general festivity, a bullock was roasted whole and filled with potatoes, and a great deal of beer with other liquors was given to the populace, all at the expense of John W. Cooper, except the 2½ bushels of flour which was the gift of Thos. Jaggard of this place which was made into puddings and dumplings; and a quantity of carrots and potatoes given by myself; and also a hogshead of good beer by John Bawtree,

Esq. It was supposed that the number of people of all descriptions assembled was not less than fifteen hundred. Upwards of seventy lbs. of gunpowder was fired away with an abundance of fireworks of different sorts. The beef was intended to be cut up and divided between the inhabitants of this parish, but, as soon as it was began to be divided the mob broke in and took it, even off the plates of those gentlemen that were eating it. Some of the most resolute amongst the rabble got large pieces, while numbers were not able to procure a morsel. A large furnace was erected near the hedge opposite the Whalebone by Barton of Wivenhoe. The bullock was put to the fire about 12 o'clock last night and taken up between 5 and 6 this afternoon and, considering the cook which consisted of the greatest part of the lower order of people in the parish, it was very well dressed, but not a seat could be found in the Whalebone or in the booths owing to such an unusual number of spectators.

October 15th. The rejoicing begun yesterday continued today. A vast number of intoxicated men, with flags flying and firing of cannon, paraded about the parish, dragging the cannon with them. About 10 in the morning the whole assemblage went to John Cooper's, where they continued for several hours drinking of punch and firing of cannon, and in the afternoon returned to the Whalebone with Cooper at their head, singing of God Save The King and other songs of victory, where they numbers of them continued in till late at night on the 17th instant. It is said and generally believed that this rejoining, expence of which principally falls on John Cooper, will cost him upwards of One Hundred Pounds.

May 17th, 1802. Another violent storm of snow and hail, so much that it covered the ground completely and in many places, where it drove, it lay more than a foot deep and continued upon the ground for several days. . . Great damage was done to the fruit trees.

Oct. 11th, 1802. This morning Mr. Wm. Simson, with his brother Edward, came and went a'shooting and, as we were returning home to dinner across Mr. T. Cooper's Stoney field, John Bawtree, the brewer, came to us and, after giving us some insulting language, threatened to lay an information. . . On the Thursday following Nandy, that keeps Colchester gaol, served us with a summons to appear at Colchester Castle on Saturday, the 16th, instant, as Wm. and I did, with Mr. Sergeant the attorney. . . Bawtree began saying we shot at his tame partridges, which we did not; he then said many other frivolous things. . . . After some conversation from Mr. Sargeant, Bawtree said that if we paid the expences already incurred, he should think no more upon the subject, which by Mr. Sergeant's advice we consented to and the business finished to the amusement of most present more than to John Bawtree's. Note. The expences amounted seven shillings each, one guinea in the whole.

Feb. 14th, 1803. This day there was much bell-ringing at Wivenhoe in consequence of them having six new bells. The parishioners invited some men from the parish of Great Tey to ring them for the first time, which they did to the satisfaction of all present, they being quite proficient in the art. The wind being at about West they were not heard very distinctly at Fingringhoe, but I being in the North Geeton Marsh, shooting wild fowl with John Gill, Esq., the sound of the bells there had a very pleasing effect.

Thurs. 21st of July, 1803, at a parish meeting at the Whalebone the principal inhabitants then assembled did appoint the different situations of persons to act as guides, conductors of teams and drivers of teams and every other kinds of cattle from off the sea coast to some more upland place, and also took the names of all the men to act as occasion may require, some with guns, others with pitchforks, mattocks, spades, shovels, hooks, axes and all kinds of offensive weapons to repel the threatening attack of our enemies, the French.

22nd. July, 1803. The Cheshire Militia marched from Colchester to Langenhoe Common, commonly called Abberton Green, and there encamped.

Friday, October 14th, 1803. Lieutenant Jones of the Royal Engineers, accompanied by 25 men of the East Norfolk Militia, began to erect a battery on Hornet Heath, opposite Wivenhoe, to protect the hardway over Wivenhoe ferry in case of invasion. . . On Sunday the 23rd was landed on the ferry bridge, Fingringhoe, the stores, consisting of shot round and grape gunpowder and other materials, and on the following day 4 pieces of cannon, two for the battery on Hornet Heath and the other for batteries at the Strood, Mersea Island. Self carted up Clovers from the Marsh below and likewise the guns and other material.

IX

JOHN CARTER, COLCHESTER TAILOR, 1804–44

Carter's merits are displayed in what he writes and in the clear, forceful way in which he writes it. Hailed by his publishers as representative of a growing band of self-educated workingmen and, by implication, presented as a credit to the new social order of early Victorian England, Carter may today be thought to have shown himself rather as its victim. His is a pathetic story. This able, thoughtful, courageous and responsible man not only failed to achieve that economic success and independence that enterprise and thrift were then said to ensure, but, in the process of failure, he ruined his own health and probably his family's happiness. Such literary recognition as he achieved was by the charity of men obviously his inferiors, yet he was so dependent upon them in his search for acknowledgement and publication that he sincerely believed them his 'superiors in all respects.'

Carter's acceptance of respectable values affected his writing. He would never have credited it, had he been told that many of his readers of a century and a half later would most have enjoyed reading from his pen a first-hand account of the working life of a tailor, both as an employee in a large establishment and as a struggling master. He could also have given interesting details of the diet, sleeping and washing arrangements and other routine matters in his domestic life. It would have been a document unique among Essex historical sources. The few remarks which he does make about his working and domestic life are so interesting that we can only regret their paucity. Again, the few glimpses given of his workmates' attempts at Trade Union organisation and of the radical politics current amongst them remind us how little we know of the outlook of the Essex working class in this formative period of its development. Perhaps there was some radical passage in Carter's own past life which he wanted to forget – there are hints of this – and he may therefore have avoided dwelling upon these controversial issues. In any case the values accepted by him led him to consider such matters hardly worthy of prolonged description.

In these *Memoirs of a Working Man* John Carter so exactly describes his own career that no account of it is needed in this foreword. For reasons unclear he did not put his name to the work and he even refers to Colchester only as 'a large and pleasantly situated market town, which is remarkable for its antiquity.' He was also the author of 'The Guide to Trade' and 'The Manual for Apprentices to Tailors', both technical works, and of 'Lectures on Taste', comprising the lectures given to Colchester Literary Society, to which he refers in his *Memoirs*. In 1850 was published a *Continuation* of his *Memoirs*.

In the following pages these parts of the *Memoirs* are reproduced: pp. 67–76, 88–90, 93–95, 114, 161–163, 166–167, 169–172, 182–184, 194–195, 206–213, 215–216, 228–229, 233. No copies of the book seem to be available locally. It was published in 1845 by Charles Knight and Co., London.

WHEN the time of my going to school was ended, the question arose how I should be disposed of so as to be made useful. I was much too feeble to be put to any very laborious occupation, while my parents were too poor to be able to apprentice me to any suitable trade. Thus there seemed to be no good prospect in regard to my future lot. I was indeed still young, being not more than twelve and a half years old; yet I felt it was high time to be learning something by which to get a living. After much thought it occurred to me that I might perhaps obtain one in the capacity of a domestic servant.

To this occupation therefore my wishes were directed, but no situation could for a time be procured. Meanwhile my mother kept me employed in the usual way; besides which I undertook the task of teaching my sister the elements of writing and arithmetic. I also endeavoured to carry on the work of self-instruction, both in these and other respects. Yet, as I saw that neither of these exercises would procure me a maintenance, I was but "ill at ease" in regard to either present circumstances or future prospects.

At length, with the consent of my parents, I went out to seek employment. I did this, however, with much diffidence, being conscious of my inability to do any work that required much strength or skill. After some fruitless inquiries, I at length succeeded in getting employment. This was to look after some horses that were feeding off the hedge-rows in a potato field. They were tethered to the hedge, and my duty was to tether them in a fresh place when they had eaten all the forage within their reach. I managed to do this pretty well, although at first with much timidity, as I was but little acquainted with the art of managing horses. Ere long, however, I acquired some courage, and, in the end, more than was consistent with discretion, for on untethering one of the horses in order to give him fresh pasturage, it came into my head that I should like to ride him for a short time. The wish was soon followed by a determination to gratify it, and accordingly I mounted him. He was a powerful beast and, as I soon discovered, of a vicious temper. As I had never been on a horse's back, I was ill prepared to control an animal like this, if he became restive, especially as I had only a halter to hold him by. The result was that he quickly threw me off and ran away, leaving me much frightened, but not so severely hurt as I might have expected to be. The horse remained at liberty until my master came into the field. I was mildly reproved for my fault and retained in my employment until all the hedge-rows were fed off, when I was discharged. From this adventure I learnt a little prudence, which was of great use to me when subsequently it became part of my duty to attempt managing a horse.

Seeing my ill success, my parents resolved to wait patiently until some suitable occupation could be procured for me; I therefore continued to perform my usual duties, with no other variety than that of an occasional journey with my worthy master, when he went from home on his land-measuring business.

At length however, a place was found for me, to which I went on July 1, 1805, at which time I was not quite thirteen years old. Here I continued until I was qualified to be my own master. My going to this situation I regard as having been by far the most important incident of my early years, inasmuch as all my subsequent experience took its general complexion therefrom. Perhaps, therefore, I may be forgiven if I somewhat minutely describe its duties.

My master[1] was a woollen-draper, in a good way of business. He also carried on the trade of a tailor, but as he did not understand this, he employed a man to

H

manage it for him. My wages were three shillings and sixpence per week, and I had a few trifling perquisites, which might amount to about fourpence more. My parents provided me with food, clothing, and lodging, so that my remuneration was small, considering the amount of labour I had to give in exchange. My duties were neither few nor pleasant; for I was expected to be ready at the call of not fewer than twenty-one persons, namely, my master and mistress, five children, two maid-servants, a shopman, two apprentices, a foreman and eight journeymen. I hardly need say that I always found it difficult and sometimes impossible to please this large number of people. I honestly endeavoured to please all, but in my well-meant efforts to achieve this, I often, like the old man in the fable, failed to satisfy any one, and consequently was in rather general disgrace, to my great discomfort and discouragement.

I eventually saw that I had been toiling at a hopeless task, and therefore resolved thenceforth to do the best I could, without troubling myself about the consequences. . . My first care was to please my master and mistress, who were very exact in all their affairs; but as I always had a strong predilection for order and regularity in everything with which I was concerned, I found no great difficulty in pleasing them.

The children were not backward in claiming my services, yet I had no reason to complain of the manner in which they treated me. One of them, indeed, treated me with remarkable kindness, both then and subsequently, as I shall have occasion to notice in the sequel.

The maid-servants were worthy persons, for whom I readily did all the little services I could, and thus secured not only their good will, but also their active kindness, for they frequently gave me what was very acceptable to a hungry boy. I had but little encouragement to serve the shopman and apprentices further than I was obliged, for they often made me do nearly all their share of the shopwork, while they were either quite idle or employed about some trifling matter.

The tailors were rough masters, but in general they were not unreasonable. Most of them, including the foreman, were very ignorant men, while all were, more or less, of dissolute habits. As my chief occupation was in matters connected with the tailoring business, I was necessarily much in the workshop, where usually I saw and heard not a little of what was either foolish or wicked. . .

I have said that my duties were numerous as well as onerous. This will be manifest when I state the various items which entered into the account of each day's labour. My regular working-hours were from five o'clock in the morning until after sunset during summer, and from day-break until about nine o'clock in the evening during the winter, abating half an hour at breakfast-time and an hour for dinner. But when work was plentiful or was wanted by any given time, I was required to be at the shop both earlier and later than the hours here named. My first business in the morning was to sweep the workshop, kindle the fire used for heating the pressing-irons, sift coals and cinder-ashes in order to get coal-dust and cinders for fuel, clean several dozens of knives and forks, and sometimes assist in opening and cleaning the woollen-drapery shop. When I had got through these jobs it was time to get my breakfast. After I had done this, I was generally employed by the tailors in fetching the irons, tending the fire in which they were heated, matching cloths or trimmings, brushing clothes, or cleaning buttons. I was frequently sent out with parcels of cloth or with clothes; in fact I was kept almost incessantly occupied until dinner-time. My afternoon's duties were not much different from those of the morning, either in number or kind, except that I was then sent, perhaps several times, to the public house to get beer for the tailors. Sometimes I was sorely annoyed by this extra duty, not only because I disliked their half-drunken frolics, but also because I was hereby deprived of nearly all the little leisure which fell to my lot; the time for this, when it did offer, being commonly in the latter part of the afternoon, which was just the time that the men chose for their drinking bouts. After they had left work it was my further duty to shut up the shop, put out the fire and take home such garments as were wanted by the customers. Before I could get through these matters it was high time to get my supper and prepare for bed.

It will hence appear that I had but little time to spare for my own use. This, however, was a privation which, of all others, I was the least willing to endure. I wanted a little reading time, and as I had none allowed me, I determined upon making some. For this purpose I arose earlier from bed, read while walking or eating and took care not to waste the spare minutes which sometimes fell to my lot in the course of my working-hours. By this means I saved more time in the aggregate than I had previously thought to be possible. It was indeed made up of fragments, yet I contrived to make it answer my purposes. I had been made the more anxious to get some spare time, because several books I had not before seen now fell in my way. This was through the courtesy of my young master, whose kindly feelings I have already noticed. He now gave me free access to his little library, in which were Enfield's "Speaker", Goldsmith's "Geography", an abridged "History of Rome", a "History of England", Thomson's "Seasons", "The Citizen of the World", "The Vicar of Wakefield", and some other books. . . . I perused each of them, but especially the "Seasons". I found this to be just the book I had long wanted. It commended itself to my warmest approbation, immediately on my perceiving its character and design. I do not go beyond the truth when I state that the perusal of this volume was of great help to me in the way of preserving me from the depraved tastes and habits of those with whom my duty compelled me to associate. When I was about fifteen years old, I bought a miniature copy, which from that time until I had reached the age of twenty years I usually kept in my pocket. It was my custom to read each poem in that season of the year to which it refers. . . The pleasure with which I at first perused the "Seasons" was much enhanced by an illusion quite natural to an imaginative and inexperienced mind. I did not then know that the poet's business is rather to present pictures of what ought to be than of what really is; and therefore I regard Thomson's beautiful and impressive descriptions of rural life and manners as being strictly in accordance with existing realities.

On another occasion I was sent to a village about four miles distant, my path to which was upon the top of a clay-wall, which kept the stream it bounded from overflowing the neighbouring marshes. It was winter-time – there was much snow on the ground – the ditches, pools, and (in some places) the river also, were covered with ice. There was a cutting wind, and I was but thinly clad. I remember to have felt cold and cheerless, as I wended my way through a scene which to me seemed dreary and desolate. When I approached the place of my destination I found that I had taken the wrong path, for the river, which I ought to have crossed at the outset of my walk, now rolled betwixt me and the place in question. The only way of getting across was by a ferry-boat; but here a new difficulty presented itself, for I had no money. The ferry-man was not to be moved by a tale of distress, but insisted on having his fare, in hard cash or goods. I had nothing wherewith to satisfy his demands, except a pocket-knife; this, therefore, I left with him as a pledge until my return. I then redeemed it, with a penny borrowed of the good man to whom I had been sent.

This journey was the means of giving my health a shock from which it has never yet recovered, nor ever will recover. My feeble and much overworked frame was ill-prepared for an encounter with the "biting frost" and the bitterly cold wind which then assailed it; and the consequence was that I soon after-wards became seriously ill. I was confined to my dwelling, and in a great degree to my bed, for five weeks, during the greater part of which time it was doubtful whether I should ever again go abroad. The chief symptoms were a severe cough, copious night-sweats, much debility and loss of appetite. I do not remember that I had any medical advice or assistance until towards the close of the five weeks above referred to. My parents did their best to promote both my comfort and my restoration to health; but all they were able to do amounted to but little on account of their straightened circumstances. These were now made still narrower by the loss of my wages, which, though small, were yet an im-portant addition to their scanty income. All they received during my illness, in abatement of their loss, was two shillings and a small piece of mutton. . . I should not, indeed, have noted down these particulars, but for the light they throw upon circumstances which, although very common, are nevertheless much overlooked. I refer to the peculiar difficulties attendant upon the illness of working people, who, when their condition requires increased comforts, are, by the failure of their income, frequently rendered unable to procure even the common necessaries of life.

The general election consequent upon the breaking up of Lord Grenville's administration, in the spring of 1807, gave me the means of adding a little more to my knowledge of the world. I could not, indeed, interpret rightly all that I saw and heard, but I could, nevertheless, understand enough thereof to see the instability of popular favour, and the worthlessness of popular applause. The gentleman who had been the favourite candidate of the people, and whom they had joyfully sent into Parliament less than a year before, was now so coldly received by his recent friends, that he thought it prudent to retire from the field without trying the issue of a contest. The watchwords which he so effectively employed at the preceding election — "T—l² and the glorious Revolution of 1688"—were now powerless, while those of his opponent—"No Popery"—appeared to have an almost talismanic influence. The worthy (?) electors seemed to have undergone a transformation which, to the uninitiated in such matters, was not easily to be accounted for. . .

The next public event that attracted my notice was the great military expedi-tion to Copenhagen. Nearly if not all the regiments of the line then in the adjacent barracks were sent upon this service; and I think it was the bustle and excitement connected with their departure that led my master's workmen to take some additional interest in public affairs. Until this time I do not remember to have heard them talk much about matters of that description. Now, how-ever, they clubbed their pence to pay for a newspaper and selected the "Weekly Political Register" of that clever man, the late William Cobbett. This journal was in the form of a pamphlet. It was chiefly filled with the letters of correspondents and the political disquisitions of the proprietor. The only news it contained was that which related to the naval and military operations of the British forces. The "Political Register" was soon thought to be deficient in matters of general interest. It was therefore exchanged for the "Courier", which in a short time gave place to the "Independent Whig". From this time the men were warm politicians—not indeed very well conversant with public affairs, but what they lacked in knowledge they made up by a rather large amount of zealous partisanship. When they were too busy to look over the newspaper they employed me as their reader—an office whose duties I found to be very pleasant.

By dint of persevering industry and attention, aided by the good offices of several of the workmen, I soon got such an insight into the business as enabled me to be very useful upon the board. Ere long my master saw that my services there were more profitable to him than they could be elsewhere; and therefore he consented to hire another, but a younger, boy, to do the greater part of the work which previously had chiefly employed my time. I also succeeded in my efforts to get an advance of wages and thus found myself in a position much more comfortable than that in which I had stood for the preceding three years.

I now had more leisure for reading and also greater facilities for getting books. Besides these advantages I had that of being able to save a little money for the purchase of clothes and other necessaries. It was at this time that I read the remaining seven volumes of the "Spectator", to which I added the "Rambler", the "Tatler" and some others of the "British Essayists". I also read the poetical works of Milton, Addison, Goldsmith, Gray, Collins. . .

[*In* 1810 *Carter went to London to work, because he wanted to see at first hand the interesting things which he had read about the capital. Though he enjoyed its amenities and was also paid higher wages, ill-health caused him to return to the quieter atmosphere of Colchester*]

I therefore was soon ready to bid, what I intended to be a final, adieu to London, and ere long was snugly quartered in my father's cottage.

My first care was to seek employment, which I soon found, because, in addition to trade being brisk, I was considered to be a competent workman, inasmuch as I had been working in London, which was thought to be the only efficient school for juvenile tailors.

My new master was, in many respects, a remarkable man. Without anything more than a brief, and necessarily imperfect, training, he was metamorphosed from what he previously was, into a working tailor, and from this he quickly graduated to the rank of a master. Several circumstances just then combining to make a fair opening for another master tradesman in that line, he adroitly and seasonably availed himself of them, and following up the advantages of his position, soon found himself to be the chief tailor in the town and its vicinity. For many years he carried on a very extensive tailoring business – working very generally, and with much repute, for the numerous military officers successively quartered in the district, which comprised several garrisons. He also contracted largely for clothing entire regiments; besides which, he was both a wool-merchant and a wholesale woollen-draper. . .

Among nearly forty workfellows there was but one with whom I could hold any intercourse beyond that of mere civility, or the neighbourly regard which one man owes to another on the ground of their common nature. For this one, however, I speedily felt a more than ordinary esteem; an esteem, which, ere long, ripened into a hearty friendship, which, in defiance of all adverse influences or circumstances, still continues.

The tenure by which journeymen tailors hold their employment is more than ordinarily slight. No workman of this craft can be sure of remaining in his present master's service after he has finished the garment he has in hand; consequently there are many and frequent changes of workfellows to him who happens to retain his station, as I did, for several years. During these years I saw many such changes, and became thereby acquainted with many different men.

I must now advert to my health, which at this time gave tokens of being much impaired; the symptoms were such as usually accompany a much disordered state of the digestive powers. My diet, occupation and amusements were alike unfavourable to my restoration, while the medicines I took for the purpose of strengthening the stomach increased the constipation of the intestinal organs and thus did quite as much harm in that direction as they did good in the other. The evil, which I judge to have been constitutional, was, I think, much aggravated by frequently suffering the stomach to go too long without nourishment, especially in the early part of the day. My work required my attention at, or before, 5 o'clock in the morning; and, as I dared not drink water, much less beer or any other heavy or exciting liquor at that early hour, and yet had no appetite for solid food, unless I had something to drink with it, I had no alternative but to brave the morning air – often raw and cold – with an empty stomach, and then work until 8 or 9 o'clock before I took my breakfast. It commonly occurred that, by this time, my stomach was unable to digest what it otherwise so much needed; as a natural consequence it frequently refused to retain the food which I then took, except at the expense of more pain than was consistent with my continuing at work; I was therefore obliged to relieve it and then I had to work for nearly five hours longer before I took any further nourishment.

My narrative has now come down to the winter of 1812–13, at the end of which I was called upon to act as a day's-man between the master-tailors of the town and my fellow-workmen in a negotiation relative to an advance of wages. This advance was rendered needful by the increasingly high prices of all the necessaries of life, together with the extra work required by the changes of fashion in making up clothes since the current rate of wages was fixed. I here saw a striking instance of the good effects resulting from acting respectfully towards the masters in the transaction of business of this kind. Our demands were moderate and were made in the shape of a request, giving our reasons for making them. They were made in writing, a copy being left with each master for his private consideration, and a time being named when his answer would be looked for. They saw by the simultaneousness of their respective workmen's movements that they were acting in concert, although in a respectful manner. They therefore soon proposed a conference, at which, after some little hesitation on the masters' side, and a good deal of trouble to keep the wrong-headed among the workmen from behaving offensively, the advance of wages was agreed upon and was thenceforth freely paid.

While, however, these more familiar matters claimed the chief part of my attention, I could not let the extraordinary events which were then almost daily occurring in the great political world pass without notice. Several of my shop-mates were quite as much struck as myself with these unlooked-for events, and, this being so, we had a good many conferences respecting them, in lieu of the balderdash, the ribaldry, or the worse-than-childish squabbling which usually formed the staple of the shop-board conversation.

These men, with several others whose curiosity began to be awakened by the tenor of our political gossip, united with myself in subscribing for a *weekly* newspaper. We would gladly have taken a *daily* journal, but our pockets would not allow of so costly an indulgence. The paper we took was called "The News". Its arrival was looked for with very considerable interest, so anxious were we to see some bulletin of the Great Napoleon respecting his military operations, with the other articles of foreign news, and the comment-aries of the newspaper editor. The perusal of the paper, with the conversation ensuing thereon, made the days of its coming a "white day" in our estimation.

Occasionally a debate would ensue between the sturdy John Bullites and those who were dazzled by the exploits of the French emperor. This debate would sometimes wax rather warm; it then naturally fell into a personal squabble, and when this was over it ended, as controversies generally do, by each of the disputants being the more strongly confirmed in his previous notions. Yet these little tongue-battles, abating the foolish personalities, were not without their use, inasmuch as they served to enliven the conversation, and further to fix the attention of the mere listeners more strongly on the matters in question.

Thus we jogged on pretty comfortably until the early part of the year 1814, when we received an accession to our numbers in the persons of about six Italians, none of whom could speak more than a few words of English, while, of course, we were altogether ignorant of
                    "Modern Italy's degenerate speech".
Yet, by the help of signs, and the occasional visits of one of their countrymen who acted as interpreter, we made ourselves mutually intelligible.

These brethren of the needle were the *picked* tailors among those belonging to about three thousand prisoners of war, who had been confined in the war-prisons of North Britain. They had been liberated on condition of engaging to serve against their old master. With a view to this service they were sent to the barracks of our town to be organised, clothed, and accoutred. The officers' clothing was made in our master's workshop. This large addition to our *usual* press of work in spring-time made us so busy that extra help became needful, and the services of even bad workmen were gladly accepted. Our foreign auxiliaries – although they might have been good soldiers, and certainly were good companions – were far enough from being good tailors; indeed, they seemed to regard work as a matter of small moment. . . They took great pleasure in singing, and as we made them understand that we thought their singing to be very good, they spared neither time nor trouble to please us. . .

In a few weeks the war was brought to a close, and all united in celebrating its termination with much seeming satisfaction. The working people confidently looked for better times, as they still continued to think that "Peace" was in-variably accompanied by "Plenty". It would have been difficult to find credence had any one asserted that a sudden change from a state of almost universal war to one of general peace could not fail to be unpropitious to a large garrison town.

During the winter I thought little about public affairs, as they were in a quiet state, except as regarded the unhappy contest with the United States of America. In this I could not take any but a painful interest, for I could not bring myself to look upon it in any other view than that of a most unnatural and profitless quarrel. As to my fellow-workmen, they took their respective sides according to the tenor of their political opinions, some wishing all manner of success to the Americans, while others felt concerned for the honour and well-being of their countrymen. . . But ere long both this and every other public affair was thrown into the shade by our hearing that the Emperor Napoleon had left Elba for the purpose of re-asserting his claim to the crown of France. This portentous, and to us wholly unexpected, event supplied us with much new matter for political gossip. Meanwhile all that had been done in the way of breaking up the garrison was quickly repaired. . . The tradespeople of the town, together with the farmers and market-gardeners of the neighbourhood, were busy in supplying the wants of the garrison and were all sanguine in their hopes of another long-continued time of prosperity.

Ere long, however, the decisive battle of Waterloo extinguished all their hopes of a long contest. Preparations were again made for a state of peace. In the course of a few months the garrison was dispersed, the barracks were demolished, and the people of the town and its vicinity were thrown upon their own resources. They soon turned out to be very unequal to the required purposes and, in consequence, there was soon much depression and adversity. Many of those who during the war had been large contractors for the supply of various articles to the army and who, therefore, were thought to be *wealthy* men, now turned out to be *very poor*. Their fine houses were abandoned, their expensive style of living was laid by, and they sank down to a comparatively humble state, in some cases, indeed, into actual poverty and want.

[*Post-war Colchester was suffering economic depression through the dismantling of the barracks and the final collapse of the cloth industry, and Carter still longed for the intellectually stimulating life of London. He therefore once more obtained work in the capital.*]

In the winter of 1815–16, I resolved upon attempting to think upon a given subject when at work and not caring to join in the shop-board conversation. I felt but small difficulty upon *subjects*, but was rather at a stand in respect of the dress or shape into which I should put my thoughts. I soon decided it should be into that of rhyme, and immediately set about tagging verses. This I did until it became so much of a habit that I have engaged in it at all times, in all places, and under every variety of circumstances. . . I thus accumulated a rather large stock of verses, in different measures and on various subjects. Much of this has been destroyed. The remainder has been several times revised. In each of these divisions it has been greatly altered and abridged. A good many pieces have been printed in a respectable although little Magazine. Several have appeared in other publications.

Towards the close of 1818 I casually met with my future wife. . . Our first intention was to have remained in London; but we were subsequently led to

determine upon settling in my native town. The chief reasons for this determination were a desire to be so near to my mother as to be able to help her
better than we could if living at a distance, and a hope that I might be able to
establish myself in a small tailoring business on my own account. I also thought
that, in the event of our having children, we should be better able to take good
care of both their health and morals in a country-town than we could reasonably
expect to be in *such* a London residence as we should be obliged to have.

About the end of May, 1819, we were married, at St. Paul's, Covent Garden,
which was my parish-church. We spent a part of our wedding-day in looking at
the Royal Artists' exhibition of paintings at Somerset House, in which we
found much that gave us very pleasant entertainment. Afterwards, as the day
was beautifully clear and serene, we indulged ourselves with a short excursion,
in a westerly direction, upon the broad and gently-flowing Thames. Within
two or three days after our marriage we went into the country and immediately
set about trying to effect our purposes. Herein we found considerable difficulty,
part of which was, for some time, insurmountable. . . Although I could not get
many clothes to make on my own account, yet I did not want for work as a
journeyman. I had obtained the promise of employment at my former master's
before I left London and therefore was so far provided for. My good wife
assisted me at the needle both cheerfully and efficiently. The first year of our
course was a rather rough one; still we had many comforts and some amusement. . .

In the spring-time of this year (1821) I began to be well supplied with work
on my own account. I thought it remarkable that while I continued to seek
master-work I could not succeed; whereas when I had long given up all thought
or hope about it, work came to me spontaneously, and from quarters whence I
should least have looked for it. . . Ere long I had so much of this kind of employment that I could not serve a master. I therefore intimated this to mine, and thus
we parted company upon good terms.

The majority of my customers found their own cloth and the other principal
materials, which, as I had no *capital*, was a great convenience. When I was
required to supply these things I found a friend in the person of my former
juvenile master. He had now succeeded to his late father's business and was quite
as willing to give me credit for what I wanted, in the way of trade, as he had
formerly been to lend me his books. . . Thus I found myself in as comfortable
circumstances as I could reasonably have expected. My increased expenses were
met by an increased income and I felt satisfied with my condition. It was needful
that I should work very closely and for many hours on every working-day, but
this was no hardship. . .

My little business continued to increase, and I made every possible exertion
to get through it without employing help. I often worked until midnight, and
sometimes to a much later hour. I had but little exercise except that which I took
when obliged to go out on business. The bad effects of this unremitting application were ere long manifest. I suffered much from indigestion and the other
ailments connected therewith. Once more my asthmatic disorder began to give
me some trouble. Altogether I was a good deal shattered and had some smart
fits of illness. These, however, for a time gave way to the power of medicine,
and thus I was enabled to keep at my business, although with less effect than
formerly. I had now frequently to employ a journeyman, not, however, so

much on account of my broken health as on account of my little business continuing to increase. In addition to the help of a man, I had that of a youth who offered himself as an apprentice. He was a very industrious, clever, attentive lad and soon made an excellent workman. He had a general notion of the business before he came into my service, having been what is called a "trotter" in a large and respectable tailoring-trade.

In the course of this summer [1824] I was unanimously elected a member of a literary society[3] which numbered among its members many of the most respectable gentlemen, professional and private, of the town and its neighbourhood. It also included a goodly number of the principal tradesmen. I believe that I was the only *poor* man of the whole number. This very gratifying mark of good-will from men so much my superiors in all respects I owed to the good offices of my old and tried friend, the woollen-draper. He told me that he wished I would take courage and allow him to propose me as a candidate. To this I consented and through his favourable representations I was elected. I now had the privilege of hearing a good lecture monthly upon some subject of real interest and was, moreover, kindly noticed by several gentlemen to whom I was previously a stranger. It was imperative upon *each* member to deliver a lecture in his turn, or pay a fine. This to me was a rather formidable matter even to contemplate; but I ventured to hope for some loop-hole through which I might retreat and thus escape the dreaded ordeal. But I was not to be thus favoured. In the spring-time of 1825 my patron, who was one of the secretaries of the society, came to my house for the purpose of telling me that I was expected to take my proper turn in lecturing. I would fain have got excused by paying the appointed fine, but found that would not be satisfactory. I therefore consented to be duly announced as a lecturer. As I was at a loss for a subject, my friend gave me one; but I felt afraid to grapple with it, and the more so because I had never read anything directly treating upon it. In fact, I was wholly ignorant of its theory. I, however, now began to get what help I could, and gave the subject all the attention I was able to give. In due time I read my lecture, and, to my great surprise, no less to my high gratification, found that I had acquitted myself to the satisfaction of the society. The issue was that many of the members noticed me in a very kind and encouraging way.

In March, 1827, my wife presented me with a fifth son, so that we now had six children, none of whom was capable of self-management. I now had three apprentices and a journeyman. Our house, therefore, was a busy scene, and the more so because our circumstances required that we should add to our income by continuing to let lodgings.

Throughout the year 1833 I was much afflicted by my asthmatic complaint; the attacks were repeated at intervals of little more than a month, and moreover were very violent – so much so indeed, on several occasions, as to threaten a fatal termination. Their effect upon both my person and my affairs was not a little injurious. Towards the close of the year, when I was slowly recovering from one of these attacks, I was considering what could be done to ward off a heavier disaster than any which had hitherto happened to us. The subject was both painful and complicated; and I knew not what to decide upon. All at once it occurred to me that there was a *possibility* of getting some help by the publication of what I had read before the Literary Society. The impression remaining with me, and growing stronger, I thought it well not to neglect it—

being inclined to regard it as an intimation of what I ought to do. I forthwith consulted the principal members of the Society; who advised me to publish and promised to assist me in getting subscribers for the book. Their generous exertions herein were far more successful that I could have looked for; I did the best I could to prepare the manuscript for the press; and in the latter part of the summer of 1834 it was published.[4] The subscribers' copies brought enough money to pay the printer's bill and also to leave a most useful and timely supply for my family. The copies remaining after the subscribers were served amounted to about six hundred. These, partly by personal exertions, and partly by the help of friends, were gradually sold. The money they produced has *oftentimes* been the means of saving us from painful privations. The sale extended over a period of nearly six years. Here then I saw the utility of having, when young, sought amusement in reading and observation rather than in the foolish or vicious pursuits which, in general, are so eagerly followed by young men of my own class.

[*Working hard to support his large family, Carter found his health deteriorating once more and so again moved to London, this time seeking to earn his living by writing, since by now he was incapable of doing so through his trade.*]

I have worked diligently at my proper business, at all times when I have not been seriously ill; but I have often been disabled. When too ill to work, I have been unable to amuse myself with a book, or even a newspaper. At the present time I am much debilitated, while it is pretty certain I shall gradually become still more feeble. I am in truth a prematurely old and worn-out man. All the physical infirmities of advanced age have come upon me before I have got much beyond my fifty-second year.

X

JOHN CASTLE, SILK WEAVER OF COGGESHALL AND COLCHESTER, 1819–71

As a silk-weaver, John Castle worked in the industry which gave Essex almost its only connection with the early stage of the Industrial Revolution. The silk industry first appeared in the county in the late eighteenth century, just when the woollen industry was collapsing, and it was soon represented in Coggeshall, Colchester, Braintree, Bocking, Halstead and a dozen other places. Many of the new businesses were branches of Spitalfields firms, which chose to employ Essex workers because they could pay them below London rates. This situation and the precarious state of the industry in general caused the lives of Essex silk workers to be anything but comfortable, and Castle escaped few of its insecurities, though, as a domestic weaver, he was not subject to the harsh working conditions prevailing in the silk throwing mills. The insecurity of his occupation must also have made him permanently apprehensive of once again becoming the victim of the New Poor Law, under the degradations of which he had suffered in his youth.

Amid hardships and uncertainties Castle showed resolution, thoughtfulness and strength of character, even in the years before religious conviction and radical politics gave him moral reinforcement. The same qualities were to secure for him the position of foreman in a Colchester silk concern and, later, that of manager of the Colchester Co-operative Society. They must also have given him the confidence to write his memoirs and thereby to provide almost unique evidence about the life of Essex workers and the outlook of their local leaders. In the latter respect he was quite characteristic of the Victorian working-class movement. Though some of his associates in the Colchester Co-operative Society were former Chartists, they, like him, had come to accept in principle the existing economic and social system, though hoping to gain within it a better life and a less inferior position for working men. Thus, in launching the Co-operative Society, he could seek the help of the editor of the local Conservative weekly paper and also the Liberal owner of the town's leading engineering firm, while in industrial relations he felt sure that the weavers' interests were best served by a recognition of their dependence on the employing class. In politics he looked to the Liberals for leadership rather than to an independent working-class movement of the Chartist type. Through the patient pursuit of these policies, Castle and his friends were giving the youthful working-class movement of Victorian Colchester the same characteristic form taken by its counterparts in other English towns, that of Co-operative Society, craft unions and pro-Liberal politics.

The memoirs were written in 1871, seventeen years before Castle's death, when he was 52 years old. I have omitted the parts not connected with Essex, some moralising passages and anecdotes, which, though set in Essex, throw little light on Castle or on local society. The original is in Essex Record Office [D/DU 490], there exist copies of a duplicated version issued by Colchester Co-operative Society at its Centenary in 1961, and, it is understood, a facsimile edition is to be published. Readers will find useful information about Castle's work for the Co-operative Society in the latter's centenary publication,

100 Up (copy in Essex Record Office, D/DU 490A). In Essex Record Office there is an essay on Castle by Kathleen D. Thomas, 'A Study of a Working Class Man of the Nineteenth century' [T/Z 38/12].

I WAS born at Great Coggeshall in the Year 1819. My father was a native of Soulbury in Buckinghamshire, my mother of Coggeshall, in Essex. When I was the age of two years and a half my father returned to his native place, taking his family, four in number, with him. After residing a little over two years at Soulbury an attack of Inflammation in the body suddenly caused my father's death, at the age of 27. My mother and family were left quite destitute and she being near another confinement. During the short time we lived at Soulbury our two sisters, Hannah and Eliza, died; my brother William was about seven years old, myself five. At the death of our father my mother's mother walked from Coggeshall to Soulbury, about 75 miles. When she arrived with my father's sister from a place called Walkern, in Hertfordshire, he was buried when they arrived. After a few days' stay they walked back, taking me with them, leaving my mother and brother behind. One month after my father's death my mother was confined with a son, whom she named Isaac. A few months afterwards my mother returned to Coggeshall. The parish allowed her seven shillings per week to bring us up. We were sent to the Church School on Sundays and to a woman's day school. My mother, to get a living, went out as nurse. At the age of eight I was sent to a writing school, where I filled only two copy books. At the age of nine I was sent to Messrs William and Charles Beckwith's[1] Silk Factory to learn to be what was called a draw boy and to clean the silks ready for weaving. After a few years the Jacquard machine from France took the place of the draw boy machine. I still remained in the factory cleaning the silk for two weavers; one of these was taking his half-pints one day. I had cleaned up the silk ready for weaving and I thought I would try my hand at weaving; having been so long in the factory I had gained a knowledge of the principle and now thought I would practise. I got into the loom and was getting on first-rate, the foreman of the factory John Bartholomew, caught me at it and ordered me to go to the Woolpack and tell the weaver if he did not come to work he would discharge him. Two or three weeks after this the foreman, who used to fill up his time by weaving, saw me at play with other boys and asked me if I had a father and mother. I told him I had no father. He asked me to clean his silk; I accordingly left one of the weavers to do his. I soon saw his motive, he told me to get into his loom and see what I could do. From that day I became a weaver at four shillings per week.

After a few months I had the care of a loom to myself, on condition that I earned 8d. for my employer and 4d. for myself, thus I was to pay dearly to learn weaving. A short time afterwards John Bartholomew died, leaving a widow and ten children. Mr. C. Beckwith took me for twelve months at sixpence out of each shilling I earned.

Soon after this an event occurred in the silk trade which caused a great change – Messrs W. and C. Beckwith failed for a large sum, which stopped the trade, throwing nearly 100 out of employment. About this time great failures took place in America, causing the silk trade to be bad all over England. I was out some months, sometimes tramping to Halstead and then to Colchester to seek for employment. I called at the Royal Mortar,[2] Military Road, Colchester, on Mr. Pain, foreman to Mr. Foot, and got a promise of employment, but the trade got so bad he could not give me any; I returned home to Coggeshall pennyless. My poor old mother would have gone without bread for me, but I had a stepfather who grudged every mouthful

I ate. My brother William was married and had one son; he was at his wit's end to get bread to eat. At last our mother persuaded us to go to the parish of our father. We were sworn to our settlement, which was Soulbury, in Bucks, near Leighton Buzzard, in Bedfordshire. We were ordered back to Coggeshall with instructions to go to one C. Smith, a baker, who was overseer at that time. We had plenty of bread for a week and then it was stopped, we were told to get work or go into the Union Workhouse at Witham. To get work was out of the question, so we packed up next morning, determined to see it out; we had nothing to lose. We arrived at Chipping Hill Union,[3] before dinner, produced our order and were admitted. We were not the first lot from Coggeshall, there were several families belonging to our shopmates. One James Cox and his wife had become bakers. As soon as they saw us they gave us a hint to put our names in as Dissenters; although he was grave-digger at Coggeshall Church and we had been brought up to the Established Church, yet we turned Dissenters because the church was close to the door of the Union. The Chapel was in Witham Street, a long way off; this gave us a good walk every Sunday.

The first day after dinner we were ordered to strip and put on the regimentals of the Union, which were composed of a pair of thick leather breeches, leather coat, low shoes, ribbed stockings, and a hairy cap with peak. I could but smile at the appearance of my brother, who was very thin; his small clothes hung about his legs. This day made me think of the words of my mother, she had often remarked – "Ah, boy, as you make your bed so you must go to it". This came true literally that day; we were ordered to go to work in a factory where stood two machines, one named the Devil the other a carding machine. Old carpets were brought to us very greasy, we cut them into ribbons and fed the Devil, who tore them into a thousand pieces. We then took them to the carding machine, put them through it, and they came out first-rate flocks. Whilst we were doing this some of our shopmates were set to sew up some bed-teaking and we had a capital flock bed, as we did not forget to put plenty of flocks into it. The work in this factory was very dusty.

The next day some one was wanted to clean boots, shoes, knives and so on, this situation I obtained, and thought it a promotion, to say nothing of the emoluments I obtained. I used to come in for a few nubbles, as we called them, which broke off the loaves of bread as they came out of the oven; these were a great relish to a hungry youth of 17. When work was done we had a large room with good fire, and about 30 or 40 of us sat round it, some talking of the days gone by and wondering where the end of this poverty would take us, others were singing or making a poor half-witted man sing, none of us seemed to be thinking that the cloud we so much dreaded was big with blessings; in fact it was a blessing that we could not see the roughness of the road we had got to travel. The days passed on.

One circumstance worth noting occurred whilst here, I was asked to stand godfather to a child whose father was in Chelmsford Gaol, by the name of James Collins. I looked upon it as a mere ceremony as no doubt thousands do; it gave me a short holiday and a pint of beer, and it passed off. I never remember seeing the child afterwards, yet I promised and vowed three things in its name. I was ignorant of the sin I was committing.

After remaining at Chipping Hill Workhouse 14 days orders came that I and

my brother, his wife and child, were to start the next morning on the Coggeshall coach for Soulbury, in Buckinghamshire. We took off our regimentals
and put our own clothes on, and walked seven miles to Coggeshall. We spent
the night with our relatives. The next morning which I think was the 7th of
February, 1837, we all started on the coach for London, under the care of a Mr.
Goodey, who was a parish officer.

[*John Castle proceeded to Leighton Buzzard Union workhouse, where he suffered
the rigours of the New Poor Law. After angering a tyrannical Guardian, he was dis-
missed from the Workhouse, but, with his aunt's help, he found work in the silk
industry in London.*]

Soon after this one morning I met the postman; he handed me a letter to say
that my brother had been to Colchester at the request of my poor old mother,
and engaged for a loom's work of satin for me, and had bargained for a loom
and even hired two rooms. All this they had done without my knowledge or
consent. They did not know but what I had work. It so happened that I was out
of employment. This seemed to me strange at the time, but after my eyes
became opened I could see a good Providence in it. I took leave of my Aunt and
Cousins Jane, Hannah, James and John Dakin also of Mrs. Owen, my old
mistress and the winders who respected me. Mrs. Owen gave me tenpence, I
believe that was the sum. I left them promising to return to London in six
months. While I am writing it is over 31 years since I promised this, but I never
returned to live in London.

I left London on the Sunday morning by railroad; the Great Eastern, as it is
now called, was only 12 miles long – it only reached to Romford then. I walked
from Romford to Coggeshall that day, 32 miles. The next day I proceeded to
Colchester and went up to the Royal Mortar to Mr. Elson, Messrs Henderson
and Arundle's foreman; he told me where my loom was and my two rooms. In
a day or two I received my cane and began to weave satin in Colchester and to
be a housekeeper, I bought one chair, one table and a bed, also one saucepan all
on trust. Thus I lived for two years getting on well.

I had not been in Colchester long before I became acquainted with the house-
maid of Mr. Newell, a solicitor of Colchester. We had kept company about 15
months when she was sent into the Hospital, and the doctors pronounced her in
deep decline; the physician said she must leave the Hospital – if she lived till the
Thursday week it was as much as she would. I consulted her aunt, who lived at
service in the town, and lodgings were taken for her by this aunt at Thomas
Seaborn's over North Bridge. To this place she was removed, but was not
expected to live. I went to see her every night. She was attended by Messrs
Nunn and Son, surgeons, but no improvement seemed to take place, neither
did she die at the time named. Doctor Nunn had a son-in-Law by the name of
Blyth, who took her in hand; he sent a blister to be put on her left breast and
ordered it to be kept on till he called. He came and asked to look at it, he turned
it up at one corner, so as to get a hold, and rent it off, skin and all. This was
cruel, to all outward appearance, but it set her on her legs again. The cough she
was the subject of seemed to come from there, and he ordered it to be kept open.
In a week or two her cough left her and she gained strength. Her friends began
to get tired. She had no mother, her father was left with ten children; she was
the eldest. Her name was Elizabeth Sandford, from Great Waldingfield,
Suffolk, the daughter of a ploughman. She had been very kind to her father and

her brothers and sisters, so that she was quite destitute of money when over-taken by affliction. Her friends persuaded her to call on the parish; she consented, believing that she belonged to St. Mary-at-the-Walls, Colchester, having lived at Mr. Bolton Smith's, wine merchant. Mr. Roger Nunn being a magistrate, she was sworn to her settlement, and it turned out she belonged to Waldingfield, Suffolk, where her father lived. One night when I went to see her, as I thought, the Relieving Officer had taken her to the Sudbury Board of Guardians and they settled 3/– per week on her to go and live with her father. I was not at all sorry to think if I ever married her I must take her off the parish. She had been very high-minded and proud, not willing to marry till she had a house such as a silk weaver could not afford, but God knew how to bring down pride, and he brought her down so that she was glad to be in a low place – even the wife of a weaver. She had been home nine days when I walked over to Waldingfield on the Saturday afternoon, about 16 miles. I found her improving in health but her father was far from well, I slept with him that night. He came in on the Sunday morning quite upset, a farmer by the name of Vince had blown out his brains; this seemed to play very much upon poor Sandford. I returned to Colchester on the Monday morning. I went again in a fortnight; he was getting worse. His daughter was well enough to wait upon him. He expressed a wish to see me marry his daughter, so I put in the banns of marriage at the Church. I went down every week to escape being published in Colchester. The last Sunday of being published I rode down with her Aunt Chignall. I thought of marrying on the Monday week, but when I went to the bedside of poor Sand-ford he had death set in his face, his eye-strings seemed broken. The Clergyman advised me to stop and marry next day, as it would be better to go from a wed-ding to a funeral than from a funeral to a wedding. We married next day, her father died the very day we intended to marry. [*This marriage lasted only a short time, ending with his wife's death in* 1844.]

I became a widower at the age of 24, after this my health began to mend. The silk trade was good. I soon began to improve in circumstances. Having a house and my wife's brother I could not get on without a woman in the house; I hired a woman as housekeeper at 1/– per week and food and lodgings. I soon found everything going to ruin – bad washing, bad bread. I consulted Mr. Herrick,[4] and he advised me, if I found anyone suitable, the best thing would be to marry again. I had thought it would be a long time before I should think of such a thing, but I found "the thought of men to be vain". I was at St. Peter's Church one Thursday evening, as was the custom of Mr. Herrick himself some times, to hear Mr. Carr; after leaving the Church, passing through St. Mary's Churchyard I passed a young woman by the name of Esther Groves, whom I had seen before but never to know her. I entered into conversation with her; I found she knew my deceased wife and had heard of me. I asked her to meet me, I wrote her a letter and we met. I courted her some weeks. As I had a house and home that wanted looking after I thought it best to marry at once. We were married by Joseph Herrick August, 14th 1844. Before I married, however, I gave up my charge of the two children. The boy Isaac was sorry to leave me, the girl, Sarah, was ill with her Aunt.

After ten months with my second wife we had a daughter born. We named her Rachel. After so many ups and downs in the world I had become the father of a fine girl. Trade soon began to get bad again, the Irish Farmine came on,

I

bread got up to four shillings per peck, sometimes no work for a week or two, sometimes we made our dinner off a pennyworth of skimmed milk thickened with flour. These things did not trouble me much as I had learnt by past experience; I was thankful if I could get bread enough, I wanted but little and I thought I should not want that little long – but it was hard for the wife who had been used to plenty at service. Time passed away; at the end of three years we had two daughters. My poor old mother just before this time, came over to stay a few days for the benefit of her health. I was taken ill with scarlet fever, my wife and child also took the fever. None of the neighbours cared to come and see us. My wife had to go a mile at least to fetch my medicine, when she was going down with the fever my mother had to work in the midst of this, yet it pleased God to give her strength and she returned home the better for her visit. After this we had another daughter Esther – two years after that had a son born and called his name John. He was a beautiful child, but he only lived three months. This we felt very much – to lose our first-born son.

I had been ten years working for Messrs Henderson and Co., No. 1 Gutter Lane;[5] trade got very bad – some of the weavers lost 13 weeks at a time, I never lost three weeks at any one time. Still everything was going to the bad – behind in rent. At last it seemed the final trouble had come which bid fair to send us to the Union Workhouse. I remembered the days of old. We had notice that the Firm intended to concentrate their trade at Braintree, a town 16 miles from Colchester. We were about 40 families in number and we had the offer to follow if we liked. But this involved an expense of at least twenty shillings and loss of time; very few out of the number could muster 20/–, trade had been so bad. I am sorry to say we had not the offer of a loan of 20/–. After ten years service this seemed to me and others not the right sort of treatment – in fact many of us could not muster enough money to move to Braintree. We met together and decided not to leave Colchester without a struggle. We decided to send two men to London as a deputation to wait upon the silk manufacturers asking them to come and take the place of Messrs. Henderson and Co. I was asked to go, but I declined unless the weavers would promise me to do all they could for my family if I failed in London – my family being my first consideration. I knew it was contrary to my present employers' wish to lose a body of men like us, and I did not care to make myself conspicuous. Well two were appointed, and then there were no funds in hand to pay their expenses.

I and two more were appointed to go round to the gentry and tradespeople of the town to lay our case before them and solicit funds. We thought it best to get some competent person to write us a petition explaining our case; a lawyers clerk was thought of, but he was not at home. I asked the question why we wanted such a person seeing we only wanted to write the plain truth? one remarked "We cannot do it grammatically enough." "Hang the grammar", I said, "Give me a sheet of paper." I wrote a plain statement of facts, such as would bear scrutinizing. We first took it to the Mayor of Colchester, which was Dr. Williams. This was in 1850. He read it carefully and asked who wrote it? I told him I did. He said it wanted a little polishing. The contents of it he considered it his duty to attend to, as it involved the loss of a trade to the Borough which if once gone could not be easily replaced. He promised if we left it with him for one day he would copy it for us. I told him I thought an unpolished document would do best, as there were to many well-polished begging petitions got up. However, we left it. Next day we called for it: the Doctor had become quite converted to my opinion – he simply wrote a note at the bottom to give us a good start. He then asked us what amount we thought would do to start it – he would give us a sovereign if we thought that would do, his opinion being that no one would like to give more than the Mayor. We told him we thought half that amount would do. He set his name down at the top and gave us ten shillings. One day was gone, and we thought we were fairly started. We went straight to the Ex. Mayor, Mr. H. Wolton. He questioned us very closely and asked how he was to know that to be a true statement? We told him Dr. Williams knew us. "Yes," he replied, "but how does he know that to be true? I cannot sign it unless I have proof of its truth. I want a note from your present employers to certify the truth of your statement." This put us in an awkward fix, as we knew our movement was not liked by them; we knew Mr. Wolton also to be a firm man, thoroughly opposed to impostures. We waited till evening and then went up to the Royal Mortar to Mr. Elson, our foreman, and he wrote us a note to take to Dr. Williams. We took it part of the way; it being an open note we read it. It stated that Mr. Elson would call on Dr. Williams. We took it back and showed our petition to Mr. Elson and asked him for a note certifying it to be true. This he very kindly gave us. We took it to Mr. Wolton, who sealed it on to our document where it remains in my possession till this day, which is over 21 years. Was this all Mr. Wolton did? No; he gave us 10/-. Two days had been lost, but we had a good start now, better than before because we had a certificate and also a licence from two magistrates to go all over the Borough to solicit funds for a good cause. Next we went to the two Banks, who gave us 10/– each; next to Sir Henry Smyth and Mr. Joseph Hardcastle, our Members of Parliament; they gave us 20/– each, Mr. J. S. Barnes acting for Mr. Hardcastle. We met with great sympathy from nearly all we went to. At the end of a week we had collected eight sovereigns and sent Messrs. J. Collier and S. Spinks off to London. I returned to my loom.

Our deputation arrived safely in London and went to work. In a day or two we received a letter to say there were hopes that a Mr. Robinson, of Milk Street, would send us work. He set our deputation fast with a partial promise: at the week's end he sent them home promising to send work. We held a Weaver's Meeting to receive the deputation. I had my fears as I had known the firm for several years. We waited till some of our weavers were on the point of finishing their work. No Mr. Robinson came to our rescue. We called a meeting and found all our funds had been spent by the deputation except a few shillings. What was to be done? Why, we had to subscribe a few shillings which we wanted for bread. There was no time to be lost. We sent one of the deputation up to London at once to ask Mr. Robinson to explain himself and decide – in case he declined circulars were to be printed and left at the manufacturers immediately, and if Mr. Colyer did not feel competent alone he was to write down and we agreed to send Mr. Piddington to join him. Messrs. Robinson declined to come to Colchester telling Mr. Colyer that they were just going to write to us. This was a poor re-compense after causing our deputation to spend £8. Mr. Colyer felt himself incompetent to do the talking part of the deputation, which required an experienced weaver. Here seems to me an over-ruling Providence for my good: instead of Mr. Colyer writing down for Mr. Piddington, as agreed, he wrote to the weavers to send J. Castle up at once. A meeting was called at midday: I had gone up to the Royal Mortar to turn on my last cane for Henderson & Co., being behind the rest of the weavers through losing so much time to get up the funds. When I returned home I found a meeting called, and I was asked if I would go to London the same night? I at once accepted the task, although I could see the danger to myself if I failed. Parliamentary train at that time, 1850, left Colchester for London at 8. p.m., arriving in London just before 11. No light in carriages. I set a friend to put my cane in the loom while I went to London. On my way to the Station I heard that I had been threatened if I did not get on with my work it should be taken away. This proved to me that I was right at first in requiring the weavers to protect me in case I was discharged for being in London to find a manufacturer to give us employment rather than to march out of Colchester in a body. Well I started for London quite low spirited, with just enough money to take me there and pay my lodgings – none to bring me home; but the weavers promised to send us a Post Office Order, which they did. I arrived at Fetter Lane, Holborn, about half-past eleven, hired a bed at a coffee-house, went to bed but could not sleep, my anxiety was so great and my hopes of success so small. Next morning Mr. Colyer came to me and found me down in spirit. Well off we went to the City manufacturers first. Mr. Colyer had issued circulars to various manufacturers. He took me down Friday Street, Cheapside, to a house nearly at the bottom – the house was closed, no one lived there. On returning back we had to pass Messrs. Campbell, Harrison & Lloyds, 19 Friday Street, the house I referred to when I first made my advent to London from Leighton Buzzard. I asked Mr. Colyer if he had sent them a circular. He replied "No, are they manufacturers, as there is nothing on their door except their names?" I replied "Yes, I knew them eleven years back; I attended that house every morning, Sunday excepted". I said "Give me a circular and follow me". I opened the door and he followed me up to the front, where stood Messrs. Harrison and Lloyd. I made known to them that we were a deputation from Colchester and our object. I told them that eleven years ago I was porter to their machine winder, Mrs. Owen. They received us very kindly. After a long stay and a long talk we were told that the senior partner, Mr. Campbell, was in the country, and we were to call in two days for a decided answer. When leaving the house a young man, the sales-man, I believe, asked where we were bound for. I told him "to other manufacturers, as I did not intend to be set fast as our first deputation was". He asked us to meet him at his lodgings at Snow Hill at eight o'clock that night, which we did. Off we went to several other manufacturers in the City; at last we reached Spital Square and next to Messrs. Vanner and Sons, umbrella and parasol manufacturers. After a long talk with those gentlemen they promised to consider the matter and write to us at Colchester. Mr. Colyer offered to be their foreman at £20. per year, as he had a pension from the Militia Staff. To be foreman never entered my mind. While in London I offered Messrs. Hickinbottom in the City to take two looms of sarsnett to weave if they would give us all work. Well 8 o'clock came and we were at Snow Hill to meet Mr. Stokes, as appointed. He took us up several flights of stairs – very high up – but his object was not very high. He tried to get us to offer to take work at less per yard than Messrs. Henderson were paying. I told him I had no power to do so, nor should I take it upon myself to do so – I came to London to get employment. My colleague expressed himself that he considered it best to take it a little less rather than lose it. Ultimately I agreed to write down to Colchester and submit the question to the weavers. We received an answer to authorize us to use our own judgment in the matter; but I had experience enough to know if I did such a thing I should have been branded at Braintree and other places as the man who was the cause of a reduction in price. Messrs. Campbell and Co. stood so high I felt sure Henderson and Co. would not pay more than they – so that the question more than concerned Colchester.

Next day after this interview I asked my friend Colyer to go with me to 19, Friday Street, and ask for an answer. I began to get tired, what with the question of reduction and the uncertainty of success. Accordingly we went and saw Mr. Harrison and Mr. Lloyd, who decided at once to establish a trade in Colchester. To the credit of those gentlemen they never breathed a word about paying a farthing less than Henderson & Co. Over 21 years have passed since the above took place and they are paying 14 per cent more now than then.

Well no one can tell the agreeable surprise I felt at such success. I felt sure we should not be played with by those gentlemen as we were by the others. We were told we might expect them at Colchester shortly. We wrote home to say we should be home next day. We agreed to keep the name of Messrs. Campbell secret as long as possible, fearing that something might be done to spoil our success.

We arrived home full of spirits, thankful to God for His good Providence. But this was a link in the chain of Providence to bring about other events in the life of one who felt unworthy of so many mercies. Well we had not been home many days before we received a letter from Messrs. Vanner & Sons to say that they should be down at Colchester on the following Monday. This caused me great anxiety, for fear Messrs. Campbell & Co. should lose the ground, as I knew they were the most suitable for Colchester. I had meantime been made Secretary to the Weavers. I called the Committee together and they ordered me to write to Messrs. Campbell & Co. to tell them we hoped they would be on the ground before Monday. They wrote to me to say they should be down on Saturday by midday train and I was to meet them. Accordingly Mr. Colyer and myself met them and took them round to a great part of the looms. They expressed themselves satisfied and desired to be taken to see Dr. Williams, the Mayor. We took them: they had a long interview. While sitting outside the door in a small lobby I overheard Mr. Lloyd say to Dr. Williams "The old gent. is out of the question. I fear the young one is not scholar enough, or there would be no question", or something as near as possible to what I have stated. I could see at once that they were discussing the question of a foreman; up to this moment it had never entered my thoughts. We saw those gentlemen off and returned home gratified with their visit. One thing I ought to say of them – they began very liberally, for they took us to the Cups Hotel and ordered us a good dinner.

The next Monday I called on Dr. Williams, the Mayor, to hear what was to be done. He informed me that Messrs. Harrison & Lloyd had left it with him to select a few names to choose a foreman from "But" said the Doctor "Don't be disappointed, Castle, it will not be you – those gentleman would have chosen you in preference to any one had you been a better scholar". Here I felt the importance of education – a chance of rising in circumstances but apparently lost from want of education. Who could I blame? My father? No; he died before I went to school. Could I blame a good mother who suffered hunger to give me as much education as cost her twenty-six shillings – or sixpence per week for twelve months? No; I dare not blame her. How many sons have cause to blame their parents for not giving them a common education. When I think of the narrow escape I had for want of education I am forced to be a strong advocate for Compulsory Education.

Well, the thought of rising in the social scale had struck me and I determined to pursue it. I wrote a note to Messrs. Campbell and Co. offering them my services in any way they thought fit to make use of me, – wholly in the loom or partly in and partly out – telling them that I had a pretty good knowledge of the manufacturing districts round about and the men who would be likely to apply for employment. I received no answer to this note direct, but went again to Dr. Williams for information. He told me he had had an interview with Mr. Elson, our foreman, to get a few names of men, the best scholars and good practical weavers; but Mr. Elson was reluctant to have anything to do with it, yet after a long talk he gave him two names – one was mine and the other S. Spinks, a very respectable weaver, but no better scholar than myself, if so good, and not at all known to Messrs. Campbell & Co. I told the Doctor I considered it not right to judge from the hand-writing a person's competence to keep books, as I considered book keeping laid in the head more than hand. The Doctor tried to ward me off of being disappointed, "for", said he "I have sent up your two names, and I have no doubt but Spinks will be the man." "Will you call in the morning," said the Doctor, "and take the authority to act to Spinks?" I told him I would, but must confess I felt rather mortified; still I was determined to bear it with goodwill towards Spinks. Accordingly I made my way to Spinks's house, which was two rooms upstairs. When I reached the bottom of the stairs I heard several voices, and as is commonly said "listeners never hear any good of themselves". I listened and heard them discussing who should be Foreman. Poor me, who had lost one week getting money for them to spend to no purpose in London and had lost nearly another week going to London and had succeeded; me, to whom the same men would have plucked out their eyes before they said I was trying to get the Foremanship, and was trying to take it from the old man, Mr. Colyer, who was out of the question from the very first; besides, said they, he has three weeks' work in his loom. True, I had; but how came that about? Why, I had lost a fortnight after them; so you may guess how disgusted I was with such men. Did I ascend the stairs after what I had heard? Not I; if I had their word would have been as smooth as butter. I turned away angry, but not without a cause. Off I went to a Public Meeting at the Room called the Bible Room, Lion Walk – a meeting called by Mr. W. R. Havens[6] to unseat Mr. Partridge, a member of our Town Council. While there, who should beckon me out of the meeting but those three weavers who one hour before were back-biting me. I went out to them. They asked me if I had any news to tell them? "Yes," was my reply; "you, Spinks, are to be foreman." He replied "not I – I would not take it – you are the proper one." "Me," I said, "What right have I to be foreman? have not I got three weeks' work in my loom? and have not I been acting deceitfully to Mr. Colyer?" Thus, I flung their own words into their teeth and they stood confounded before me. Spinks said "I won't take it." "Mind you said it," I replied, and I left them disgusted, with everything concluded in my own mind that I would finish my work and go to Braintree, and have no more to do with men so deceitful. But God had something better in store for me. I cut away at weaving a rich satin – took no more trouble after Dr. Williams nor the foremanship.

Several days after I received a letter from Mr. Harrison expressing a surprise that I had not informed them as to whom among the weavers wanted work. I was surprised at this letter, because Dr. Williams had told me no one could act unless he instructed them. In a few days Mr. Harrison came down with silks . . . to my house. This was about the beginning of March 1850. Scales and weights were sent down and my house was used for a warehouse till Mr. Elson removed to Braintree, when Messrs. Campbell & Co., hired the Royal Mortar and I removed into it. Thus you see what the changing scenes of 13 years had brought about – at that time I was a poor tramp calling upon the foreman at the Royal Mortar asking for employment and failed to obtain it; now here I am blessed by the good Providence of God to be living there as Foreman. Many had been my trials and afflictions, but out of them all the Lord had delivered me up to that time. One thing used to be a trial to me – that was, I could not keep my rent paid up, I owed my landlord several pounds and other small sums. I had often wished some kind friend would lend me about five pounds so that I might pay all my debts and have but one creditor. Even this friend I found in Messrs. Harrison & Lloyd, they lent me the money and it was deducted from my wages. Thus I entered upon a new life of bookkeeping and a variety of things quite fresh to me – forty or fifty weavers had to be got to work, winding machines to be set to work. The responsibility was great and almost overcame me at times; and some of the men before spoken of tried from envy to put all the stumbling blocks in my way possible. I was like the Poet who said –

"Ahead, then, keep pushing, and elbow your way,
Unheeding the envious who wish you to stray;
All obstacles vanish, all enemies quail
In the path of their progress who nev'r say fail."

With all the obstacles I had had to contend with, I had gone ahead, and was very thankful for mercies received, but I had not got beyond the troubles of this life. My poor old mother was sinking and never likely to recover. I was so full-handed in my new occupation that I could not devote myself to her affliction as I could wish, she being about 10 miles off. She died two months after I had got my situation. I went to see her several times and hope and believe she died simply trusting in Him who died for sinners; she felt her need of a Saviour.

Mr. Harrison had two rooms fitted up for his accommodation at our house and used often to come down, and for several years I and my wife and family used to count the hours when we expected him and Mrs. Harrison to spend a few days at the house – their kindness was enough to win any one, especially one who had seen the adversity I had.

Before these events we had to leave our country house, the Royal Morter. The government decided to make Colchester a military town again, and Messrs. Campbell & Co., were offered £50 to give up possession of the house. They allowed me to hire No. 2, Abbey Gate Terrace and a small Factory in Stanwell Street. We had all our machinery removed too.

Soon after this trade got very slack, and I had read a deal about politics and Co-operation; I had raised a weavers' Club[7] and it had done good, but through bad trade it had broken up. I felt tired of taking a leading part in politics or anything else among the working people – they did not seem to appreciate what anyone might do for their good, especially if they saw anyone advance themselves above them in the social scale.

A friend named Dand used often to call and see me: he was a man who desired to see working men raise themselves in the social scale. He often discussed Co-operation and urged me to call a meeting of the working people on the subject, but I would not. At last, he prevailed on me to say I would attend a meeting if he called one. He accordingly called a meeting of about 12 respectable men at Thompson's Coffee Room, Short Wyre Street. This was the beginning of 1861. Mr. T. Rawlings,[8] H. Arnold, myself, Mr. Dand, R. Taylor, with several others were present. We discussed the desirability of a Co-operative Society in Colchester and decided that it was quite necessary that something should be done to elevate the people: this was not the only reason why it was necessary to raise a Co-operative Society – some of the Bakers were selling what they represented to be a 4 lb. loaf, but which I proved more than once only weighed 3 lbs 10 ozs. This dishonest system seemed to me to arise out of unfair competition one with the other. We also discussed the evils arising from the "trust" system, and many other reasons justified us in starting a Society. But the shopkeepers might say and often have said to me "You did not take into consideration the customers you would be likely to take from us." "No," I replied, our chief aim was to benefit ourselves and families. I calculate that is, or should be, the motive of all persons who set up in business – every new beginner must take his customers from some other tradesman – such is life that no great good can be done without a small amount of injury." We adjourned our meeting to the Committee Room at the Public Hall. We mustered 28 about the third meeting and agreed to pay down one shilling each as an entrance fee. This was our first capital 28/-. We chose a Committee to get up the rules to submit to the body. Mr. James Paxman[9] invited the Committee to meet at his house: we accepted his kind offer. Mr. W. Munro, our Secretary, wrote down to the Parent-Society at Rochdale for a copy of their rules, which having received we commenced in good earnest, and when our rules were forward enough we submitted them to the members, who, with a few alterations, adopted them. They were sent up to Mr. J. Tidd Pratt, and Certified. Our subscriptions by this time amounted to enough to have them printed. We gave the printing to Mr. J. B. Harvey,[10] Printer, High Street. Mr. D. R. Hunter, who was a member, then offered us the use of his room for our Committee meetings; we accepted it for a few weeks when the Committee requested me to see Mr. John Taylor proprietor of the "Essex Standard" newspaper and ask him to let us some empty premises in the Back Lane or Culver Street. These rooms Mr. Taylor, and several other gentlemen had devoted for a working man's club and reading rooms, the work people only paying one penny per week for every privilege the Club afforded. A good deal of money was spent about the Club, but it failed, the people not appreciating so good a boon. I was one of the Committee of this Club. As I expected, I was kindly received by Mr. J. Taylor, who was ever ready to listen to anything that would do good to his fellow man. He very soon saw that our motives were good-intentioned and capable of raising our fellow-creatures, however low their position in life.

Well Mr. J. Taylor let us his premises at 4/– per week. We very soon got capital enough to commence business. About the 2nd of August, 1861, we bought a sack of flour, borrowed scales and weights – I lent a basin which answered for a flour scoop. Thus we started in a small business, which was destined to grow very fast. The first week we took about five pounds, the week I am writing, June, 1871, we took over one hundred and forty pounds. I was made one of the Trustees, and the Committee asked me to buy the goods. I had no wish for office – this I declare; but did not like to refuse to try my hand at anything that might tend to help on the Society. We only opened at 5 o'clock in the evening – one of our members, R. Lee, who understood a little about grocery, helped us. We bought a little grocery, but we grew so large we were forced to look for a better shop. We had a social Tea Meeting, several addresses were given upon Co-operation. This gave an impetus to the Society – over fifty joined us at one time. I saw some premises at the back of St. Nicholas Church; it looked a tumbled-down old place, called "Blomfield's Butchery." But the site was good. We discussed the hiring of it, some being opposed to it. At last I hired it at £24 per annum. The old shop contained eight rooms and a Butcher's shop and good slaughter house. After a while we opened all day as other tradesmen, employing a Mr. James Nevard as our shopman, a concientious servant who had been employed many years by Mr. Moore, grocer. We increased both in members and takings. Our dividend rose to 1/6 in the £. We soon found the necessity of baking our own bread, therefore set on a determination if possible to buy the old premises, which were freehold. I was appointed to wait on Mr. R. Blomfield for that purpose. After several interviews the property was offered to us for five hundred pounds. We decided to have it on condition that it was conveyed free of all lawyers fees. The bargain was struck. We called a large meeting, who sanctioned our proceedings. Our Bankers, Messrs. Mills, Bawtree, Errington & Co. offered to lend us two or three hundred pounds if we should want it; but to our astonishment shares came in so fast that we had enought to pay for our Building and two or three hundreds over, so that we invested the surplus shares at the Bank. Mr. J. S. Barnes kindly consented to inspect all deeds, conveyances, or anything needed as to title deeds or mortgage deeds for the sum of two guineas.

Mr. Henry Wittey, Magistrates' Clerk, solicitor of Colchester, was the owner's solicitor; both those gentlemen acted well and were very courteous to me as the representative of the Co-operative Society. Many were the journeys I had before it was finally settled. Once I wanted to see Mr. R. Blomfield to hasten on the conveyance. He lived at Cold Hall, Bromley. Off I went from 12 to 14 miles there and back. There I found out that it was necessary to advance £250 to release the poor old house from bondage. This we did and the title deeds were soon handed over to us. We turned the slaughterhouse into a bakehouse, built a large oven, and commenced baking our own bread. I had declared that when we got our oven I would know what the bread was made with; for I would get in the oven and look but what I would see that the bread was pure and sold full weight. Some of the Committee caught me one evening in the bakehouse and demanded, in a joke, that I should keep my word and get in the oven and look round. I was not to be done in joking, so I got a wisp of straw to sweep away the dust and in I went.

About this time we had a social cup of tea at the Public Hall, and to my astonishment an address was given by Mr. W. Munro, our Secretary at that time, and a beautiful Timepiece was presented to me as a token of the goodwill of many of the members and others who were not members had subscribed for, with a silver plate on its front, dated August 22, 1862, with a suitable inscription on it.

About 12 or 18 months after we had started, Mr. J. Nevard, our much-respected shopman, was taken ill with a fever, and died; this was a great loss to our Society. The Quarterly Meeting voted five pounds to his widow. Afterwards we had various shopmen and bakers, and, like most Co-operative Societies, we had to trust our business to the management of men who had no sympathy with the movement, and several times had it not been for a Reserve Fund, we must have paid a small dividend. On this account we had to get rid of several men.

Our shareholders increased and our capital flourished, so that the Management Committee considered it time to build New Stores. A shareholders' meeting was called and it was decided to form a Building Committee, and our Mr. J. F. Goodey, the Secretary, being a builder, was set to get out plans for New Stores. His plans were approved, and we set to in good earnest. At this time I had become Treasurer, Purchaser, and Manager. I felt over-anxious that the undertaking should be a success, but in spite of all our efforts bad men got among us with questionable characters, although well recommended. While our new Building was going on we came to a very large deficiency in profits, and I acted as a detective and traced two of our shopmen to houses of ill fame, so that they had to leave us.

We completed half our New Stores, leaving half standing to do business in while we built. We then had a social cup of tea at the Public Hall, Mr. Henry Pitman came up from beyond Manchester to Colchester in one day; he was quite exhausted. He had travelled that long distance to address us upon the subject of Co-operation, yet was not able to say much, but his very presence did us good. We found him to possess a spirit rarely met with – one that is destined to have a good influence over those it comes in contact with, if they have a kindred spirit, especially none could fail to see his self-sacrificing spirit.

We went on increasing for a year or two, at last we determined to complete our Building. We did so, erecting a large Assembly Room, 45 by 26 feet at least, also a Reading Room with Library to which Mr. J. Taylor presented altogether 80 volumes. At the completion of our Building we decided to have an Opening Day. The Committee deputed me to see the Mayor, Mr. P. O. Papillon, and ask him to take the chair, and declare the Co-operative Building completed. We also invited Dr. Brewer, Member of Parliament for Colchester, to our opening, as well as Dr. Williams, the gentleman whom I have had occasion twice before to mention. The whole affair passed off well. After tea we all adjourned to the Town Hall, kindly lent by the Mayor, Mr. P. O. Papillon. This was a great success, our trade increased, our capital also, the 28 shillings subscribed the first meeting night had become as many hundred pounds. We had a noble building with every convenience.

At this time the silk trade had become so diminished that I thought if I could succeed in gaining an appointment as Rate Collector it would fill up my spare time. At length the Collectorship of the First District, comprising the parishes of St. Mary's, St. Giles', St. Leonards and part of St. Peter's Colchester, became vacant, I canvassed the 24 commissioners with great success, and sold one of their wives a silk dress at the same time; when coming from this latter commissioner, I met Mr. Sayers Turner, the Town Clerk, who called me to him and told me the commissioners had elected me twelve to one to fill up the vacant Collectorship and gather the outstanding rates, which had been neglected by the last two Collectors; Between £300 and £400 remained to be collected and the time had expired when the rate ought to have been all got in. I was taken by surprise when told I had been elected so suddenly. Mr. H. S. Goody, the clerk to the Commissioners sent for me to commence collecting at once. This I did not feel at liberty to do, as I had not had time to consult my employers, who had consented for me to take such an appointment if I could get one. I at once went to London and informed my employers what had taken place. Mr. Harrison readily consented for me to fill up my time as Rate Collector, and gave me a letter to the Commissioners to stand Bond for any loss on my part. I returned home thankful to think I still had the confidence of my employers and also of the Commissioners who had elected me to fill such a responsible office.

Well I set to work in earnest to gather in the Lighting and Paving Rate. I was elected July 3rd 1871, consequently there were only 28 days for the Commissioners, the Rate Collectors, Surveyor, and all Officers to remain in office, anyone being at liberty then to contest any of the offices. I soon found an organized opposition to myself. A certain Baker stirred up the bakers and other tradesmen against me, putting it about that I was the cause of the Co-operative movement in Colchester, which was against the interest of the bakers and others; such was their spite they sent circulars to the bakers calling a special meeting to consult as to how they could overthrow me at the Annual Election on July 31st. The Commissioners encouraged me to go on and collect as much of the back rates as possible, telling me that they never knew the Ratepayers to upset an arrangement made by the Commissioners, especially after two Rate Collectors had been chosen by the Ratepayers who had both become defaulters; it was thought high time a Collector be found that would carry out the duties with credit to himself and to the Commissioners that chose him. I am proud to think I had their confidence. A month's experience proved to them they had not misplaced that confidence. I had collected £137.8.4. of small rates, some of two years standing. While I was doing this my enemies were busy seeking my downfall, and four other candidates were busily canvassing every £30 Ratepayer. I had 400 circulars printed and sent one to nearly all the voters offering myself for re-election; I could not feel right to neglect collecting rates to make a personal canvass. No doubt this was a part of the cause why I did not succeed in being re-elected, but I found another cause – one candidate was going to his friends the Conservatives setting before them his father's long standing as a tradesman and the support he had always given the party. The Conservatives took him by the hand with the exception of about a dozen, who, to their everlasting credit be it said of them they acted for what they considered the good of the Ratepayers, and shut their ears to those who would upset a town – yea, a whole nation – to answer their own selfish ends. It was suggested to me to make a party canvass, but I scorned to act as a party man where a whole town was interested. I can say with truth I preferred to lose rather than make a political question of it. Some of my Liberal friends acted liberally, but one in particular promised me he would vote for me and falsified his promise. This was anything but liberal. The chief baker who exerted himself against me was called a Liberal – God forbid I should be guilty of calling him so. He does not live far from the baker's whom I found out cheating me six ounces in every four-pound loaf at a time when I had eight in family and my consumption was at least eight quarters per week. This was cheating me to the tune of over 40 quarterns of bread per year, and yet as a working man I ought to have held my tongue and worked on and said nothing, leaving the bakers to undersell each other and cheat the public. I hold my tongue! No, not I – I dare not. I and a few more like myself met, as I before stated, and formed a Co-operative Bakery. This cured their short weight as far as we were concerned. Hence, you see, comes this enmity to me. Well, God forgive them; I hope the Chief Baker who acted against me will not come to the same end that Pharsah's Chief Baker did.

Well, I was voted out and I have no doubt but my opponents rejoiced to think they had done me evil according to their way of reckoning – but I have a strong impression it is for my good. I feel thankful to God in His Providence to allow me to attain to such a position of trust. I had the confidence of the Commissioners and the goodwill of many of the Ratepayers. It was the general belief that I had lost the office through my connection with the Co-operative movement. Be this as it may, I rejoice that my fall from such a position was because I had aimed to raise my fellow-man morally, socially, and physically!

JONAS ASPLIN, DOCTOR OF PRITTLEWELL, 1826–28

In 1825 Jonas Asplin returned from Paris, where he had long been doctor to the English residents, and resumed his practice in the Southend district. He had grown up nearby at Little Wakering Hall and had been apprenticed to a doctor in the neighbourhood. As the eldest son, he seems to have occupied Little Wakering Hall after his father's death, but he had at some time been succeeded there by his brother, Charles, perhaps when he had left for Paris. He and his wife, Eliza, on their return took a house opposite Prittlewell Church and, with his brother still at Little Wakering Hall, his sister Lucy at the Lawn, Southchurch, and his mother also in genteel retirement nearby, he had no difficulty in taking his place once more in local society.[1] Though now fifty-four years old, he retained great vigour and zest, dining out with friends or entertaining them at home, often until late in the night, occasionally enjoying a day of sport, and relishing regular visits by coach to London.

As a doctor he appears knowledgeable and confident. He stood in a transitional position between an addiction to bleeding and the ability to perform a mastectomy, then a very rare operation. Though a majority of his visits were to middle class patients, he treated poorer people, whenever called upon, and sometimes operated on them in the parish workhouses, which seem then to have been used as hospitals for all people unable to pay for treatment. He writes of many of his poorer patients with a detached but real sympathy. His attitude to his own kind was not uncritical. While applauding the transportation of offenders against the social order, he denounced strongly the grasping ways of the chief landowner of neighbouring Foulness. He was a moderate Tory, voting for his party but willing to support a Whig when the alternative was less attractive, and deploring extremism even on his own side.

His diary, which covers the years 1825 to 1828, is tidy, systematic and detailed, so detailed indeed that many entries about his visits, both medical and social, have had to be omitted here. It ceases in 1828 for reasons unclear, though he continued to practise at Prittlewell and later at Rayleigh where he died and was buried in 1842.

The original manuscript is held by Colchester Borough Library. An article by L. F. Matthews in the *Essex Review* (Jan., 1957), 38–46, contains interesting biographical details as well as extracts from the diary. Asplin's will is at the Essex Record Office [D/AER 36/494].

1826

Jan. 1 Prittlewell, Essex. Very wet and cold wind E. The independence of the Spanish colonies is fully established and to some of them we have just sent regular Ambassadors. The Greeks seem too much divided amongst themselves to form any just notion of the probability of their emancipation.

The numerous failures of the London and Country Banks has caused severe private distress in every part of England, and that of Crickett and Co. at Chelmsford to this county in particular, and which is not a little increased by the stoppage of one of the oldest houses on the Corn Exchange, Ryland and Co. In Dengie Hundred I am told it is dreadful, for there Crickett's notes chiefly circulated and from thence also the principal consignments of their corn was to Ryland's house.

Rode to Rochford about noon and Mr. Marsh accompanied me to Canewdon to visit a Mrs. Coe. We went through Mr. Barrington's yard (Doggits) and passed by Hyde Wood, where my recollection was most agreeably called to the numerous lovely spring mornings I have been by its side, anxiously waiting the breaking of cover – and, Alas, with numerous friends, most of whom are now lieing quietly in their graves.

This part of the country, if not classic, is at least sporting ground, and the numerous beautiful runs we have had across it, in the heyday of health and pleasure, can only be appreciated by a real lover of sports.

The roads are every where greatly improved. Nothing can exceed the excellence of the farming, where heavy, wet, land, though deluges of rain have lately fallen, is now lying as dry as a bone.

After visiting Mrs. Coe, Mr. Marsh returned with me to Rochford and I rode on by Sutton to Southchurch. Met Rev. J. Sumner who had been doing duty for Mr. Scratton at Barling.

Visited Mrs. Matham at Southchurch and then home to dinner.

Eliza was at Church and we expected Mr. and Mrs. Burchell to have gone with us to Church, but the weather is so unfavourable they did not come.

Received a note from Bathurst respecting a bill formerly given to Limner, a glazier at Rayleigh, which is likely to give me much trouble, and probably it will be necessary for me to take the case to the Assizes.

Jan. 2. Fair. Took an early dinner and afterwards rode to Rayleigh Mills to visit Miss Audley and her sister. Went on to the town and stopped at Withams at the Lion. His family are all settled. One of his daughters is married to Crisp, a son of Mr. Harridges, one to a shopkeeper opposite and one to a son of Mr. Byass, the surgeon. It is reported that the firm of Joyner, Surridge and Joyner, Bankers at Romford, are declared bankrupt.

Rode home by half past nine – night fine.

Jan. 3. Dined early and then rode by Wakering. Visited Mrs. Matham at Southchurch and Mrs. Harrison at Shoebury. Rode round by the church at Wakering and enquired for Sharp who kept the shop late Stringfellow's and who owes me for attending his child, found he was gone to reside at Leigh. Called at my mother's and then went down to the Hall. Took tea there and at 7 accompanied Charles to the club at the Lion.

Home by Eleven. Wind fresh.

Jan. 4. A cold comfortless day. Did not go out, nor did anyone call.

Jan. 5.   At one rode to Rochford, called at Gullocks and saw Merryfield to whom I gave the only note I held of Crickett's Bank.

Hear of nothing but the distresses occasioned by the Bank failures.

Asked Mr. Giles to dine with us tomorrow. Home to dinner.

Jan. 7.   Received an invitation from Mr. and Mrs. Prentice to dine with them on Wednesday next.

Jan. 8.   A hard frost. Wind continues E. and very cold. At 11 went to Church with Eliza. Mr. Taylor and Mr. and Mrs. Thorn called after church. Dined at One.

Mas. Henry and Miss Davis called from Leigh. Captain Scallon also called. Eliza to Church at 3 and the Little Davis's returned home.

Very few people at Church, the wind is so cutting.

Jan. 9.   Everything in the garden is cut up, the young lettice completely and all the early peas.

Jan. 10.   There is a funeral this morning of some woman who died from the Custom House cutter, S. End.

Took an early dinner and then drove with Eliza by the beach to call on Mrs. Lodwick, saw all the family and young Ramsden there – he is the *cher ami* of Lodwick's eldest daughter. Thence on to Wakering Hall, where we remained till Eleven.

Jan. 11.   Thomas Barnett (a very severe case of ophthalmia with ulceration of the Cornea) called.

The state of the country from the failure of the Banks, particularly at this time of year, is dreadful.

Mr. Audley from Rayleigh called.

At 5 we drove to Mr. Prentice's to dinner. Met there Mr. and Mrs. Comport and the Reverend Mr. Wallington, Rector of Hawkwell, Captain and Mrs. Scallon, Mr. Tabor from Rochford Mill, Mr. Hardwick and Miss Boosey. We spent a very pleasant evening and walked home with the Scallons about 1 in the morning.

Jan. 12.   Rode to Rochford, met Mr. Edmund Taylor, who is connected with the Oyster Fisheries, learn that the oysters are suffering much injury from the frost.

Saw Charles at Rochford who talks of going to London on Monday.

Dined at old Mr. Thorn's and rode home by 7.

Jan. 14.   Mr. D'Aranda sent her servant for a consultation.

Jan. 15.   We walked to South End and took tea with Mr. and Mrs. Thorn on the Terrace. Home by 11.

Jan. 16.   Mr. D. Thorn called and we rode together with his son and Mr. Abraham Thorn to Leigh to see an estate of Mr. D. Thorn's just beyond the town which he has greatly improved. Went over the brick field on this side, by Mr. T. Carr's, where preparations are making on a large scale.

All the oysters on the shore are destroyed and Mr. Osborn, a principal merchant, has failed at Leigh.

In the pits, where the flat fish are kept, they do not break the ice. If, after they are frozen quite over, the ice is broken, the fish are disturbed and they are then sure to die. I always thought they died if air was not afforded them.

Jan. 18.   Several patients called this morning. At 1 we drove and called on Mrs. D'Aranda in the Hamlet. Mr. D'Aranda was thrown over in his gig a day or two since on Hadley Common. The horse, too, fell. From there we drove to Southend; Wind W. and cold. Called on the Ramsdens on the Terrace, on the Watsons and met Scallon there, on the Lilburnes and thence by the beach to Mr. Lodwick's. It is hard frozen and the sand in general bears the wheels. From thence, after visiting Mrs. Harrison at Shoebury, we drove to Burchells; they being out, we drove home to dinner at 6. Mr. and Mrs. Kebbell called.

Jan. 19. At 1, rode to Rochford. Went only to Gullocks. Monsr. Fregnier, the schoolmaster at Rochford, met with a serious accident yesterday near Barling, from a vicious horse by which he was thrown from his gig and much cut.

Jan. 20. Mr. and Mrs. D. Thorne called with their son Daniel for a consultation. We asked them to return and dine with us at 4 o'clock, having a fine hare which Mr. Sopwith sent. The affairs of one of our great men near Rochford are talked of as being in a very precarious state.

Jan. 24. I intended driving to Rochford and calling on Mr. and Mrs. Kebbell, but the fog is too dense.

After dinner rode to Wakering to call on Charles. Saw Cobb at Southchurch, of which parish he is vestry clerk, as also of Great Wakering, these parishes having Select Vestries under an Act of Parliament passed since I left the country.

Jan. 27. A Mr. Boice, an officer of the Coast Blockade, residing at Shoebury, came for a consultation.

Jan. 30. Mr. Carr called for a Poor Rate of One Shilling in the Pound. Paid him 25 shillings.

Feb. 1. Mr. Fitch from Hockley called for me to visit his daughter at Rayleigh who keeps a Ladies' School there.

Feb. 2. Death of old Wm. Potter at 82. He was formerly in my troop of Wakering Volunteer Cavalry.

Feb. 3. Visited Mrs. Matham—this poor woman cannot survive many days. It is a case of consumption in its last stage.

Feb. 6. There is a parish meeting today. Busy in my garden, cutting trees. Did not go out. At night it blew a hurricane.

Feb. 8. Mr. Hardwick called and left the Morning Chronicle of yesterday. Mr. Prentice, Scallon, Mr. Hardwick and myself take in this paper and I receive it regularly at 9 o'clock.

Feb. 9. Rode to Rochford. Found two patients waiting for me at Gullocks.

Feb. 10. Old Prior, the gardener, is pruning the vines and fruit trees in the garden.

Feb. 13. We have a party to dinner today. At 5 Mr. and Mrs. Prentice, Captain and Mrs. Scallon and Charles and his wife came to dinner and departed about half past one.

Feb. 17. Blew extremely hard towards morning. Mr. Lewin called. He says a boat was lost off Shoebury from Foulness this morning with two men in it. The men of the Coast Guard saw the accident but it was nearly an hour before they could get off to it. The men were still clinging to the boat, the one quite dead, the other nearly so but recovered on being brought ashore.

Feb. 18. Took an early dinner and then rode to visit my sister, Mrs. C. Parsons, at The Lawn.

Feb. 20. Wind sunk at night and in the garden it was as mild and as serene as on a Summer's night.

Feb. 21. Washing day.

Feb. 22. Amongst the accidents of the day, my poor cat Minet is very ill. I had her a kitten from the Hall on my return to England. Rode to The Lawn to visit my sister. Returned home about 12, and my poor little cat died soon after.

Feb. 23. Examined the body of my poor Minet. She died in great agony – it was inflammation of the bowels. Buried her in the garden. Altogether a dismal day.

It may seem ridiculous to lament severely the loss of a favourite animal, but I have felt it impossible to pick up my spirits the whole day.

Feb. 27. Received an invitation from Mr. Kebbell of Strood Green to a Coursing party in Wallasea Island on Wednesday.

Feb. 28. Messrs. Joyner, Surridge and Joyner, Bankers of Romford, are in Saturday night's Gazette.

After dinner rode to Wakering, called on Lucy and at my mother's and thence to the Hall and took tea and walked across the fields to the Clubb. Home by Eleven.

March 2. At 9 sent William to Mr. Kebbles in consequence of having given the servant, who brought my horse to the door, a sovereign instead of a shilling. He returned with the sovereign.

Messrs. Sparrow and Co.'s Bank have suspended payment. The astonishment excited by this is extreme and the inconvenience to many very great.

Visited a Mrs. Harvey (bakers) a bad and desperate case of cancer. Mr. Marsh called and accompanied me to Mrs. Harvey's and, as she seems inclined to submit to an operation, agreed to see her on Saturday and decide upon its practicability.

March 4. There is a meeting at Chelmsford on the subject of Sparrow's Bank.

March 7. Washing day. Am sent for to visit a poor woman at Paglesham. Called and took tea at Mr. Grabham's. A Miss Harridge and her brother came there and another brother Edward, who came by coach from London, being unwell; he is studying Physic. These are children of the late David Harridge, who was in my Corps of Cavalry, and are a generation sprung up since my stay on the Continent.

March 8. Busy gardening all day. Sowed carrots, parsnips, onions, and spinnage. Evening at home.

March 11. Mr. Maclaughlin, who married Miss Bullen, and Mr. Gepp have opened a bank at Chelmsford, but do not intend issuing notes.

March 12. Eliza to Church. At 2½ was sent for to a case of Hernia. William drove me to Gt. Wakering, whence Miller accompanied me to the workhouse at Little Wakering, where the subject of the case is. Operated on a strangulated femoral Hernia in the case of Mrs. Fletcher, formerly Germany, and then kept the Anchor at Great Wakering. Left her as well as possible.

March 13. Revd. W. Benson Ramsden, Rector of Stambridge and Vicar of Little Wakering, has failed, with such an income as renders it impossible to frame an apology for him. Saw Mrs. Wade at Stambridge, where Ramsden is the sole topic of conversation.

March 14. Rode to Lt. Wakering and visited Mrs. Fletcher, who is going

K

on well. Rode to the Hall and dined with Charles and walked up to the Club in the evening.

March 18. Busy sowing seeds and trimming trees in my garden all day. Sowed some Arbot India from Mr. Colclough's garden at Versailles and acacias from the Bois de Boulogne.

March 20. A meeting of Mr. Ramsden's creditors was held at Rochford today and the glorious offer of two shillings in the pound was made, and this not to be paid till Michaelmas twelvemonth.

March 23. Rode to Rawreth and visited Mrs. Smith. Mr. Smith returned from fox hunting with Lord Petre's hounds. They threw off at Woodham and left off at Benfleet and had a good run.

March 26. Have a fine nest of young chickens this morning.

March 27. Received a letter from the Honble. George Wynn of Warley announcing himself a candidate to represent the borough of Maldon.

Rode to Little Wakering to see my patient, on whom I operated for Femoral Hernia; she is perfectly recovered.

Attended a parish meeting at the Castle.[2]

April 1. The Honble. Mr. Wynn called on me yesterday, whilst at the meeting.

April 3. Attended a Vestry meeting. They pay the medical men so badly in this Parish for attending the poor that no one will take the parish on the terms offered. £60 per annum is demanded, the parish offer £45 and have risen to £50.

Mr. Hardwick called in the evening; he tells me that someone from Rayleigh is about taking the parish.

April 7. Rode by Southchurch and called on Lucy, and on my mother at Wakering, who is very poorly. At $1\frac{1}{2}$ rode with Charles Miller by the Stairs to Havengore and visited Mr. ———. Then to Foulness[3] up Asplin's head and on to the Mill House, where I visited one of the men employed on the Coastal Blockade, thence to Cotes End and visited Mrs. ———, formerly Blois, an old servant of my Mother's. The Signal Station and the Semaphor are both standing in Foulness. Came out by Sexton's Head and reached Wakering at nearly dark. It was high water at Twelve o'clock and we had to wait at the Stairs for its leaving the black grounds. I here observed a largish track of saltings taken in on Jennings's Farm.

April 9. Our servant maid attends the funeral of her sister today at Rayleigh.

April 12. Preventive Service. A Lieutenant Dyer was shot the other day at Hythe in Kent by one of his own people for not answering when hailed. The same might happen at night to any person walking on his own land near the Sea Coast. This service reminds me so much of the power and system of the Douaniers of France that I hope to see it put a stop to. It is odious.

April 13. Am so ill today that I cannot go to Rochford.

April 14. Being sent for to Little Wakering, I determined on going, though certainly not in a state to go out.

April 15. In bed all day. Mr. Grabham called and bled me. Several kindly sent to make enquiries.

April 17. Bled myself to 22 ounces.

Mr. Wilson of Rochford Hall failed on Saturday. He has a family of thirteen children.

April 18.   Mr. Wren called and came upstairs. Paid him his half year's rent, due Lady Day last.

April 24.   The King's Birthday kept, and apparently most stupidly.

Mr. Wren called and introduced a fatt young clergyman, who does duty at Hockley.

April 26.   Visited Mrs. Johnson, glaziers; her husband in prison and herself confined with her 4th child and in a most dangerous state. On my way home was called in to another patient of Miller's at Wren's old house at Southchurch, who was also confined; she is dying and not much above 19.

April 27.   At 11 drove to Wakering, called at Southchurch and found the poor young woman died about 2 in the morning. Her infant died just before I saw her last night. She appeared to be a very fine young woman.

Visited Mrs. Johnson, of whom I have no hopes.

April 30.   Revd. Mr. Nolan called after church. He sent me his book, which he has just published, entitled "The Assyrian expectations of a deliverer".

May 5.   In the evening a Mr. Henley called to consult me. He is a straw-bonnet manufacturer and book vendor at Prittlewell.

May 6.   Death of old Mrs. Kemp. In her earliest days lived at Wakering Hall. She was amongst the very few of the old standards of Rochford Hundred remaining.

Mr. Gason brought us a kitten from the Hall last night, the same breed as the last.

May 7.   Ministers are now letting loose about 300,000 or 400,000 quarters of bonded foreign corn upon the Agricultural Interests of the country and are asking for the power of importing 500,000 more, paying a duty of 12 shillings the quarter.

May 9.   There is a meeting of a benefit clubb here today. They go to church and afterwards dine together at the Spread Eagle.

I apprehend a change in the weather from a large number of vessels which were windbound in Leigh roads having got under weigh at high water and proceeded down Swin.

May 12.   The weather here has been and still is so cold that nothing grows.

May 18.   The report of the day is that Lieut. Eikin, who married Giles Bell's widdow, committed suicide in the King's Bench and that his family are on Thundersly parish, where he hired a large, poor, heavy land, farm.

May 19.   To Mr. Burchell's, who had a few friends to shoot the young rooks.

May 22.   The first morning we have sat down to breakfast without a fire. Rode to Southend, saw Captain Green by the Hotel.

Unless we have rain very shortly, the crops on the hot lands will all be spoiled, and, as to hay, it is not thought of.

May 25.   At 8 drove to Wakering Hall to meet Sir John Tyrell and Mr. Gepp, who departed after breakfast for Rochford. Sir John wears well and looks extremely well.

May 27.   Are in a great bustle today with chimney sweepers and clearing up after raising the kitchen and dining room chimney 5 feet. The kitchen before smoaked abominably.

May 29.   Lady Sidney Smith, wife of my friend, Sir Wm. Sidney Smith, the Hero of Acre, died lately at Paris.

Being the anniversary of King Charles's restoration, the Church steeple was well decorated with oaken boughs and the bells rang a merry peal.

June 2. Mr. Lennard's party have a supper at Prittlewell tonight and Parliament is expected to be dissolved tomorrow.

June 3. Went to Southend and set a broken collar bone for a son of Mr. Braybrooke, the consequence of the electioneering suppers given by Mr. Winn, Mr. Lennard and Quintin Dick, candidates for the Borough of Maldon.

June 8. Rode to Southend. Find the numbers at the close of the poll[4] yesterday were

For Mr. Lennard 436, Mr. Winn 291, Mr. Dick 198.

June 9. Poll at Maldon last night was for

Honble. Mr. Winn 864, Lennard 794, Dick 608.

June 10. State of the poll

Winn 1130, Lennard 1009, Dick 799.

June 11. Winn 1286, Lennard 1073, Dick 892.

June 13. Winn 1313, Lennard 1095, Dick 917.

June 14. Old Scallon is hay making. Planted some celery today.

Winn 1478, Lennard 1225, Dick 1076.

These parties are running one another to a great expence. It is not less than £500 per day to each of them.

June 16. Called at the Library, to which I subscribed for the season for 12s. It is still kept by Mrs. Renneson and Miss Terry.

Received a note from Thos. Barrett Lennard, Esq. requesting my assistance at Maldon tomorrow.

June 17. In consequence of Mr. Lennard's note, I determined on riding to Maldon today. Poll yesterday evening, ninth day,

Winn 1561, Lennard 1283, Dick 1166.

At 11 rode to Maldon by Fambridge Ferry, put up at the Blue Boar still kept by Mr. Shinn. Saw Colonel Kersteman who introduced me to Mr. Winn, for whom I polled. There is not much bustle today, it seems to have exhausted itself. Took a chop at the Inn, where Mr. Thos. Hunt called upon me. Left Maldon before 4 and started gently home.

June 22. Mrs. Kemp from Rayleigh called with her daughter. Drove to Mr. Wrenn's and to Merrill's, near there, to engage a female servant. Home.

In the evening we walked by the cliff and on to Southend. Called on Mr. Thorn's and saw Mr. Hore, who once kept a school in Southend, there. To the library. Home by the brick house.

Maldon Election

Yesterday, 13th day. Winn 1698, Lennard 1390, Dick 1325. It will terminate on Friday at 3 o'clock.

June 24. Called up to a man at Southchurch who has fallen from a stack. State of the poll at the close of Maldon election,

Winn 1747, Lennard 1454, Dick 1401.

June 26. The first day I have thrown off my flannel waistcoat.

June 27. It is said a scrutiny will be petitioned for by Mr. Dick against Mr. Lennard.

July 1. In the evening drove with Eliza to Southend and called on Miss Morgan at No. 4 Grosvenor Place, who was just going to Leigh by water to see a whale they have brought up there. Drove to Leigh to see Mr. Davies.

Walked down the hill and saw the whale, which [is] of the shark-headed kind and 47 feet long.

July 2.   Took the chaise and drove to Wakering Hall to dinner at 3, where my mother came to tea.

July 5.   Too hot to go out, except in the evening.

July 7.   Find Beard, the thatcher, died this morning. He was a good reed thatcher and came originally from Orsett. He was the oldest in this part of the country and taught Loyd and others, whom I used to employ.

It was nearly eleven o'clock before I reached home, when I met my man William, coming for me in consequence of my being sent for to Wakering to Bailey, the carpenter, he having received a kick from a horse this evening by which his scull is fractured. My horse was just brought out, when a second messenger arrived to say he was dead. He was an ingenious, usefull man and has left a wife and seven children.

July 11.   Not being much engaged, I think of taking a run up to London tomorrow by the early coach, if fine.

July 12.   Rose about half past 3 and got upon the early coach for London at 4; it passes through here. Found Mr. George Vandergee on the box. Morning very fine, but weather suspicious. At Billericay it came on to rain and I got inside, as did Mr. Vandergee. Reached the Bull Inn, Whitechapel, about half past 9. Breakfasted there. Mrs. Nelson still keeps the house. Lunson, the shaver at the corner, is dead and a stupid son of his has succeeded him.

First went to the Tower and found Mr. Croft in the Ordnance Office – he is now Chief Clerk under the Treasurer. Thence to Headingtons. Walked to the Strand and found Mr. Benfield at No. 39, corner of Buckingham Street. To Park Place, Westminster, No. 4, to Mr. Tennyson's. Returned across the Park, to the Horse Guards. . . Returned to Headingtons by seven, heartily fagged. Slept there.

July 13.   After breakfast Mr. Headington walked with me to Bedford St., Bedford Square, to a French bookseller there. Returned to Headingtons, took a lunch and proceeded to the Bull Inn, Whitechapel, and I had the mortification to find the coach quite filled, but taking a fiacre to Stratford, I there got upon the S. End coach, as it passed, as did Mr. Wright, my old patient. I reached home about 8.

July 14.   They are busy preparing for the Fair.

July 15.   Morning very fine. Arranged the stalls in front of my house. The fair is a very decent one and an exhibition on our right of a giant, giantess, an Albiness, a native of Baffin Bay and a dwarf, very respectable. We had a learned pig and punch on our left, and in front some theatrical exhibition, all in very good order. Everything was quiet, orderly and decent.

July 16.   In the afternoon we went to church.

July 17.   Prittlewell Fair 2nd day. The fair does not commence till two or three o'clock. Mrs. Prentice and Miss Nelson called and I accompanied them to the shew on our right.

Parsons, Lucy and Christopher and Mr. and Mrs. Watson came to tea.

Night very fine and we saw most of the shews depart about one for Brentwood Fair, which is tomorrow.

July 18.   Very fine. Wheat harvest began. Brentwood Fair. It is 40 years this day since I entered the profession, when I went with my father to Brentwood and at Mr. Marston's met Mr. Miller, with whom I remained six years.

July 19. The day being very fine, I determined on going to the True Blue Club at Maldon, of which I have been a member about 30 years. At 12 rode the young horse to Fambridge Ferry where Mr. John Scratton and Mr. Davis came in a gig and we crossed together. The Club is greatly increased – about 140 dined. The Honble. Mr. Winn, M.P., in the chair, Sir John Tyrell, Mr. Bramston, Col. Tyrell, Mr. Dick, Mr. Horace Twiss, M.P. for Wotton Bassett, Cummings Parker the present Mayor of Maldon, Mr. Gepp and Geo. Gepp. . . Mr. Dick's party were numerous and noisy. We had a very good dinner, but the party too large to be pleasant. Mr. Codd, John Wright, Mr. Crabb, Charles Parker and Rev. Mr. Brooksby were also there. About 9 the chairman departed and so did I. Sir John kindly asked me to take a bed at his house, but I preferred going home. Barrington and his son crossed the ferry with me and I reached home very tired, from riding a young half broken in horse.

July 25. Wakering Fair. The Fair consisted only of three stalls and the music and dance in the barn might be enquired for in vain.

July 28. Called on Revd. Mr. Stafford at Shoebury, who with Mr. Burchell was thrown out of a gig, returning from a Visitation at Maldon.

July 29. Charles called this morning and brought me a young cuckoo who was reared in a haulm wall at the Hall by two water wagtails. I purpose taking it to London with me on Monday to Mrs. Headington who is fond of these things. The harvest is generally very forward.

July 30. Sent William to Southend to take a place for me by the coach to London tomorrow morning at 4 o'clock. Sent for to Mrs. Packman to South Shoebury. Mr. Packman died this forenoon, I believe from a broken heart. He had taken a farm in Foulness of Lord Winchelsea at an extravagant rent (Old Hall Farm).

July 31. Very fine. To London and return the same day. Rose at half past 3. The Monitor Coach came through a little after 4. By Rochford and Rayleigh, where we took up Mr. J. Scratton. Breakfasted at Billericay. Mr. Silver and Mr. Jackson were from the inside. Arrived in London 20 minutes before 10. Went to Northumberland Street, Strand, No. 8, and found Smith. Invited Smith to come and see me at Prittlewell tomorrow. Very hot in London. Made some purchases, called again upon Headington and returned at 3 by the same coach to Prittlewell by $\frac{1}{4}$ past 8, at the rate of ten miles an hour, stoppages included.

Aug. 4. Read of the death of Earl Winchelsea, which took place on Wednesday. No loss, and had it taken place earlier, it would have been better for this part of the country. He owned fine farms in Foulness[3] and has demanded such rents as to oblige the old tenants to leave them and will ruin those who have taken them. Old Mr. Packman . . . is an instance of it.

Aug. 6. Called on Lucy on my way home; they returned from Chatham Races yesterday.

Aug. 9. Miller having mentioned the death of Jonas Thornborough in the Island and his being an interesting case of Angina pectoris, I determined on endeavouring to examine the body and accordingly rode this morning to the Hall to breakfast by 8, and Charles drove me over to Foulness. Found the body of Thornborough in such a state I could not inspect it. At 12 we took sands again and got off just as the tide reached us.

Aug. 10. Rode to Southend. The steam packet came in. The Theatre opens this evening. Had my horse exercised in harness.

Aug. 11. Had my horse put in the cabriolet for the first time and, with William, drove him to Southchurch.

Aug. 13. Visited Mrs. Nashe's little girl at the workhouse.

Aug. 15. Mrs. Cause called with a sick servant maid.

Aug. 18. Went to the Hall at 2, but Charles was at a meeting at L. Wakering in consequence of the death of Mr. Pizzy, their late Overseer.

Aug. 21. Visited Mr. Austin, the Dissenting Minister there [Gt. Wakering], with Miller and drove again to Southend by 10. Played a rubber and returned home by 12.

Aug. 22. The harvest is in general got in, but the dryness of the season has made hay very scarce and consequently dear. Meadow hay is now £5 per load. Bought a load of Mr. J. Scratton.

Aug. 23. Sowed more turnips in my garden. The fly takes off everything.

My poor mare at Wakering Hall was killed on Saturday last. I saw him on Friday, reduced by his pulmonic complaint to a skeleton.

Aug. 27. To Rochford, called on Revd. Dr. Harris, another Dissenting Minister.

The harvest is finished everywhere. The peas and beans are a wretched crop, oats also, and are likely to be very dear.

Aug. 30. Read of the death of Cristopher Heley Hutchinson, Esq., M.P. for Cork, an old patient of mine when at Versailles.

Sept. 1. The birds are very plentifull and the whole country clear.

Sept. 2. Charles and Margaret called on their way to Chadwell and for Barnett Fair on Monday.

Sept. 3. To church – a charity sermon and a collection for the school[5] took place.

Sept. 10. Whale's son, George, is to be married to a daughter of Goodman's of the Crown Inn, Billericay, and the young people are to have the White Hart Inn at Bocking, I am told a good house.

Sept. 11. Brought home a brace of birds.

Sept. 13. Was called up at 2 to go to Mr. Audley at Rayleigh. Rode there. Night not dark and very fine. Day break before 4. Saw Mr. and Mrs. Kingsland on my return about ½ past 4 in the road, waiting for the second morning coach to London.

Sept. 15. Rode to S. End and operated for Hydrocele on Mr. D. Thomas' infant, the only case of the kind in an infant I ever saw.

Sept. 18. My horse still lame. Sent William to Whales at Southend and hired a horse.

Mr. Edward Taylor, having bespoke a play this evening at S. End, we drove there and, though a wet night, there was a good house, almost entirely of the country people, and put us in mind something of old times. They are very respectable performers and under Mr. Verrall. The play was Paul Pry and the Turnpike Gate. Our cabriolet was ready at the door when we came out. Home by 11.

Sept. 21. Clay from North Shoebury workhouse called for me to see his wife. Visited Mr. Harvey, the baker, and arranged for an amputation of part of the foot tomorrow.

Sept. 22. Rode to Rochford and performed an operation on Mr. Harvey's foot, Mr. Fairchild and a Mr. Thos. Smith of Nottingham present.

Sept. 26. Mr Winn called. He is going round to thank his constituents for their votes at Maldon election.

Sept. 27. Drove to South End to the Dinner at the True Blue Clubb, the Honble. Mr. Winn, M.P., in the chair. About 80 dined and the party was very respectable and free from those ebullitions of political feeling which have so much shewn themselves at former meetings, particularly at Maldon and Billericay and which made them anything but pleasant. We had an excellent dinner and the whole passed off extremely well. The West Essex Militia band attended.

Sept. 29. A Mr. Tomlinson from Maldon has set up at Wakering as an apothecary this day.

Oct. 4. Mr. Thorne having offered me his great horse, I availed myself of it to ride to Maldon from Rochford. Took an early dinner at Mr. Thorne's and then rode for Battlesbridge. Called on the Revd. Mr. Ray at Hockley and left my card. Went on to Battlesbridge where it came on to rain. Stopped at the Plough beyond Rettendon Common till the rain was over. Rode on to Chelmsford. Saw Mr. Crabb at Baddow. The road from Baddow to Chelmsford is altered and improved since I was last there. Went to the Black Boy, which is still kept by Bacon, and the old Hostler is also there. Wished to see Mr. Guy, but he is in London. Rode to Maldon by 7½. Some showers and the night rather dark. Went to the King's Head, now kept by one French, Kensett and his wife being both dead.

Oct. 5. At Maldon. Morning fine but quite cold. Called on Mr. Bugg and about 11 set off home by Woodham Mortimer and Hull Bridge where I was obliged to ferry, being too late for the tide by a quarter of an hour. Home to dinner. Lieut. Hales dined with me. Captn. Scallon came afterwards.

Oct. 9. Rode to Southend and called at Whales for two tickets to Miss Fisher's benefit at the Theatre tonight.

Tea at D. Thorne's and thence to the Theatre. Saw the Comedy of Who Wants a Guinea? and an excellent afterpiece called X,Y,Z.

Oct. 10. About 11 this forenoon our Vicar, the Revd. F. Nolan, passed by in a post-chaise to the church and soon after came Mr. Scratton's carriage full of ladies, muslin and lace, and stopped also at the church gate. This was the first intimation we had of a wedding and it turned out to be that of our parson to Miss Boon, a sister of Mrs. Baynton Scratton's and daughter of a bookseller in London.

Oct. 17. Received a letter from Smith, my Paris taylor, to say he is settled in London.

Oct. 19. At 11 drove by S. End, called at Mr. D. Thorn's. Saw Sheehy who goes to Chelmsford Quarter Sessions tomorrow respecting a row between himself and another paddy, O'Riley. To Rochford. Settled with Trotter for my furniture, paid Mr. Salmon for wine and Mr. Edwin Sumner for coals, and took Mr. Wren's receipt for my rent.

Oct. 20. Amputated a finger for Mr. Nunn from Eastwood. Mrs. Bennewith from Wakering called with an order from the parish of Foulness for me to attend her daughter with an old case of Fistula Lachrymalis.

Picked our quinces after dinner.

Oct. 23. Dined *en famille* at the Hall.

Oct. 25. To Shopland and visited James Adams, who has a concussion of the brain and has been three weeks under the care of a medical man without being once bled!

Nov. 6. It being the celebration of Gunpower plot, we had a terrible noise all night from the boys erecting a pole for the Bon fire at night.

Rain continues and the season is excessively wet. Many have not quite done sowing and the land is in a terrible state, but this refers only to a few, for in general the new wheats look very fine. Sad night for the bonfire.

Nov. 8. Lucy purposes going to London for change of air on Saturday.

Nov. 12. Parsons and Christopher dined with us on a very fine pig.

Nov. 17. Visited the man at the Anchor. Left my card at Mr. Tomlinson's, the new apothecary at Wakering – he is from Maldon.

Nov. 20. Mr. Carr called and I paid him a Poors Rate of 1s., being 25 shillings.

Nov. 21. Drove to Southend and visited Pritchard, the boat builder.

Dec. 4. To the Hope at S. End to enquire at what time the early coach goes for London and took my place for 4 o'clock. Very cold.

Dec. 5. The coach came about ten minutes past 4. It snowed, but did not continue long. Reached London and breakfasted at the Blue Boar, White Chapel. Went to Charing Cross, purchased some medicines in the Poultry at Winstanleys. Strolled into the different Law Courts in Westminster Hall and then through the Abbey. Thence to Bedford St., Bedford Square, and bought some books. Dined at the London Coffee House on Ludgate Hill, being very tired from walking so far. Thence to Headingtons, where I slept.

Dec. 6. Took a coach to Great Georges St. and saw Mrs. Lettson at Sir Wm. Garrows. Learn that the Duke of York has been operated upon for Dropsy and is not likely to do well and that the King is anything but in a healthy state. Walked back to Headingtons to dinner by 4 o'clock.

Dec. 7. Walked to Swans', the surgical instrument makers, and ordered a lancet razor for a case of burn at Little Wakering. Bought plated candlesticks and other articles and at ½ past 10, or near 11, left the Bull Inn, Whitechapel, in Nelson's coach for S. End. At Billericay called on D'Aranda whilst they changed horses. Reached Rochford by 5 and found William there with my cabriolet. No one wanting me, I went on with the coach to Prittlewell – had no one inside but myself.

Dec. 19. Dined at the Hall and went up to the Club in the evening.

Dec. 23. No newspaper came today.

Dec. 25. Dined *en famille* at Mr. D'Aranda's and slept there. Sent my chaise to the Crown.

Dec. 26. Lord Petre's hounds are assembling here this morning. They are very strong dogs, and most of the horses very fine ones, strong and well bred.

Dec. 27. Sent for to Mrs. D'Aranda. Opened an abscess for her in the throat, brought on by her own bad treatment of herself.

Dined at Wakering Hall.

1827

Jan. 1. As to the state of the country, farmers are not better off than they were last year. The ports are open for foreign grain, which has the effect of not merely lowering the price of corn, a circumstance sufficiently lamentable after the serious losses sustained last year by the breaking of the banks and the continuance of high rents, but of rendering that of our own growth unsaleable.

Loads and loads of wheat have been sent from hence to the London market, not only without being sold, but have been absolutely brought back again in the barges to save expenses.

Jan. 7.   His Royal Highness Frederick, Duke of York and Albany, died on Friday evening. It is supposed the Duke of Wellington will succeed to the Commandership-in-Chief.

Jan. 13.   Mr. Firmin called and paid me his rent for two pieces of land in Milton Hamlet.

Jan. 16.   William thatching the pig stie.

Jan. 17.   Rev. Mr. Nolan and Mr. Hardwick called for subscriptions for the distressed manufacturers. Had a pig killed this morning. Planted some cabbages.

Jan. 18.   Saw Mr. Gepp, there being a meeting of the Foulness Island commission.[6]

Jan. 20.   The funeral of the Duke of York takes place today. The bell tolled here in the morning at 10. The shop windows are shut and at night a dead peal was rung, which had a melancholy effect.

Jan. 24.   Clearing away the snow.

Jan. 29.   Mr. Burchell and his daughter called; the latter returns to school to Mrs. Gisborn's in a few days at Enfield.

Feb. 3.   Henry Davis called; he goes to School on Tuesday to a Dr. Nicholas at Ealing.

Feb. 7.   Jackson of Rochford has stopped payment.

Feb. 8.   Mr. Brown from Rayleigh called and I made his will for him.

Feb. 13.   Our young chickens, now a month old, are going on badly – four have died.

Feb. 20.   The Earl of Liverpool was taken with a fit on Saturday and, being Prime Minister of a Cabinet anything but united, his loss creates a great sensation and particularly as some important measures are about to come before Parliament. Mr. Canning, too, another Secretary of State, is at present also so unwell as to be unable to attend to business.

Feb. 21.   To Stafford's sale. Mr. Robjent has bought the corn bins for me. Thence to Barling to Miss Lambert and returned to the Hall to visit Charles' servant maid.

My mother and brother Peter and his wife, who are staying at Parsons', came there to tea, as did Parsons, Lucy and Christopher, thus meeting an unexpected family party. Night fine. Home by two.

Feb. 22.   Rode to Rochford. Visited Harvey. Others came to me at Gullocks. Wren called on me there and named the price I am to give for the mare I now drive.

At 3 to Wakering Hall to see the servant maid. Dined there. Mr. Mayston, an Uncle of Margaret's, was there. John Parsons came in the evening and we had a rubber.

Feb. 26.   A miller residing next door to us, named Watson, was found dead in his bed yesterday. He was an elderly man and subject to fitts.

March 3.   Mr. Codd held his inquest on old Watson at 8 and breakfasted with us at 9.

The alterations proposed in the Corn Laws on Thursday are not so great as apprehended.

March 5.   In going home, my horse could hardly get along with the Cabriolet. Jackson sent us a card table for our sitting room.

March 8.   Blows quite a hurricane. Rode to Rochford. My hat was blown off and went into a ditch of water and got quite filled.

March 15.   Making asparagus beds.

March 16.   Beautiful morning. Busy in the garden. Prior pruned the Jessamin in front of the house thoroughly which has not been done for many years. Miss Taylor sent her piano here.

March 18.   A large ship was totally dismasted by the hurricane and is lying at the Nore.

March 26.   Parish meetings are general today.

March 30.   Rose early and prepared for a journey to London. Drove with William to Rayleigh and called on Mrs. Barnes by Audley's, who is better. At 10 took the S. End coach, inside, and reached London about two. . . Walked back to Walbrook and slept there.

March 31.   Agreed not to return home till tomorrow and to dine at old Mr. Headington's at 5. Hired a gig and drove to Mrs. Hodson's, Norton St., No. 36. To Ballier's the French bookseller, Bedford St.; thence to Westminster and called on Mr. Tennyson. Bought Army and Navy lists for April. . . Returned to Headingtons and at 5 accompanied them to Mrs. Headington's, Spital Square.

There is some disturbance just now about there among the weavers.

Played two rubbers and returned not late.

April 1.   At 12½ left Headingtons for the Bull Inn, Aldgate, and then found the coach does not go till two. Had a fine beef stake, which I think they dress nowhere so well as in London.

Had no companion inside, till we got to Shenfield when the rain drove in Mr. Lazarus of Leigh. At Rochford the coach was filled.

April 5.   By Barling to Little Wakering workhouse to see Goff's daughter.

April 6.   To Thundersley, where I visited Mr. J. Thorn, who keeps the only public house there. The ride to Rayleigh was extremely warm. The woods behind Hadley Turnpike are now converted into cornfields.

April 7.   Received a note to attend Mr. Deeley at Battlesbridge Mills.

April 8.   Miss Taylor and Mrs. D. Thorne returned with Eliza from church; there seems to have been a full congregation today. The carriages were Scrattons', Heygates' and Hopes'.

April 9.   Old Mr. Harridge escaped from all injury from his horse running away today, down Wickford Hill over the bridge, through the village and round the next corner by the blacksmith's, where some timber carts and carters assisted the progress of the horse. He was in a four-wheeled chaise. The escape is a narrow one to a feeble, old man of 87. His servant is a strong powerful man but he lost all control of the horse.

April 10.   Drove to Wakering. Morning very fine, something of a white frost. After the blustering weather we have had lately, it was something to see the smoke from every chimney of the village ascending tranquilly in a direct line.

April 13.   Eliza to Church, it being Good Friday.

The increasing demands of enormous rents has induced Mr. Wren to relinquish the fine farm of Eastwood Bury and it is advertised in this day's County Paper to be let.

April 14. The morning being so very fine induced Eliza to ride with me to Battles bridge. Things are getting quite green and we had a nice ride.

April 18. Lucy went to town this morning by the coach. Found my favourite cat Minet had produced two little cats this morning. She was very uneasy when we came home from Rayleigh.

Called on Goff's daughter and John Harvey at Little Wakering poorhouse, both of them subjects for an operation on Monday.

April 19. I rode smartly to make my visit first to Shoebury, but my horse not liking to leave the Prittlewell road at the Three Ash turning I pressed him and had nearly cleared the turning, when he became so suddenly and unexpectedly restive, I was taken completely off my guard and thrown out of the stirrups on to the pummell of the saddle with so much violence as to render me quite shiftless and, the horse continuing to plunge and kick with the utmost force, I was thrown upon my back upon the hard gravel and received so much injury that, though I was able to get up upon my legs, I had no power to move and was almost immediately obliged to lie down again which, with the assistance of a man and a boy who were hoeing in Mr. Lodwick's Hall field and came to my assistance, I was enabled to do on some grass between the two roads.

I soon had plenty of assistance, it being about the time of returning from market. Brody's man took my horse home to come back with my cabriolet. D'Aranda came to me and many others, and after about an hour William came with the chaise, but I was not then in a state to be got into it. Grabham was with me but I could not bear to be moved. Swain's carriage was sent for and he kindly came with it. At last with assistance I was enabled to crawl or rather draw myself into it and, my legs being gently lifted so as to allow the door to be shut, lying like a log and in great agony, in this state I was removed to Prittlewell with as large an escort as has been seen from some time. Mr. John Scratton of the Priory and Mr. Baynton Scratton were particularly attentive; the latter with Mr. Swain's coachman were the two who got me upstairs. Indeed nothing could exceed the kindness and attention of everyone who could make themselves useful.

April 23. After plentiful bleeding and leeching, I am this day enabled to turn myself in bed, but still have no power to move the right leg or thigh. My bruises are most severe. Saw some patients at my bedside. Nothing can exceed the calls and kind enquiries of, I may say, the whole Hundred.

April 26. Got up for the first time.

April 27. Up. Mr. Byass, surgeon from Rayleigh, called also and consulted on the case of Mr. Deeley of Battlesbridge. Mr. J. Thorne from Thundersley came for a consultation.

April 30. Very hot. Miss Robinson, a nice looking girl from Dengie Hundred, came for advice in, I fear, a hopeless case of pulmonary consumption.

May 1. I do not get on nicely. My right hip is so much injured.

May 3. Ventured out for the first time, to visit old Mrs. Parsons at Shoebury.

May 6. Christopher came. He brought me a pair of spectacles which Lucy got for me in London.

May 11.   Miss Harvey died. Her father formerly lived at Wakering Hall and has taken me to school, then at Witham.

May 13.   At 5 drove with Eliza to D'Aranda's. Met Mr. Carter, Mr. Clayton and Mr. Taylor there. D'Aranda very poorly, and these three trying for their lives to smoak him, I suppose, into good health again.

May 15.   Sopwith's son accompanied me to Little Wakering, having two operations at the workhouse there.

May 17.   Visited my surgical patients at the workhouse, thence to the Hall and dined there.

[*Entries are missing for May 21–Nov.* 15]

Nov. 16.   Mr. Alfred Wedd came over this morning from Wakering with a fractured arm. He dined at Wakering Hall on Wednesday, after attending a tithe meeting at Wakering, and, on getting upon a young blood horse to return home, he fell off.

The Vicar of Wakering, The Revd. Mr. Pritchard, of The Red Lion memory there, has only sold his living twice and both parties had served notices on the parish.

Nov. 20.   My birthday. At 5 Mr. Parsons, Lucy and Christopher, Mr. and Mrs. John Parsons, Mr. Edward Sumner and Lieutenant and Mrs. D'Aranda and Miss D'Aranda, his sister from Billericay, dined with us. We did not break up till near two o'clock.

Nov. 24.   There is a great mortality about Sheerness from some sort of remitting fever.

Nov. 27.   News from Constantinople, four days after the defeat of the Turkish fleet was known, states all to be quiet.

Dec. 2.   Mrs. Sumner called in the afternoon after Church and told us of a fracas at Boreham House, which was alluded to in the Kent and Essex Mercury of Tuesday last. Mrs. Sumner has today received a letter from Mrs. Gepp in London, stating that there is but too much truth in the report and that the lady has gone off to Cornwall with a Revd. gentleman (d'Aubyn). . . It does not appear . . . that she has returned; on the contrary the reports are that the parties have gone for Paris.

Dec. 8.   The Yeomanry Corps are disbanded, except in districts where they are essential to the police. The officers are to retire with their respective rank.

Dec. 11.   A fellow was hanged yesterday at Chelmsford for a murder about a fortnight ago at Colchester of Patrick, a publican; he was an old offender but would not make any discoveries. In France they would have managed better.

Dec. 13.   The only topic today is a robbery at Grabham's by a woman formerly his house servant.

Dec. 15.   Mrs. Sumner called with a letter from Mrs. Aikin respecting her children being attacked with the Hooping Cough and wishing my instructions, but I decline attending to any of these cases where I cannot see my patients.

There is no doubt of Mrs. Tyrell being on the Continent, but where is not known.

Nov. 19.   Old Goss, who has lived here many years, died last evening. He received a fall at Rochford from his cart and fell upon a scraper which wounded the scalp severely. The external wound was carefully cleaned and put up, but the inside of the head scarcely thought of—*vide* the consequence.

Dec. 20.   Up at 5 and, being very fair, drove with Willm. in a light gig of

Mr. D'Aranda's to Foulness. Went up Rugwood head and a worse drive to Church-end could not be wished for. Breakfasted at Archer's and returned so as to take sands at 10 and got off before 11, when the tide was over the brooms.

Dec. 22.   Gullock called and brought the information of the death of old Abrey in Rochford workhouse this morning, a happy release.

Dec. 24.   Old Abrey, it seems, had not been in Rochford Workhouse above four hours before he died.

Dec. 25.   Xmas. As usual, had a miserable serenade about 3 this morning. Eliza went to church and the Thornes called afterwards. Mr. Jas. Taylor also called. At 5 we drove to the Hamlet[7] and dined with Lieut. D'Aranda; did not get home till 3.

Dec. 26.   To Foulness. Found my patient better. The riding through Foulness is just now terrible.

Dec. 31.   A poor man came from Canewdon; he is just out of St. Bartholemew's Hospital.

To the Hall for dinner. Saw the New Year in and reached home about 4.

Almost every shrub is budding.

1828

Jan. 1.   We saw the Old Year out and the New Year in at Wakering Hall and further kept it up by dining at Southend today at Mr. D. Thorne's on the Terrace, No. 14.

The agricultural state of the country is as flat as possible. Rents are still excessive, but down they must come, however reluctantly on the part of the landlords, who appear, in general, regarding themselves only and their tenants as nothing. Foulness is nearly new peopled and the change in the Uplands is almost as extensive.

The present administration . . . is too motley a group to last long, and the absolute necessity of retrenchment in the public expenditure will make the situation of any ministry not very enviable.

A war of some sort with Turkey appears inevitable. They obstinately hold out against any concessions to the Greeks.

Jan. 13.   Hurricane of wind and rain. Eliza to church, but there was scarcely six people there.

Jan. 14.   Had coals in from Lazarus at Leigh at 40s. per chaldron delivered here.

Jan. 15.   The Thames Tunnell has broke in again and 6 men drowned.

Jan. 16.   Charles came and brought a fine hare, which he stopped and partook of.

Jan. 18.   Operated on the burnt arm of Goff's daughter.

Jan. 24.   Some worthies from Barling were transported for seven years at the Sessions last week, one Cook, Murrell and Scott, the latter a son of Scott, otherwise Matthews of Little Wakering (a bad family). Home to dinner.

Jan. 25.   Mrs. Collins, otherwise Old Jane, died last Saturday at the Wall House, South Shoebury. She was an excellent cook and an old servant of ours and married Collins when both were in my service at Wakering Hall.

Jan. 27.   The Duke of Wellington is now at the head of the Administration.

Feb. 1.   Saw a large East Indiaman being towed up head to wind by two steam boats, one on each side.

Feb. 6.   A Mr. James Wilson (of Hermes memory in 1814) is appointed Surgeon to the Coast Guard here.

Feb. 8.   Traced my relationship to Stephen Jackson, formerly of Doggets, near Rochford, where Barrington now lives. There is a tomb to him in Rochford Churchyard. He died 24 December, 1705, aet. 52. He was my great-great-grandfather. His daughter, Susanha, married Francis Woodfield, my great-grandfather, had issue Elizabeth who married Jonas Asplin of Rochford, my grandfather; their issue Francis, my father, who married Mary Kennett of North Shoebury; their issue myself and several others.

Feb. 21.   Rochford churchyard resembled something of the Fête de Morts in France today. Some fellow was taken up yesterday, suspected of disinterring dead bodies, but nothing was proved. Enough, however, was fancied to induce every one to enquire after their dead grandfather or grandmother and to poke sticks down in their graves.

Feb. 24.   Read of the death of Mrs. Losack, wife of Admiral Losack, at Bern. We knew her well at all Paris parties as a determined Ecarté player.

March 1.   A new theatre in London, the Brunswick, fell in during a rehearsal and destroyed several people on Thursday; it was only just finished and performed in only once.

Mr. Thorne has a coursing day on Monday in Havengore.[8]

March 3.   Morning being very fine, determined on joining Mr. D. Thorne's party. Rode the roan mare and about 8 overtook Mr. Francis, Mr. Severn and a young friend of his and Mr. Thorne near the S. End road. The Severns and Mr. Francis rode with me by Wakering Stairs. Never knew the road to the Stairs worse than just now. The head way on to the sands is very good.

Met a largish party at Havengore. Had very good sport. Killed — hares and very few got away. After a hearty lunch we took Sands at ½ past 3, being high water at 1 o'clock today, we could not have taken them earlier. Home at 6. Turned in early, very tired.

March 5.   James Gardner from Gt. Wakering came; he has just received a hint of his mortality by a partial loss of speech.

March 13.   Grabham's servant maid, who robbed him, is transported for seven years and the man with whom she lodged, for receiving, fourteen years.

March 14.   A woman, Argyle, from Foulness, sent by the parish to be under my care.

Mr. Stallybrass and Christopher have just returned from Chelmsford Market. Turnip and coleseed feed is so plentiful from the forwardness of the season that in some parts of the county it is given away, in others money has been given to have it fed off by a certain time!!

March 17.   We have at present no Equinoctial gales, nor any wind since the gale of the night of the 4th. which threw up a very high tide on Wednesday, the 5th, higher than has been known for a long time; it run in at the headways at Foulness and came over the Walls very generally.

March 26.   Mr. Watson, a surgeon at Southend who never had any business there, is about to leave it.

March 28.   Drove to Little Wakering to dine at the parish meeting at 3 o'clock.

May 10.   A shift of wind to the Westward, and warmer. Mr. G. Vandervord called. At 11 rode to visit Mrs. D. Knapping. Called at the Workhouse on Mrs.

Radford. Saw Mr. John Scratton and Mr. Sheehy. The guns are saluting at Sheerness, I suspect the Duke of Clarence is there. Met Miller at Mr. Knapping's. Saw Charles going to Foulness. My grey mare was to have been sent there today, but I cannot spare her. Saw Lucy and her friend driving on the Common, arranged for their coming to us on Wednesday. Visited Burchell, called on Rev. Mr. Rays and then home to nurse my cold. Very fine out, but the wind has again got to the Eastward and is cold. Mrs. Knapping's case is, I fear, hopeless.

May 16.   Rusley Island.[9] They are boreing for water there and have now got to the depth of 413 feet and are still in a soapy black clay.

May 18.   Am very unwell. Bled myself largely.

May 19.   Charles called with little Lizza. Miss Lester came from Wallace Island and a Mrs. Thorby from S. End, whose breast I condemned for amputation.

May 20.   Drove to S. End to Mrs. Thorby at 10 to make arrangements for an operation which has not been performed in this country for 40 years (Mrs. Andrews at Rochford) and then not by any surgeon in the country. Saw Sheehy and appointed 4 o'clock tomorrow afternoon for the operation. Wrote to Mr. C. Miller and Mr. Tomlinson at Wakering and to Mr. Grabham and Mr. Marsh at Rochford, inviting them to be present.

May 21.   Find Sheehy has kicked up some hubbub as to the proposed operation today, which however has no effect upon my determination.

Waited till after 4 for Mr. Grabham. Drove to Whales and there met him, Mr. Marsh and C. Miller. We then proceeded to Mrs. Thorby's, opposite the Baths.

Removed the whole breast, being diseased from cancer, and succeeded extremely well.

Saw her again at night, and then home.

May 22.   Drove to S. End and visited Miss Leith and Mrs. Thorby; the latter has passed a good night.

May 25.   Mrs Thorby is doing delightfully.

May 31.   The Brazilian Ambassador has taken lodgings at S. End.

June 1.   Visited Mrs. Thorby, which case cannot go on better.

Saw Mr. and Mrs. Cattlin at Whales; they go to Greenwich by the steam-packet in the morning.

XII

Elizabeth Fry of Warley Lodge was the granddaughter of Elizabeth Fry, the prison reformer, who is referred to in this diary as 'dearest grandmama'. Born a Friend, the grand-daughter was, when sixteen, christened in East Ham parish church, perhaps because 'dearest Papa', John Gurney Fry, was a Justice of the Peace and an Anglican. Elizabeth was a studious and independent-minded girl, with a cultivated taste in literature, who expected the same degree of intellectual self-reliance in others. She was also very religious. On June 24, 1842, she wrote, 'My birthday, having completed my sixteenth year. May I feel it an impressive time and feel more and more the necessity of preparation for Death, with an increased knowledge of my Maker and growth in grace and wisdom.' Twelve years later she had died in childbirth. Happily, in the intervening years a less sombre outlook had allowed her to write a 180-line poem, 'The Lynn Regatta', and a story, 'The adventures of a kitten written by herself'.

The diary is for the year 1842 and I have selected entries for January, April, July and October.

The diary is in Essex Record Office, along with its author's other papers [D/DU 353]. There is also an essay by Mrs. V. Clarke, 'Time and Women, 1815–56' [T/Z 38/18], which includes a discussion of Elizabeth's life, and there are typescript notes on the West Ham associations of families referred to in the diary, compiled by the Borough Librarian of West Ham [T/G 86].

Journal
Commenced 1842

WINTER

JANUARY 1ST. We commence this year at Upton Lane, where all our party are staying, enjoying a visit to our beloved Grandpapa and Grandmamma;[1] the latter I grieve to say is very far from being in good health, which circumstance throws a gloom over the beginning of this year; her illness is much felt by all and is a cause of anxiety to many but we trust that a kind Providence will watch over her and restore her once more to her usual state of health. I greatly enjoyed taking a short walk in the garden with dearest Grandmama but was struck by her weakness, she only being able to take three turns up one short path and then seemed quite fatigued on reaching the house.

This afternoon Maria and I accompanied our dear Aunt Louisa Pelly and Harry to see a poor old man and his wife; they were wretchedly poor and seemed delighted with my aunt's kind present of some tea and a warm shawl for the old woman; a small debt they owed was also paid for them to their infinite satisfaction. Uncle and Aunt Joseph Fry dined with us this evening.

Janry. 2. Sunday. We had an interesting meeting this morning; dear Grandmama prayed and spoke beautifully; being the commencement of a new year, I think she seemed to feel it a solemn time.

Janry. 4. Passed quiet morning with dear Mamma and Sisters. Rachey still poorly. Walked in the afternoon to Aunt L. Pelly. In the evening an agreeable dinner party. We acted a good charade in the evening with Harry and Frank.

Janry. 5th. I returned last night with Uncle and Aunt Raymond Pelly and spent this morning with my dearest Aunt; in the afternoon we walked together to Vandrants at Stratford and dined in the evening at Ham House, where we enjoyed ourselves thoroughly, the youth amusing themselves by dressing up and playing at Blind man's Buff.

Janry. 7th. Dearest Grandmama is decidely improving. I fancy I see a change for the better every day, her strength seems mending and she speaks more cheerfully respecting herself. We dined this evening with Cousin Sam and Ellen and met the Gurneys and passed a very pleasant and cheerful evening. Cousin Ellen has invited us for Wednesday and a Juvenile Party, which we have accepted.

We have had and shall have, numerous engagements, though being among our dearest Uncles and Aunts, I feel they do no harm.

Janry. 9th. Sunday. . . In the afternoon we did not go to Church but remained at home and passed, I greatly regret, an unprofitable afternoon; for *all* the children were in the drawing room and totally prevented reading quietly, and if we had gone to our rooms, they would have followed us.

Janry. 10th. In the evening some of Uncles and Aunts dined here, and Uncle Joseph greatly entertained us by singing some of his Scotch ballards.

Janry. 13th. A quiet morning and in the evening a large party at Uncle Robert's where we had some nice dancing and music. Agreeable as these things may be at the time, I cannot help feeling the total unprofitableness of these parties, so entirely devoid of any real use or sense, consequently great waste of time. (I say perhaps too much as the sociable meeting of friends together is pleasant and gives satisfaction to many.)

Janry. 14th.   I returned last night with Uncle Gurney and Aunt Sophia to Harley Place and today has passed quietly and pleasantly. I fear however I have indulged too much in reading foolish, silly books, and not employed my time well by solid, good works. A novel is engrossing and amusing at the time, but I feel afterwards more fully the utter emptiness and uselessness of such works, which often, I think, do harm.

Janry. 17th.   The morning alone with Aunt S., saw Mamma and Aunt Katharine on their way to London, Mamma to see the laying of the first stone of the Exchange and Aunt to a grand dinner, given at the Mansion House by the Lord Mayor (Mr. Pirie) in honour of the before mentioned event. Dear Grandmama is going, together with dear Papa, and Uncle Gurney. We hear that Grandmama and the Lady Mayoress will sit in grand chairs, one on each side of the fireplace in the Mansion House drawing room to receive the visitors. The dinner will begin at five, and Grandmama we hear will be near the top of the table.

Janry. 18th.   This morng we three came by the railroad to Warley, I must say to our pleasure, for *home* always has indescribable charms... We have heard a little more about the grand dinner of yesterday. We hear that Grandmama sat between Prince Albert and Sir Robert Peel, with whom she had a great deal of conversation; they were particularly attentive and polite. Papa liked it extremely and thought Prince Albert one of the handsomest and most pleasant looking men he ever saw. The dinner was splendid. Papa looked really well in his Court dress and not so ridiculous as we expected... This afternoon we took a drive in the carriage to see Lady English and the Hirsts, after which we proceeded to the station and brought home Miss Worsley, with whom we shall recommence studies tomorrow.

Janry. 20.   This afternoon we spent at Lady English's, principally on her pond, it being frozen. Katey in high glee, sliding with Augustus.

Janry. 21.   Papa yesterday told us very sad news, the most grevious and melancholy deaths of the three excellent and brave commanders of the Expedition up the Niger, together with the deaths of most of the crew, the return of the vessels, and consequently the total failure of the Expedition... Uncle Buxton will doubtless feel it acutely, he has had so much to do with it and it has always been a very favourite project of his.

Janry. 22nd.   A pleasant evening enjoying Shakespeare.

Janry. 23rd. Sunday.   Went to our village Church in the morning, played the Seraphine, but found myself out of practise.

Janry. 27th.   A quiet evening with dear Papa and Mamma. We enjoyed ourselves again with one of Shakespeare's plays.

Janry. 28th.   A large party in the evening when many of our neighbouring friends were with us... We had a most pleasant and merry evening, charades, games, dancing and singing. I hope our friends enjoyed themselves; I really believe they did.

Janry. 29th.   I pay for last night's dissipation with a very bad headache.

Janry. 30th.   In the evening an express came from Upton to say we were *all* to be there the next day to meet the King of Prussia, who is now in England and who intends visiting our dear Grandmama.

Janry. 31st, Monday.   This morning we started at eleven and after having stopped for refreshments at Aunt Louisa's, arrived at Upton Lane at about half past one. All there were in a great bustle, busily making preparations for the reception of the King, who was expected at about two. Before that time were collected in the drawing room *all* the brothers and sisters, I mean all the children of Grandmama, while the upstairs rooms were crowded with grandchildren and nurses, the former all dressed in their best and looking extremely pretty and blooming. Expectation was on every countenance, and many were the exclamations of surprise and disappointment when three o'clock came without any signs of the King's approach. The King was during this time at Newgate with Grandmamma, where we heard he passed a most interesting and edifying time. Grandmama read a psalm and prayed, the Royal visitor with his suite all kneeling around her. On leaving, he expressed his particular approbation of the cleanliness of the prison and its inmates and of the other arrangements generally. At Upton Lane the house was decorated with flowers, and a most elegant collation prepared in the dining room. All the company was most tastefully dressed and looked extremely nice. All the windows looking up the road were thronged with children and those who would not meet the King in the drawing room, who beguiled the weary hours by watching the movements of the crowd assembled round the gates, and by various surmises and conjectures as to whether his Majesty would honor us with a visit or whether he would not. At last a state coach drove rapidly up, from which descended Grandmama, the Lady Mayoress and two Sheriffs. These were followed by one of the Queen's private carriages containing the King, Lord Hardwicke, Chevalier Bunsen and a German lord, Count Stolberg. Grandmama then conducted the King into the drawing-room and introduced him to all there assembled, consisting of her sons and daughters with Sir Fowel and Lady Buxton, Sir Henry and Lady Pelly, and Mr. Hankinson. His Majesty then retired to wash his hands, and in the meantime all the grandchildren were marshalled into the room and arranged in a group; his Majesty shortly after entered with Grandmama on his arm, and on seeing the pretty smiling assemblage of youth before him, lifted up his hands with delight and surprise and kindly noticed many, appearing astonished that all were grand-children. He then conducted Grandmama into the dining room to the déjeuner, where he remained about a quarter of an hour, during which time all the little children were taken out of the drawingroom and the numerous party of cousins, nephews, neices, etc., came in; to these his Majesty was introduced on again entering the drawingroom with Grandmama. A small party of friends, assembled for the purpose, then read an address to the King, at which he appeared affected. Shortly afterwards he went to his carriage, accompanied still by Grandmama, to whom at the door of his carriage he gave a most affectionate and tender farewell, his eyes filled with tears and apparently finding it a great pain parting with her with whom he was so delighted. He then entered his carriage and, unable to control his feelings, threw himself back in the seat, but a moment after, as if wishing once again to see our beloved Grandmama, he leant forward and looked out of the window, but was too late, Grandmama having already entered the house.

The King had said to Grandmamma in the course of the time "When I next come, I shall hope to bring my Eliza with me", meaning his Queen. When the King first entered the room, I naturally scrutinized his person very partic-ularly; he has decidedly a very pleasing, kind countenance, although far from handsome, he is rather tall, but has a bad figure, dresses badly, and has slovenly manners.

This has been indeed a most interesting and never-to-be-forgotten occasion, one which will ever be remembered by us with feelings of infinite pleasure, gratification and interest.

SPRING

1st April. Amused ourselves this morning with making April fools and succeeded admirably in taking in everybody.

2nd. Mr. Williams never appeared this morning, so we employed ourselves with drawing and received a visit from Johnny, who occasionally peeps into our schoolroom.

3rd. Sunday. Went to Church and played the Seraphine, which was placed last week in the galery. Enjoyed a delightful sermon from Mr. Pearson. . . Pleasant evening, though I think it might have been spent more profitably.

4th. In the evening a dinner party. . . Minnie and I sung and played a great deal.

5th. Walked again part of the way to the station with Mr. G. Tanqueray and in the afternoon accompanied Mama to Childerditch to visit a poor woman. Papa and Uncle S. at Chelmsford, they returned rather late; Papa has been made a Magistrate.

6th. Papa, Uncle Streatfield and Mr. Tanqueray went together to Chelmsford in order to be present at the trial of a man who had been stealing Papa's ducks.

8th. A regiment of recruits came to the barrack[2] yesterday where they remain till tomorrow morning, when they will embark for India.

12th. Had a half holiday and took a delightful long walk with cousins, played at King cards on our return. The Hirsts came to dinner, Ellen and I dined downstairs, rather against our inclination, although it was nice to join the party. Music, dancing and much merriment.

16. A lovely day, took a charming ramble with Papa and sisters, while Mamma and Katie went to Brentwood in the carriage.

17th. Sunday. A quiet, pleasant day, went to Church in the morning, but remained at home in the afternoon and enjoyed Milner's Church History.

18th. This day poor little Gurney Cresswell left his home and friends to go as a midshipman on board the ship Agincourt . . . bound for China.

Started early this morning with Minnie and Papa for the Mansion House (London), where a grand fancy bazaar is to be held tomorrow and the next day. Grandmama and her family are to have one very long stall next to that of the Lady Mayress and M. and I went up today to assist in laying out and arrange our things. After that fatiguing business we returned with Aunt Katharine to Upton Lane where we shall remain for three nights, thoroughly tired and both with bad headaches. Dearest Grandmamma not at all strong but cheerful.

19th. Took my place as a seller about 12. Most of Aunts were busy selling with many of our friends, Uncles kindly exerting themselves as stewards. . . Dear Grandmama was an object of great interest, all crowding to gain a glimpse of her and her text books with her autograph in them sold capitally. We all returned home, of course, thoroughly knocked up.

21st. Returned home this evening with Papa by the railroad, heartily delighted to leave the bustle, dirt and din of London. To our vexation, instead of enjoyed [*sic*] a nice evening with dearest Papa and Mamma, they went out to dinner and left us alone with Miss Worsley.

23rd. Went with Papa and Katie in the afternoon a delightful ride on horseback. . . We rode by Brentwood, Hutton, Shenfield and home by the Scrubs.

24th. Sunday. . . Quiet evening with sacred music. Walked after late dinner to the kitchen garden.

25th. A lovely day. Passed the afternoon on the lawn reading and in the evening a pleasant musical party.

30th. Passed all the afternoon reading on the lawn, while Papa and Mama and Katie drove out in the Phaeton. My book was Don Quixote, a volume which I am glancing, as it were, thro'; for it is in most parts very tedious, although extremely clever. I but rarely read it and then as a little relaxation from works of a graver nature. In the evening Aunt Cresswell with her three youngest boys . . . arrived; the dear boys are charming, fine and healthy.

[SUMMER]

July 1st. Walked in the afternoon to the kitchen garden, thence to visit Mrs. Bannister with her daughter who is very ill.

2nd. This morning Agatha, Mary and little Emmy left us, much to our sorrow. . . I took a quiet walk with Mama. Drank tea at Lady English's and walked home in the evening.

3rd. Sunday. Went to Church morning and evening as usual.

4th. Went to Brentwood with Mamma and Minnie in the afternoon, where we heard another report of a third attempt to shoot the Queen. It is really absurd to make such a fuss about a trifle as this seems to be. Some poor wretched boy in weak imitation of Francis snapped a pistol at the Queen as she passed and, tho' it appears there was nothing in the pistol except a little powder, yet the newspapers are full of it and all London is in an uproar. If no notice was taken, these silly attempts would not be made; for it seems wholy for the purpose of gaining notoriety and good keeping for life.

5th. After a quiet morning drove in the carriage with Mamma and Rachey and Katey to Herongate where was a cricket match between the Herongate Club and the B——[3] Club. After watching for some time with great interest Mama and I went to call on Mr. and Mrs. Button, leaving R. and K. with the little Pearsons. Mama then returned home with Papa and we three remained for the rest of the evening. It is very interesting and amusing to watch this game when one has seen it all; to drop in in the middle is remarkably dull. Mrs. Pearson and Miss Browne were quite excited and truly I think I partook of their feelings. We screamed and laughed with joy at any occurrence favourable to our side and sighed and groaned for the success of our enemies. Our side, the Herongate men, were however fairly beaten by 18 runs. We then drank tea at the Pearsons and jogged home in our "Bus"!

6th. Left home to pass a few days with Mr. and Mrs. Tanqueray. Met the latter at Stratford and came here in her poney chaise. . . Went over to the Forest in the afternoon.

7th. A deplorably wet day. Quite unable to leave the house but took a nice little drive in the evening. Amused ourselves with drawing, working and reading.

8th. Went in the evening with Mr. T. a funny sort of scramble over hedges and ditches, ploughed fields, potatoe and corn fields, etc., and returned home wet from a pouring shower.

11th. Spent the day with cousins at Wanstead and tho' amused and interested, yet felt fatigued by the incessant gossiping and discussions on dress, etc. but I suppose this is partly unavoidable as the wedding will take place tomorrow fortnight.

12th. Passed the afternoon at the Forest and were a very merry party, enjoyed a little music, etc.

13th. This morning left our kind friends (to whom we feel really grateful for their hospitability) and joined Papa and Mama on their way to town. . . Went to many shops with dearest Mama, who is I am thankful to say better, and after much deliberating and discussing settled the mighty matters of dresses, cardinals, bonnets, etc., and returned altogether home and truly glad am I to be there again.

14th. In the carriage to Brentwood and also to see the Hirsts who returned yesterday from Brighton. They came and drank tea and passed the evening with us. We were a most merry party tho' I think there was too much giggling and trifling talk.

18th. to 24th. The last few days have been passed quietly at home without visitors.

Sunday. Went to Church as usual morning and evening. The weather intensely warm, and general headache and languor prevailing amongst the party.

25th. Started off this morning in the carriage with Mamma and Sisters for Upton Lane.

26th. This morning at an early hour wedding preparations commenced and at ten o'clock Mama and I in our bridal attire went with Aunt E. Reynolds over to Wanstead where we had a peep and a kiss of the dear bride, who looked lovely, dressed in white satin with a white crape bonnet, lace fall and feathers. Being joined by more bridesmaids we proceeded to the Church. . . Agatha went thro' the ceremony admirably and repeated the responses distinctly, Mr. Bland appeared rather nervous. The happy pair then led the way to the vestry, followed by the six pairs of blooming maidens. . . After Mr. and Mrs. Bland's departure most of the party retired to their respective rooms or homes and met again in the tent at six to tea, after which we danced on the lawn all the evening, a capital band playing all the time.

27th. . . We came home to Warley, having much enjoyed our trip.

28th. A quiet day.

29th. Dearest Papa's birthday, he is 38.

31st. Sunday. A warm and pleasant day. Went to Church together in the morning, and in the afternoon M., R. and myself accompanied Papa and Mama to Horndon Church where we heard an excellent Charity Sermon from Dr. Robinson.

October 1st. This morning dearest Aunt left us with little Harrie. Uncle

Streatfield remained and passed the day shooting with Papa. . . A pleasant quiet evening.

3rd.   Went all of us to East Ham, lunched at Aunt Streatfield's and thence proceeded to East Ham Church where Uncle Joseph's and Aunt Alice's dear little baby Frederick William was christened. There also myself with my dear sisters were baptized, a most interesting, impressive and I trust never-to-be-forgotten occasion. Being born as Friends and consequently never having been Christened our beloved parents deemed us at a fit age when we should become members of the *visible* Church on Earth, and earnest is my prayer that we may be also members of Christ's *invisible* Church, in heart and deed true Christians and humble followers in his blessed footsteps.

4th.   Last evening dear Papa left us for Mr. Bramston's where he is going to pass a few days for the purpose of shooting.

5th.   Minnie and I went with Mamma to London. After having accomplished some shopping we called on Mrs. Bland and took lunch with her. We were much pleased with her little house, which is elegantly furnished. We then drove to the Orphan Adult Institution, where Mamma saw Miss Smith, a governess whom she has engaged to come to us, and sincerely do we hope she will prove suitable. We visited the bazaar and were much pleased by the gay scene, tho' I felt much tempted by the pretty things.

6th.   Passed a quiet day at home, walked in the afternoon to call on Mrs. Lewis and saw some of her paintings, which are beautiful. She is a very peculiar person, one whom I think however will improve on acquaintance.

7th.   Johnny and Gussy English came to dinner, passed a merry evening playing at chess, draughts, etc.

8th. . . Mrs. Blakiston . . . arrived this morning to pass a few days with us. Mrs. B. is a very charming person, full of life and spirits, with plenty of good sense; she has a straightforward way of speaking which pleases me and which I so far prefer. I also much like Caroline Abbott. I think (tho' I am not qualified to judge) that she possesses sound judgement with good sense and energy of character. Passed a very pleasant evening, Mr. Abbott's turn for drollery greatly enlivening our party.

9th.   Went to our village sunday school. . . Enjoyed a nice reading of Milner; the more I know of this delightful book, the more I like it and long for more time to devote to the study of it.

10th. . . Miss Smith, our new governess, arrived. I do not wish to judge from appearances and can therefore say little; her manners are very quiet, too much so perhaps, simple and ladylike, but wholly void of animation.

11th.   Spent the morning with Miss S., looking over books, etc. I can get her to say nothing, and to talk to her is like pumping from a dry well. She seems to have no ideas of her own, nothing to say on any subject, unable to give her own opinion, devoid of general information, and on the subject of books, studies, etc., without the slightest energy or power of mind.

But I am judging hastily, for no doubt she is nervous at first and her good qualities will in time develop themselves.

Took a long walk in the afternoon, with our agreable visitors, Mamma and Miss Smith, over the gap and thro the Magpie Wood—The country is looking lovely; every day is marked by visible changes and soon we shall see the bright warm lines of Autumn give way to the sombre tint of Winter. But when the cold has really come and Winter has fairly set in, there is a charm in the social evenings, the merry parties round the glowing fires, and such pleasant cosiness causes the gloom without to be forgotten. Some prefer Winter to Summer, but I do not there agree. Sweet Summer with her birds and flowers has ever charms for me, dearly as I love the sports of Winter.

12th. . . Miss Smith improves on acquaintance.

15th. . . Took a nice walk with Miss Smith.

17th. . . Evening spent pleasantly with chess and music.

19th. . . In the evening Mr. Hand joined the party. We younger ones with Harry acted a capital charade—the word was Bohemian—and the scenes caused roars of laughter from the spectators, who seemed highly amused. Music and draughts succeeded.

20th.   In the evening a rather formal party—Sir T. Neave, his daughters.

23rd.   A pleasant quiet evening, Sacred Music and poetry.

24th.   A wet day, unable to go out, read "Charles O'Malley" instead and I confess much enjoyed it.

27th and 28th.   Very fine days. Took some pleasant walks and passed the days quietly.

29th.   Accompanied Mamma to Sir Thomas Neave's to see the consecration of the Chapel in his parish.[4] It was a very interesting ceremony, performed by the Bishop of London. The Church, which was dedicated to St. Thomas, is very pretty, though *externally* peculiarly plain.

30th. Sunday.   Went to Church as usual. Our sermon in the morning was on a subject, caused by the Visitation last Friday, that of reviving in the Church many old customs, which have lately fallen into disuse. Many of these decidedly border on Popery, and at a time like this, when the English Church is so much torn and agitated by contending parties and by various opinions, it is perhaps unwise to introduce these new regulations, which place too much dependance on outward forms, not sufficiently savouring of spiritual things. In all things a due degree of order and form should assuredly be kept up, but with more simplicity and purity of manner—for after all, if but in heart and deed we truly and sincerely serve and worship our Great Creator, it little matters where or how our adoration and supplication is offered or with what outward signs it is accompanied.

XIII

William Wire's diary testifies to the standards of self-education to be found in early Victorian times among Colchester's skilled artisans, to which class as a watchmaker he belonged, but his intellectual curiosity and erudition would have been outstanding in any social group. Though his range of interests was extensive, it was to the study of Colchester's Roman past that he devoted his main effort amid difficulties which would have crushed the spirit of less dedicated students. These difficulties included his own poor health, a very large family and the continuing financial burden incurred when he acted as guarantor for a friend who failed in business. Another was the resentful attitude taken towards this self-educated, radical Nonconformist by well-to-do antiquarians of the district, most of whom he far excelled in archaeological knowledge.

Wire came from a family of radicals and from 1835 to 1839 himself took an active part in Reform politics. Disappointed by the results of the 1832 Reform Act, he organised the poorer supporters of the Liberal cause into an Independent Reform club, thus anticipating the Chartist movement of 1838, to the Colchester branch of which he gave tentative support until in 1839 the increasing militancy drove him out of Chartism and, indeed, out of active politics altogether. During his commitment to the Reform cause he characteristically emphasised the central importance of adult education as the prerequisite of social progress. In a lecture to the town's Chartists, then organised in the Colchester Working Men's Association, he said:

'May we indeed be guarded against the crime of drunkenness and let it be seen to the world that the working classes, who meet for mutual instruction, are no longer influenced by intoxication. . . It may be asked, what are we to do with our time? I will tell you. There is a Mechanics' Institute in the town, open every night; the subscription is only 2/– a quarter, and every member can go and read the newspapers and periodicals, and have the privilege of taking home a book to read to his family. That would be a much better way of spending your time – in pursuit of knowledge. 'Knowledge is power' and you can command it; you would also be instructing your children and making yourselves better men for society, and doing everything to render you worthy of your franchise.'

After his withdrawal from politics he intervened in one matter of public policy only, but he did so most effectively. The town's Grammar School, then situated in Culver Street, was an offence to Wire's party, because it was then an Anglican foundation, with Tory trustees and a narrow curriculum. Its history was not without periods of considerable success, but in Wire's day it had declined to the point where only one free scholar was attending, a boy who happened to be Wire's own son. In 1842 Wire sued the Master for assaulting his son and, though he lost the case, he had in the process brought before the public the poor state of the school. He next proceeded to ask the Bishop of London to use his powers to institute reform. Wire wanted him to change the curriculum so as to provide a commercial training for free burgesses' sons, but, instead, the Bishop enlarged the range of subjects taught and ensured that the Master took a greater number of free scholars. Indirectly Wire's initiative also caused the school to be provided with new buildings on a pleasant site, which it still occupies, and the consequent building operations afforded him additional archaeological material. The school's success in the years following would probably have been achieved in any case, but Wire's initiative certainly hastened the process of reform.

One cause of Wire's withdrawal from active politics was his growing pre-occupation with Colchester's history as a Roman town, new light on which was being shed almost weekly by the mass of objects discovered in the course of the numerous building operations then taking place. He acquired many of these objects and, by selling what he did not want, was able to add to his collection articles in which it was deficient. When his efforts to bring about the establish-ment of a public museum proved unsuccessful, he set up his own in 1840, only to have to sell many of its contents to support sick members of his family. When his troubles decreased, he resumed his archaeological work, maintaining it until his death. He recorded his acquisitions from the start of his diary in 1842, noting, wherever possible, the location of their discovery, so that the geography of Roman settlement in Colchester cannot be fully surveyed without this information.

Wire died in 1857. He had for some years been earning his living as a postman and, being unable to find a substitute to deliver his letters on an April day when he had influenza, he insisted on delivering them himself. Soon after his return home he died. The *Essex Standard* described him as a 'zealous and useful antiqu-ary . . . highly esteemed for his uprightness and integrity' and it held a sub-scription for his wife and the four children still dependent upon her.

The diary records his experience of the years 1842 to 1857 and is therefore lengthy, despite the paucity of entries at certain periods within those years. Details of archaeological and historical interest predominate and from these I have selected only as many as seem necessary to illustrate his work in this field. The majority of the entries included here are those telling of Wire's life and outlook or showing the town's expansion in an important period of its develop-ment. It is in the latter connections that his diary has most value for those with-out a specialised concern in the details of Colchester's Roman archaeology. Wire himself strongly exemplifies the Victorian ideal of the self-educated, self-reliant, sober and thoughtful artisan, while Colchester, similarly, is seen as a town which, through its own voluntary and civic efforts or the enterprise of individuals, macadamises its streets, expands into new housing estates, attracts the services of railway and steamship, and acquires a public cemetery and new Town Hall.

JOURNAL of events transpiring in the Borough of Colcr., kept by William Wire. 1842

May 23. Called upon Mr. John Taylor, jun., when he kindly gave me Sparrow's plan of Colchester and shewed me several pictures and sketches of different parts of the town.

May 25. While the laborers were digging on the East side of North Hill to lay down a drain of gutter bricks, when opposite the church gates, they dug on to a foundation of the same character as the Town Walls, that is a soft stone with a mixture of broken Roman tiles, which was found to run up the hill 10 feet; at the termination was a Roman road, 10 feet in width and which appeared to cross the hill.

May 30. Mr. John Green, bricklayer, informs me that he discovered a tesselated pavement on the premises of Mr. Salmon, linnen draper, No 50, High Street.

June 17. Purchased of a railway laborer, who found it near the viaduct, Lexden, a silver gilt hand-in-hand mediaeval ring with following legend engraved on it, JESUS NAZARENE.

August 26. Mrs. Alston of London shewed me a first brass coin of Hadrian, very much corroded, said to have been found in the rampart near Lexden Lodge, when cut through for the Eastern Counties Railway in July last.

August 28. Went this afternoon to hear a sermon preached at Trinity Church by the Rev. D. F. Markham in advocacy of the claims of the committee, who had built a school room for the parish children. . . He pleaded the cause well, but the inculcating passive obedience was the chief doctrine.

August 30. Went to the rail road, found they were getting on with the station, which appears from its slight construction to be but for a temporary purpose. The "navvies" continue digging but find nothing.

September 2. Received a letter from the Rev. H. Jenkins containing a few particulars respecting a Roman villa discovered by and being explored under his auspices at Gosbeck's Farm, Stanway.[1]

September 5. Went to see the foundations of a Roman villa in Cheshunt or Chesnut field, Gosbecks, near the Brick-Wall farm, Stanway, which is being explored under the superintendance and direction of the Rev. H. Jenkins, Rector. The following measurements were obtained by me, 400 feet wide from S.S.E. to N.N.W. and Mr. Jenkins sends me word that the Crypto Porticus is 305 feet long; this ran the whole length of the building.

September 14. Purchased of Mr. Fincham, gardener, a few Roman brass coins, very much corroded, and a lead seal, which I suppose was used as a voucher for the quality and quantity of a parcel of bays manufactured here.[2] See Morant's Hist. of Colchester.

Received a letter from A. J. Kemp, wherein he endeavours to combat my opinion respecting Colchester being the Camulodunum.

September 16. Went to the railway and was informed by one of the company's police that persons not engaged on the work was not permitted to visit them and he told me that the day before he had ordered Mr. Green, the banker off.

September 19. Went on the Court and laid a complaint against Mr. Dunningham, Master of the Free Grammar School, for assaulting my son,

William, who was on the Foundation. . . Likewise appealed against the power of Mr. Dunning's suspending my son.

September 22.   Sold an ancient British coin to a lady.

September 26.   A person who gave the name of Hunt Temple, London, called upon me, to whom I presented a few local Provincials and in return he gave me two Stycas found at York 1842. This person is one of the gang who travel the country selling forged coins.

September 28.   The first zebra I ever saw rode in public and which seemed pretty tame, was in the procession of Mr. Batty's horses and company who are now exhibiting in the Castle Bailey.

September 29.   Mr. Cuthcent gave me an iron cannon ball found in the field adjoining the railway station, which was probably shot from the town during the Seige.[3]

October 5.   A man working in the Hythe river called and shewed me a 2b coin of Claudius, rev. Ceres sitting in a chair, which he said he found in the river below the last granary.

October 17.   Left with Mr. Bray, Sudbury carrier, a parcel . . . being my gift to the Sudbury Museum.

October 27.   Purchased a Roman ring key found in a field, north side of the London road, opposite the second pump, which is being converted into a cricket ground.

October 31.   Mr. Braithwait, engineer in chief to the Eastern Counties Railway, kindly sent me a pass so that I can inspect the works at any time.

November 11.   Mr. Stephen Clubb, millwright of North Street,[4] called this morning and shewed me a sample of barley stripd of its skin, for which he has constructed a machine. This is the first attempt in this town to prepare barley in this way for puddings, etc.

November 20.   Went to the railway on Tuesday last, when I was informed that the day before that a fluted Roman Urn had been discovered in a field south of the Station.

November 27.   The milk man informed me that a fire had been discovered at Mr. T. Daniel's, West Bergholt, between eleven and twelve o'clock last night. . . It is rather a singular coincidence that several of the fires in the neighbourhood have taken place on a Saturday night.

Nov. 29.   Mr. Henry Vincent,[5] who is employed as a missionary at the expence of — Sturge, esq., to advocate the Complete Suffrage system, delivered a lecture on that subject at the Large Room, Lion Walk, to a very large assembly, who were delighted with his address, which, as I am informed, was a very eloquent one . . . of two hours duration. The meeting ended in the electing of Mr. J. B. Harvey, printer of this town, to be a delegate to the ensuing meeting of delegates to discuss, watch and report which will be the most efficient way to obtain their object, viz. Universal Suffrage, paid members of Parliament and other matters connected therewith.

December 1.   It was customary some years since for the Corporation to appoint someone styled the Bellman (an office quite distinct from the Town Cryer) whose [duty] it seems to have been originally to call people up to their work but now dwindled down to nothing. In my recollection he used to begin his nocturnal vocation immediately this day commenced by ringing his bell as soon as the clock had struck twelve on the last night of November and recite the following dogorel verse at various parts of the town:

> Cold December is come in,
> The poor men's backs are clothed thin,
> The trees are bare, the birds are mute,
> A pot and a toast will very well suit.

The last Bell-man died some years since... At Christmas he used to go boxing, when he presented each person who gave him a "box" with a copy of verses.

December 2. The Town in a state of excitement in consequence of a fire at West Bergholt Heath; the engines went between 7 and 8 o'clock in the evening.

December 7. Mr. Harvey, gaoler, informs me that Jas. Fenning, Town Cryer, has obtained the Mayor's consent to serve the office of Bellman.

December 9. There is an enlargement being made on the South side of the Waterworks engine house.

Mr. Winch, sub-secretary to the Mechanics Institute, informs me that, when the offer to read a paper before the Mechanics' Institute on the study of History was made ... by the Rev. King, Catholic Priest, the President (Mr. G. Stokes) said that if the Roman religion was touched upon, he would withdraw his patronage.

December 15. Attended a lecture delivered by Mr. Underwood at the Assembly rooms, Three Cups Inn, on the application of Phrenology to Education and, if the science is true, the arguments advanced by the lecturer went to show that, if attended to, the advantages to society would be great.

December 19. My father, who is 72 years old, says that the "Red House", formerly the residence of Dr. John Bastwick, stood on the site of the present Baptist chapel and that it was used as a cow house in his memory.

Called up Mr. Dunthorne[6] at Winsley's Alms houses, when he informed me that all his father's local portraits were parted with sometime since. He is 85 years of age.

December 22. A fire occurred at Mr. G. Sadler's, Lt. Horkesley.

The butchers' show of Christmas beef.

December 24 ... a district church is to be erected near the Leather Bottle Inn.[7]

December 26. Christmas Day falling on Sunday, the shops were closed this day and a holiday was kept generally by all excepting the Quakers, who refused to shut up their shops when others do.

Went for a ride to the railway viaduct, Lexden; walked on the top which is covered with a pitch-like substance to prevent any damp penetrating the brick work. Down each arch is a funnel, opening near the bottom, for conveying off the surface water.

Another fire occurred this evening in the direction of Stoke-by-Nayland; it was distinctly seen from this town to burn for three hours.

December 27. Intelligence arrived here that the fire ... was at Red Barn ... where Corder murdered Maria Martin.

December 28. A new cricket ground is being made in a field North side of the London Road nearly opposite the second pump.

December 31. It is intended by the Wesleyan Methodists to establish a day school on the Glasgow system.[8]

1843

January 2. Walked to Mr. Balls, Sheppen Farm, to clean his clock and accompanied him to the second field south of the house called Fort field to look at some places discovered by him. . . There is a great quantity of fragments of Roman pottery along the bank. The place that was opened in my presence was floored with concrete, and portion of some bone was found in it but whether human or animal I am not competent to say, and some fragments of Roman pottery. These places by compass bearing are S.W. by N.E. He informed me that he had discovered a number of such places on the farm. . .⁹

January 3. Sold Mr. Bolton, traveller, 16 forged silver coins of Anglo Saxon, Anglo Danish and English and 10 silver Greek coins in silver that I purchased before I understood them.

Purchased a 3B coin of Constantine the Great in excellent preservation and another in a fair state found in the Roman burial ground, back of Mill Place, Butt Lane.

January 9. Mr. Gilbert informs me that he and the Rev. H. Jenkins of Stanway had been trying to discover what Roman roads diverged from this town and that they had in a great measure been successful, one of which he said passed through the centre arch of the railway viaduct, Lexden.

January 19. A report is current that Mr. H. Nye Fenner, schoolmaster, of Head St. and one of the Town Council, has absconded, being very much in debt.

January 21. Mr. Henry Thorn, Sen., informs me that the parish books of Holy Trinity parish were destroyed by one Barnes to enable him to defraud the almshouses called "Trinity Poor Row" in that parish of some garden ground belonging to and adjoining them.

January 22. The news reached here that Sir Robert Peel had been shot at.

February 2. Mr. H. Thorn, Sen., tells me that, when he was a boy, it was customary at the Wilderness fair, held at Easter and Whitsuntide in Middleborough, to throw custards at each other and that he has partaken in the sport himself.

February 6. It is currently reported that a railway train, drawn by an engine, is to arrive at the station, but no such thing took place.

February 10. A train drawn by an engine arrived at the Station here.

February 14. Went to the railway viaduct, Lexden, and saw an engine drawing the muck waggons.

February 21. This day a writ of ejectment was enforced at Stockwell Chapel in consequence of a dispute in money matters between the Rev. J. Herrick and some of his congregation, who had withdrawn from the Chapel and attended the Round meeting, when the Sheriff's Officer, who got possession and turned out all the books, hassocks and cushions into the street, locked up the doors and would not permit the Rev. J. Herrick to preach there.

February 24. Went to the railway station and saw the directors arrive per rail, accompanied by General Paisley, the Government Inspector, before whose inspection and approval as to its completeness no railway can be used for public conveyance.

February 27. The town in a state of excitement and the bells ringing in consequence of a report that the railway directors and shareholders were coming by the rail in four carriages drawn by the engine.. Went to the station and, after waiting there two hours, finding they did not make their appearance, came home, after which it was reported that a bridge at Mountnessing was not considered safe to cross. Daresay there was two thousand people collected . . . and much disappointment prevailed.

Several men were discharged from the silk factory of Messrs. Brown and Moy, and this week it is closed two days in a week in consequence of the depression of the silk trade.

March 1. The Railway Directors arrived from London by rail, walked in procession headed by a band of music and flags flying, bells ringing and other demonstrations of joy to the Three Cupps Hotel where they partook of a cold collation.

March 2. No. 64 Railway Policeman informed me that luggage trains commenced running this morning for the conveyance of goods to and from London and intermediate places.

March 11. Received a vote of thanks from the Society of Antiquaries for the exhibition of a small bronze figure of Mercury and a book of drawings of antiquities discovered in this town.

March 13. Mr. John Cant lent me a ms. journal of Birth, Deaths and Marriages and other occurrences which took place in this town from 1764 to 1773.

March 14. A lecture was delivered this evening in the public room, Lion Walk, on the distress of the country by the Rev. Thos. Spencer, perpetual curate of Hinton Charter House near Bath.

March 15. Commenced obtaining subscriptions for the republication of a scarce tract entitled "Colchester Teares."[10]

A party of ladies and gentlemen came down by the rail, the former proceeded to see St. Botolph's Priory . . . then returned to the station when the two carriages they came in were set out, dinner spread, and they enjoyed it during their return to London.

Mr. Stephen Club of North Street[4] informs me that the pond in the Mile End Road nearly opposite the Railway Hotel was unenclosed and always considered a roadside pond till it was enclosed within his memory and that a man going to water his horses found the gate locked and without any ceremony put his horses to it and pulled it down.

March 16. Miss Posford waited upon me for a contribution to raise the fund for redeeming Mr. Herrick's chapel called "Stockwell Chapel" from the hands of the Mortgagees, when I gave her sixpence. There is a party of ladies who have undertaken to go from door to door the town through on the same errand. During the time of Mr. Herrick's expulsion from the Chapel he performed the Sabbath Day duties in the Lion Walk room.

The Rev. S. Carr kindly granted me permission to visit the field he has purchased behind the present Vicarage where it is hoped some interesting Roman antiquities will be discovered, as in the same field . . . some years ago a beautiful mosaic pavement was discovered and covered up again.

March 19 . . . a piece of ground belonging to the Union House and lying on the North side near the Water Works was sold . . . to the Rev. J. Round for £110 . . . for allotments for industrious labourers and artizans.

March 22. A ball at the Angell Inn, Ladies tickets 1/6 each and Gentlemen's 2s.

March 23. Went and looked over the Castle, but had not time for a minute inspection.

March 29. Opening of the railway for passengers through to London; the first train . . . left the station here at nine o'clock. . . A great number of people went to the station to see the trains arrive and depart.

April 1. Another fire occurred this evening at Mr. Lambert's, West Bergholt—most probably incendiarism.

April 2. Rev. Joseph Herrick has regained his Chapel and preached in it this day for the first time.

Missionary sermons at the Wesleyan Chapel; £19 was collected.

April 4. Lecture at the Mechanics' Institute by Mr. Burt on the principles of Machinery and the Mechanical Powers.

April 17. On Friday last, being Good Friday, a Tea meeting in aid of the Town Mission was held in the Lion Walk Room . . . the proceeds amounted to sixteen pounds odd.

April 21. The old North Bridge is being pulled down.

April 24. To remedy the inconvenience caused by North Bridge being impassable, a temporary bridge is erected on the West side of it by a company of gentlemen and to pay for it the following charges are made for crossing it, viz. for a horse, or a cart drawn by a donkey, 1d. . .

March 25. Received a letter from Mr. J. Adey Repton, Springfield, expressing a hope that the Norman Arch at the Moot Hall will be preserved.

May 1. Signed a memorial to Sir G. H. Smyth and R. Sanderson, the Borough Members . . . to vote against Sir J. Graham's Educational Bill.

May 5. Mr. Fitch, Ipswich, favoured me per post by the loan of Mr. Morant's pen and ink sketches of the earth works in Lexden . . .[11]

New premises are being erected in Church St., St. Mary atte Walls for the Savings Bank.

May 8. As the "Retaliator" 4-horse coach, driven by Mr. Flack, was coming over Mile End Heath to the railway Station, the horses ran along with the coach and continued their speed till they came to the temporary North Bridge, when the coach, coming in contact with the rails, was upset and the passengers receiving no other harm but a few scratches and fright.

May 9. Mr. T. Stribling, coachmaker, North Hill, is insolvent.

May 11. When I was walking up Balkon Hill, I saw that a portion on the North side of the Balkon Fort[12] had been destroyed in order to build additional rooms to the King's Head Inn to command a view of the railway. What a pity that one of the best preserved remains of Roman times should be destroyed to administer to the sensual pleasures, as it may be considered only as a decoy to induce persons to enter the house to drink.

May 12. The Old North Bridge is taken down . . . and the workmen are standing still waiting for Mr. Braithwaite, the Engineer, to give orders as to whether the old piers are to remain to support the bridge or taken up and new ones erected. Report says that the plan of the new bridge is too short by four feet. As usual, all public works executed in this town, especially bridges, are sure to have something amiss. . .[13]

May 14. In passing through the Castle Bailey, I see that the cow sheds, erected against the West side of the Castle and a disgrace alike to the builder and proprietor, are removed.

M

May 20. Received a vote of thanks from the committee of the Sudbury Mechanics' Institute for an elephant tooth, etc., sent to them for the Museum there.

Between twelve and one o'clock at noon, in consequence of the drivers neglecting to chain the wheel of a laden timber carriage belonging to Mr. Hawkins . . . , it overcame the horses and went down North Hill at a fearful rate. . . No one can calculate on the mischief that must have been done by it, had the hill, it being market day, been as full of vehicles and pedestrians as it was just before and immediately after.

May 23. The Rev. J. Jenkins of Stanway called upon me and said it was his opinion that the Temple of Claudius, mentioned by Tacitus, stood near the Castle, if not on the same site.

May 24. Mr. Wollard informs me that some years since there was a wilderness near the Castle Inn, North, which belonged to the original Lexden Park, where was a maze or labyrinth and from this the Fair held annually at Easter and Whitsuntide takes the name of Wilderness Fair.

May 27. The "Wellington" coach is taken off the London road in consequence of its not paying, after having run from this town to London for many years.

Three tumblers exhibited their feats of contortion, jumping or ballancing each other on North Hill.

May 29. A new or the old "Wellington" coach started this morning . . . to London . . . under the name of the "Golden Path", by the same proprietors, Messrs. Shuttleworth and Co. . . . Fare to London, inside ten shillings, outside six shillings.

Mr. S. A. Philbrick lent me some Mss, squibs relating to the affair of unroofing the Old Chapel in Helen's Lane, in consequence of a dispute between the pastor (Rev. J. Herrick) and the members of the church . . . and a list of the contributors to the clothing and other expences of the "Royal Colchester Volunteers, 1803".

The bells of St. Peter rang a peal at various times . . . in commemoration of the restoration of Charles II. But how altered it is. Within my recollection some years since an oak bough was placed before most of the houses and he who failed to yield to the custom was considered disloyal and in the afternoon the boys, assisted by some men, used to take them away to some favoured spot and in the evening with a tar barrel or two make a bonfire, which burned most furiously; fire works were let off during the evening. On this occasion a few were exhibited.

May 30. Mr. John Cant, gardener, lent me a private journal of some of the events . . . in this town between 1795 and 1830.

May 31. The Rev. S. Carr, when asked where it was the Baptists held their meetings in the Parish of St. Peter, he did not know.

Mr. Woolmer informs me that a Roman urn containing a deposit by cremation was discovered under the concrete foundation of the North buttress of the old bridge.

June 2. The tenders for the erection of a new Town Hall were opened.

June 4. Mr. Hardy, who resided at the Blue Boar, West Stockwell St., was buried with Odd Fellows' honors at St. Gyles' Church. The brothers, arrayed in all the paraphernalia of the Lodge, walked six abreast, preceded by an officer carrying a Bible on a black cushion.

June 5. Attended my Benefit Club feast, a very good plain dinner for which 2/6 was paid the meeting night before.

June 6. Mr. James Farren informs me that several of the members of the Lion Walk Chapel have separated themselves from that church and have hired the large room opposite and purpose having a preacher that will expound their doctrines . . . till circumstances permit them to erect a more convenient place. The leading men amongst them is Mr. D. Morris, surgeon, and R. M. Savill; the latter attended the Wesleyan Chapel for some time. This is another specimen of the evil arising from the Dissenters' plan of electing their own minister, but doubtless it would work well if they were embued with the Christian doctrine of Loving their neighbour as themselves.

June 8. Purchased of a laborer, who found them in John Street, a blue glass bead, a bone pin, several fragments of Samian ware and Roman glass vessels and of bronze. It is as well to observe that all the antiquities noticed above and subsequently as discovered in John Street were found from No. 5 to the East end of St. John's Terrace, unless stated to the contrary.

June 10. During the time I was standing to see the men at work on the north side of the river they dug on to a Roman pot which fell to pieces immediately it was exposed to the air.

June 16. The "Swift Sure" steam vessel arrived at this port, being the first steamer that ever delivered goods at the Hythe wharf.

This morning an attempt was made to close the path leading from Magdalen Green to Moore Lane, by fencing up the entrance to Childwell Alley near Magdalene Church, which was no sooner done that Mr. Thomas Moore's men demolished it, so it remains open.

Two omnibuses, one from the Red Lion and one from the Three Cupps Inn, a one horse fly and two cabs called Brohams continually keep plying between the railway station and various parts of the town at the fare of sixpence each person by the two former and a shilling each fare by the latter.

June 20. Anniversary of the Blue Coat and National School. The day was ushered in by the ringing of the bells of St. Peter's. The children walked in procession from the Bailey to this church, preceded by the Town Council of which only twelve attended. The Mayor was dressed in a scarlet cloak wearing the gold chain. . . Some of the boys carried banners of blue silk with the following on them in letters of gold: CHURCH AND STATE. THE QUEEN, then followed two made with pink silk, having inscribed on them OUR NATIVE TOWN. OUR PATRONS. . . Money collected £73. 9. 6. The bill of fare, which consisted of 14 rounds of beef, twenty three legs of mutton, 50 baked plum puddings, forty boiled plum puddings, a barrel and a half of beer, etc., was supplied by the liberal contributions of the town's people and was as usual eaten in the Bailey.

June 26. The hoard is put up before the old Town Hall, preparatory to taking down.

June 27. Workmen are taking the roof off the houses west of the old Town Hall, but adjoining it, preparatory to removing them.

Mr. Rumball, the Phrenologist, gave a lecture to prove there is no truth in Mesmerism or Animal Magnetism.

June 30. Mr. John Taylor, jun., and other persons are purchasing antiquities for a museum without either judgement or discretion.

July 3. The Anti-Corn Law League are very busy distributing tracts in this town, preparatory to a meeting to be held on Saturday next, when Mr. Cobden is expected.

July 7. Mr. Moore gave a Free Trade lecture at the Mechanics' Institution, preparatory to the Free Trade meeting tomorrow.

July 8. Took a walk this morning to see where the public Anti-Corn Law meeting was to be held, when I saw preparations for it in a meadow near the tan-yard, East Bridge. Bills are posted about the town, forbidding the holding the above meeting in the High Street by order of the Mayor. . . Went to the Anti-corn Law meeting . . . but did not stay 10 minutes, as I merely went to see. Mr. Cobden, the great Free Trader, was addressing the meeting which was not so large as I expected.

July 10. In consequence of some misunderstanding between the lessee of the Theatre and the lessee of the gasworks . . . the latter is having the gas fittings taken down. The Theatre passed its prime some years since; in fact this is not a theatre-going town now.

July 13. Went to the station. . . The seven o'clock train, coming at the rate of 25 miles an hour, the brake not answering left it to pursue its rapid course past the station, when it ran into the engine which was standing at the extremity of the rails and drove it off down the bank. Providentially no injury was sustained . . . except a little fright to the passengers.

20 July. Visited the bridge works . . . report says the iron work is cast 8 inches too short; if so, it is Colchester all over.

July 21. At Chelmsford Assizes one Woodard was found guilty of arson at West Bergholt and sentenced to transportation for life.

July 23. Boatswain Smith, alias Penzance Smith, treated the Colchester folks with his annual sermon from a cart near the remains of the old Town Hall, accompanied by his small band.

July 24. The Colchester Total Abstinence Society walked in procession up the High Street to spend the day in the park [at] Beerchurch, preceded by a band of music.

The foundations are in course of being dug out for a gasworks in a garden immediately west of the silk factory, Dead Lane.

July 27. The field south of the railway station is being divided by wooden rails for the reception of cattle going by the railway.

Purchased an Elizabeth sixpence found near the brick kilns, Mile-end.

August 1. Last night two prisoners escaped from the Borough Gaol. . . It appears they escaped by wrenching out the bars of the window and let themselves down by their blankets tied together.

August 5. A short time since an additional part was erected to the King's Head, Balkon Fort, when part of the old wall was taken down on the north to put a window in.

August 7. Sent a letter to the Bishop of London respecting the Free Grammar School.

August 8. Gas pipes are being laid down to light up the railway Station and Hotel.

August 11. Had some conversation with Mr. J. H. Church, solicitor of the Town Council, respecting the Free Grammar School in this town and, when it was stated that, as it at present stood, it was a disgrace to the Town Council, he said that the rebuilding of the Town Hall had occupied the whole attention of that body and asked me what would be the best plan to adopt; upon which I said to make a commercial school of it was thought to be most advantageous to the greatest number of qualified children. He then asked me whether it should be thrown open to the town at large; my reply was, to the sons of freeburgesses only and that my opinion was the Bishop of London could make the necessary alterations in the statutes without going to the Court of Chancery and that according to the Charity Commissioners' Report the Town Council are the Governors.

August 24. Took the freeman's money, seventeen shillings; why two shillings less than the two preceding years no reason was given by the Town Treasurer.

The Cupps omnibus passed over the new bridge this day.

August 31. The Mail Coach had a narrow escape from being upset at the new bridge last Tuesday night.

August 14. The streets are lighted by gas this evening for the first time this season.

August 15. Mr. G. H. Garrard has contracted to light up such public oil lamps as remain at thirteen and ninepence each for the season.

An experiment was made in front of Mr. Bryant's house with the "Bude" light in a glass lanthern sent from London for the occasion; it failed to exhibit that brilliancy that was anticipated from two causes; firstly the jets were too high in the lanthern, secondly the contractor for the public gas lamps put on a greater pressure, which caused a greater light from them, a jealousy being created for fear the "Bude" should eclipse their lights – in fact I do not remember seeing so much light proceeding from them before.

August 17. Received a letter from the Bishop of London, stating he would attend to the Free Grammar School in September next and requesting a copy of the memorial I presented to him in October last.

August 23. Miss Alicia Barker kindly presented me with a list of the plants and shrubs growing in this neighbourhood and of the butterflies and moths caught here.

September 1. The independent dissenters who meet in the Large Room, Lion Walk, to worship God, have purchased a house in Black Boy Lane, opposite the Brewers' Arms Inn, to convert into a chapel; it is now and has been for some time in the occupation of a notorious bawd. . .

September 10. . . The Bishop Blaze Inn,[14] now the Locomotive, in Duck Lane. . .

Sept. 11 Mr. David Morris, surgeon, informs me that the liberal party of this town have purchased the Essex and Herts. Mercury newspaper to be their organ of publication. . .

September 13. The first stone of the new Town Hall was laid by the Mayor; the Freemasons walked in the procession. The bells rang a merry peal during the day. There were a great many people in town but they were very much dissatisfied.

October 2. Mr. Catchpool, ironmonger, High Street, has had the bow windows taken out of his shop and a flat front put in.

October 4. Mr. Mordecai Levy, a Jew residing in this town, informs me that the Jews' synagogue was in a court, West Stockwell Street, at the back of the Quakers' meeting.

October 8. The Rev. H. Norton, Wesleyan Minister, preached at the Independent Chapel, Lion Walk, instead of the Rev. T. W. Davids, who is going to preach at the new Wesleyan Chapel, Gt. Bently, it having been opened on Thursday last.

October 11. Agricultural show at the Castle Bailey and a ploughing match in a field down Maldon Lane. Wet all day.

October 20. The pavement is being taken up in Middleborough to macadamise it.

St. Dennis Fair was proclaimed by the Mayor but not with that parade it used to be previous to the passing of the municipal reform bill.

November 6. The anniversary of the discovery of Gunpowder Plot is still kept up as usual by boys and lads, who go from house to house, some with an effigy, others with another boy dressed up with his face blacked. . . Fireworks . . . were let off in the High Street and an empty tar barrel was set on fire in the inside and rolled up and down the High Street to the amusement and danger of the people congregated.

November 14. The gas works, Dead Lane, are set to work for the first time. The railway station first lighted by gas this evening.

November 16. The "Golden Path" two-horse coach to London was taken off the road last Saturday in consequence of not paying and the Hadleigh branch coach came . . . last Monday for the last time.

December 2. Miss Smith, residing at the Castle, informs me that the Revd. H. Jenkins, in company with Professor Buckland and other gentlemen, visited that building a few days since, when the Professor gave it as his opinion that it is a Roman structure.

December 25. Shops closed as usual, excepting the Quakers.

December 27. Mr. Henry Thorn, the present proprietor of Buxton's receipe for candying eringo root,[15] informs me that from Buxton it went into Mr. Chas. Great's possession, at his decease to Mr. Chas. Keymer's, from him to Mrs. Crane, when she died to the wife of the present proprietor.

1844

January 15. Received a copy of the Anti-Corn Law League newspaper, when the postman told me that 2000 came to this Post Office, which accounts for him being at my house a quarter nine in the morning instead of a quarter to eight, his usual time.

January 29. This evening the town was alarmed by a fire at Ardley Hall and another near Harwich. Mr. Abrey of Ardleigh tells me that an unsuccessful attempt was made to fire Ardley Hall last Saturday week.

February 17. For some time past Phrenology has been all the rage in this town; now it is nearly supplanted by Mesmerism.

March 3. Attended the Wesleyan chapel; Mr. Lythe preached. After the service he gave notice that a public meeting would be held . . . to form schools in each circuit in the Wesleyan connection.

March 17. Sermons were preached at the different dissenting places and collections made on behalf of the Scotch Free Church. . . The united congregations, for this evening only, of the Lion Walk chapel and the Lion

Walk room at the Round Meeting. . . Sum total collected £98. 5. 0½.

March 30. North Hill is watered for the first time this season.

April 8. Mr. Thomas More, wholesale grocer, Barrack St., has hired Magdalen Green and is having it enclosed by a brick wall for a garden.

April 27. Mr. Tracy of Lexden, who is between 60 and 70 years of age, informs me that there was formerly a wooden post near the Ramparts, Lexden Heath, which was used as a whipping post to secure the soldiers to during the time the camp was on the heath; that it was removed when the heath was enclosed some years since.

The Essex Standard newspaper . . . contains an account of the alterations in the Statutes of the Free Grammar School.

May 16. The minister, accompanied by the Churchwardens, other parochial officers and parishioners and schoolboys, perambulated the bounds of St. Peter's parish.

May 22. Signed a petition to the House of Commons in favour of a railway to Harwich from the station here. The two contending parties in favour of Lock's or Braithwaite's line, both of which were lost by a decision of a committee of the House of Commons after having spent a great deal of money, have now become amalgamated to enable them to try again.

May 29. Two oak boughs up at the shop of Mr. Chignall, butcher, North Hill; it was a faint attempt to imitate the celebration of the preservation of Charles II in the oak tree. . .

June 11. Attended a private meeting at the Cups Hotel to take into consideration the propriety of forming a society for reclaiming and maintaining the common field walks in Colchester and its neighbourhood, when resolutions were passed that such a society was highly necessary.

June 13. Trade is very dead here. The town is Mesmeric crazy.

July 9. About 30 years since Mr. Simons, who resided . . . on North Hill, made a collection amongst the townsfolk to defray the expense of putting down steps at King's washing place, keeping the bank in order and trimming the grass near on the Town side of the river.

July 23. A board is put up at the Middleburg end of Dead Lane changing its name to St. Peter's Street.

July 26. A spring that rises under the Town wall opposite the great gates of the water works and which runs at the foot of the wall some distance, then cross the road into the old tanyard, has been diverted into a well in the yard of the waterworks company. The spring is boarded over but a small trap door is left in it for the people of the neighbourhood to get the water from.

August 3. Report says that Messrs. Charles and George Bawtree at the Rectifying Office, Culver St.,[16] are insolvent for £40,000 and that they have offered a composition of nine shillings in the pound; Mr. Bawtree is an alderman . . . but . . . he resigned.

August 5. The street gas lamps lighted up for the season.

August 7. This evening the town in a state of excitement in consequence of a fire seen from the North at the farm of Mr. Mortimer, Nayland. The news was brought by two men riding horses who started in so great a fright as not to stop to put on either waistcoat or coat.

August 8. The Town Council go the bounds of the River Colne this day and afterwards to Mersea Stone and have dinner; several who are not members of the council go there and have a day's recreation, but the excitements attendant on it has in a great measure subsided, as formerly the old Corporation invited their friends and paid the expence out of the Borough funds. Now all that go, not members of the body politic, have to defray their own expences.

August 19. Went to London by the Luggage Train, paid the fare, four shillings, started about half past one in the morning, arrived there a little before 4.

Agust 21. Came down by the luggage train, started from Shoreditch about 20 min. past 6 p.m. and arrived there about half past eight.

August 22. Took breakfast at the Victoria Hotel (which was opened last Monday).

August 28. Some earth is being removed to widen the road leading up to the railway station in consequence of the "Criterion" Stowmarket coach being upset by turning the corner too abrupt.

August 29. The performers at a circus now being erected on the north side of the Castle in the Bailey came from the King's Arms Inn, Crouch St., and paraded the town, one of them driving eight in hand and turning corners with as much ease as if driving only four. . .

The newly erected Chapel in Chapel St. is opened this day.

September 2. According to annual custom the agricultural labourers at the conclusion of the harvest call upon different tradesmen in the town and solicit "larges" . . . get what money they can and get drunk with it.

September 10. Pears are to plentiful they are hawked upon the streets a penny a quarter a peck.

September 16. A meeting convened this evening at the Cupps Hotel by Mr. Wolton, grocer, to take into consideration the necessity of closing the shops earlier.

September 18. Signed a paper . . . with most of the tradesmen . . . to shut up my shop at eight o'clock in the evening from March to September . . . and at seven o'clock for the remainder four months.

September 20. The measles are very bad in some families.

September 21. The time of closing the shops is altered to eight o'clock all the year round, excepting Saturday evening when it is to be 10 o'clock.

September 23. Shops shut up this evening at eight o'clock for the first time by all the tradesmen in the High St. excepting Mr. Fairhead, pastry cook, and another.

September 28. So great a quantity of cattle in the market that for want of room in the High St. some stood below the church gates, North Hill.

October 2. Mr. Van Hamburgh made a procession through one part of the town with his trained horses and tamed wild beasts, which were in caravans. . . The elephant did not walk in procession as on a previous occasion but down North Hill alone to the place of exhibition in a field opposite the "Globe" Inn, North Street, The performance consists of feats of horsemanship and exhibition of the animals in the caravans, the dens of which Mr. Hamburgh enters and commands animals to obey him in the performance of several tricks.

A field, lately glebe, called "Golden Acre", which was this year exchanged for one lying behind the present vicarage of St. Peter's, situated between the Globe Inn and Sneak Lane, North Street, was in part sold in lots of thirty feet frontage and a hundred feet in depth and averaged forty shillings a running foot, that is only the frontage is paid for, the depth is given in. At this sale not quite half of it was disposed of. . . Had the whole been sold, no doubt the proceeds would have realized a thousand pounds.

October 5. The shop of the corner of High St. and Head St. has had a new front put in of brass mullions and plate glass and was opened this day by Mr. Nicholson, hatter. This is the first shop in the town lighted by French reflectors.

This morning a fire supposed to be the work of an incendiary broke out on an off-hand farm of Mr. R. Bradbrook which consumed the barn and its contents.

October 9. Agricultural show held in the Bailey by which the thorough-fare is blocked up.

October 21. The Weavers' Arms public house, Middleborough, last licence day was altered to the Spread Eagle. Most of the old signs in this town have been changed.

This day the penny a mile train started from this town but at such an awkward time—five o'clock in the afternoon—that it is very problematick if it will confer that benefit on those it was intended by the Parliament.

October 29. Attended No. 25 Druids' Lodge, held at the King's Arms, Crouch St. . . There is another in the town, but, being a rebel lodge, it is not open.

November 6. Rode with Mr. Jno. Brown of Stanway to Hitcham to spend the day with Professor Henslow. . . We were treated with the utmost kindness and shewn his museum.

November 10. Collection at Wesleyan Chapel for Kings-wood and Wood-house schools.

November 16. . . when a cesspool was dug at Beverley Lodge a few days since, an urn was discovered.

November 22. Walked to Mr. Fairclough's, West Bergholt Heath . . . and cleaned the clock, when I embraced the opportunity to enter into conversation with the woman left in charge of the house respecting the late fires in the parish. . . There appears to be no sympathy for the farmers, she having made an observation to the effect that they . . . do not suffer from the fires and, when I said it was a serious thing to destroy food, she made no reply. She likewise said that Bibby, who was apprehended on suspcion, was made drunk at the White Hart Inn, Bergholt Heath, by Mr. Ratcliff and the police to draw a confession from him, which she said was the reason he told so many different tales.

November 24. Collection at the Wesleyan Chapel on behalf of the day-school attached to it.

December 13. Visited Essex Street and the other thoroughfares now forming on part of Mr. Cant's garden ground.

December 19. Attended a public meeting at the Cups Hotel, convened by the Mayor who was in the chair, to take into consideration the best way to form and permanently establish a public library and museum, when resolutions were passed to that effect. Several persons set down their names for shares in the building, others for donations. . . There was only two or three clergymen in the room, they as a body being opposed to it, likewise the bankers, the former for reasons above stated,[17] the latter having so recently erected the new corn exchange.

December 25. Christmas day, shops closed as usual, except the Quakers'.

1845

February 7.   Bought a large brass Roman coin found in the old Laboratory, now converted into tenements between Dead Lane and Duck Lane.

February 13.   Visited Langinghoe church; nothing in it of any interest if a stone front is excepted.

February 17.   Rode to Braxted. On returning, called at the "Sun", a beer shop at Feering, to look at some carved work, which it is decorated with, which seems to be of the 15 cent. In the lower room, used as a tap room, there is round two sides of the cornice 28 carved heads of different sizes and various dresses of the hair and caps on.

February 23.   A collection was made at St. Botolph's church after the three sermons towards paying for a new organ.

March 7.   The severity of the frost having prevented bricklayers and their laborers from working, the latter have ranged the town, calling at each house soliciting aid; one of them informs me that 60 were out of work.

March 8.   The journey[-men] gardeners are going from house to house begging, being unable to work because of the frost.

March 19 . . . people are skating . . . between the bridge and Middle Mill.

March 22.   An agricultural laborer, who works at Langinghoe Hall, informs me that on the marshes belonging to it there are two hills—tumuli—formed of a reddish earth and that others have been carted away. . .

April 11.   Mr. Brown of Stanway informs me six Ancient British coins have been found at Walton on the Naze. . .

May 1.   The new Town Hall was opened. The procession which met at the Castle walked in the following order—the Town Council, clergymen, tradesmen, and subscribers and the children of the National and British Schools, headed by the regimental band of the East India company from Warley Barracks.

A holiday given to the shop men by the closing of the shops at five o'clock in the evening.

July 29.   The foreman of Mr. Batty's circus which is going to perform in Cheeping field drove seven pair in hand through some of the streets of this town.

November 28.   In Mr. Bryant's garden, east side of North Hill, abutting on a new street on the North, a Roman tessellated pavement has been discovered, composed with red tesserae one inch square. Several fragments of fresco house wall have been found.

December 5.   Went into Mr. Bryant's garden and took a rough sketch of the pavement as far as discovered.

1846

October 10.   Received per post a letter of invitation from Mr. Charles Bailey to meet him at the Red Lion Hotel in this town tomorrow, as some of the members of the British Archaeological Association were coming on Monday next to take an antiquarian tour of inspection through the town. Sent word by return of post that I could not conscientiously meet them on the Sunday but would on the following day.

October 12.   Accompanied the archaeological gentlemen in their pedestrian visit.

October 14. Agricultural show held in the Castle Bailey.

October 28. Carried to the Town Hall, where a room is set apart for the reception of articles of virtu forming the nucleus of a Town Museum, a pair of hippopotmus tusks and a Spernacity whale tooth.

Walked to Little Horkesley Church and took rubbings of two monumental brasses there.

November 5. As usual, many effigies stuffed with straw are carried about the town. . . Bonfire and fireworks in the High Street in the evening. On occasion of public rejoicing, there are collected a number of idle and loose characters, fully ripe for any mischief. So it was this evening; about forty such paraded the High Street, armed with great cudgels and walking six abreast to the annoyance of the peaceable spectators.

1847

January 1. The publicans raised the price of London porter from twopence to twopence halfpenny, but they were soon obliged to reduce it to the old price, as most people left off drinking it.

January 18. A public meeting held in the Town Hall in aid of the distressed Scotch and Irish, when a good subscription was entered into.

February 16. A fire occured at the Grammar School, Culver Street, but was extinguished as soon as discovered.

April 1. The branch of the Stour Valley Railway from the Hythe to the Eastern Counties railway opened this day.

April 3. Potatoes are selling at five shillings a bushel.

May 5. Flour rose this morning five shillings a sack and bread is selling at tenpence halfpenny the four pound loaf.

May 9. Bread rose again one penny the four pound loaf.

May 25. The Colchester Horticultural Show held this day in the new Corn Market.

July 30. Mr. Hardcastle and Sir George Henry Smith of Berechurch Hall were, after a hard fought contest, returned members of Parliament, the former in the Liberal and the latter in the Conservative interest. Mr. Sanderson, the old conservative member, was on the occasion rejected.

August 10. Mr. Hughes and his trained animals came into the town early this morning and proceeded as far as Beverley Lodge where they waited till the time of entering the main streets in procession. It was really an interesting sight to see an elephant nibbling the grass that grew on the bank and eleven camels lying down nearby.

August 16. Great consternation was created in the town by the news that Mr. Sanderson, late M.P., had suspended payment.

October 1. Sent a registered letter to the Hon. R. C. Neville, Audeley End, containing two brass coins of Cunobeline found in this town.

November 1. Municipal election. Two liberals returned for the first and third wards, in the second ward they were rejected. There was nearly as much of the usual bustle as is created at a general election.

December 29. The Town Treasurer has become insolvent for between 20,000 and 30,000, chiefly borrowed money of different individuals, whereby some of them are reduced to great distress. It is whispered that his Town accts. are dificient some £600, which his sureties made up.

1848

March 23. A laborer working at New Quay in the channel brought in a 1b coin of Marcus Aurelius.

April 12. Wombwell's Menagerie came into the town this morning, when the sight loving folk had their taste gratified by the Lion Queen riding in a seat on the back of an elephant through the principal streets, followed by the caravans in train.

May 17. Mr. Green, the celebrated aeronout, ascended in his balloon from the Botanic Garden about half past three o'clock p.m., and a splendid sight it was, the wind blowing from the south-west with a gentle breeze by which he was wafted gradually to the opposite point of the compass for a short distance, when he began to ascend gradually and was carried to Diss in Norfolk where he descended between five and six o'clock in the evening. . . What added to the splendor of the sight was a clear sun, shiny day.

July 5. Pineapples are hawked about the town from one shilling to two shillings according to size. This is quite a novelty here.

August 10. Purchased the seal of Thomas Great, candier of Eringo root.

1849

April 23. A street sweeping machine first used in this town, by being applied to cleanse Head Street. Popular opinion being against it in consequence of its depriving several men, who did the scavenger work, of employment, it was soon returned to the proprietor.

May 24. Mr. Green, the celebrated aeronaut, made his 410 upward trip in his balloon from the Botanic Garden. The wind blowing from the N.W. caused it to go in the direction of Fingringhoe, in which parish it descended and was brought back to the garden in the evening.

September 10. A barrel drain has been laid down from the Anchor Inn, Magdalene Street, to and down the yard of Messrs. Hawkins, Timber Merchants. Another up Hogg Lane as far as the great gate entrance to Kendall's Gift homes and another from the Colchester Arms Inn to Magdalen Street, but nothing was found.

1851

February 26. A fire broke out at Mile End Hall, by which [the] greater part of the farming produce and out buildings were destroyed.

March 31. This day the census was taken.

July 5. Prince Albert passed by the railway on his return to London from Ipswich. A great number of persons were attracted to the station in consequence of a report that he would visit the Idiot Asylum. He did not get out of the carriage. . .

July 21. Purchased "A new and exact Prospect of Colchester taken from the North east, 1724", dedicated to the officers and members of the Corporation by John Prior. . . This is the only copy that has either been seen or heard of by me.

July 31. Went to the Rural Fete, held in Wivenhoe in aid of the funds of the Mechanics' Institute. Rustic amusements were entered into by those who felt inclined – Vaulting, Archery, Quoits, Football, Cricket, Swings, Traps, etc.

1852

July 6. Purchased of a lad some fragments of Roman pottery and a plain Samian ware bottom, potter's mark PRIVA, for 2d., found at West Lodge.

Gave a lad 3d. to bring me a portion of Roman brick having three impressions of a stag's foot on it, which I selected from the fragments of Roman bricks found at the Botanic garden.

Died on Tuesday . . . Mr. Alderman Vint of St. Mary's Lodge, London Road. He has left all his antiquities to this town, providing there is a fire proof building provided for their reception in three years; if this condition is not complied with, they are to go to the British Museum.

July 16. This night between 10 and 12 o'clock a dreadful hurricance blew, which injured more or less all the wind mills in the neighbourhood. Butt Mill had the sails torn off and sustained other damage. Mr. Poppy['s] Mill in the Mersea Road sustained very little damage. The large mill in the Military Road is very materially injured by having the top near the sail shaft lifted up, which caused a good deal of injury to the working gear, and had some of the vanes stripped of the sails. . . The smaller mill had some of the vanes rent from the sails. The distillery mill, Greenstead mill, St. Ann's mill all have had some damage done to them and so has Birch mill. The rag-mill of Mr. Club, North Street, had the top and sails thrown to the ground.

August 12. Sold Mr. Acton a lot of antiquities.

August 18. Went to the excavations going on preparatory to building the new grammar school next the hospital, when the laborers informed me that he had instructions from the Rev. J. T. Round, who is acting for his brother, C. C. Round, one of the Trustees, to save everything found for them.

August 20. Walked up to the Grammar School works. Nothing found but a few fragments of common Roman pottery and an iron nail 8 inches long.

August 23. A new school is being erected for the British and Foreign school in Moor Lane.

August 24. Dr. Duncan called this morning and invited me to attend at the Local Archaeological Society meeting at the Literary Institution on Wednesday week.

September 1. Went into the meadow back of Rev. T. J. Round's to meet the local Archaeological Association and inspect the remains discovered there. They consist of a drain of graduating size and depth built with tiles and in some places arched over with the same and floored with them, in fact of the same character as that part of it discovered outside the walls and noticed before. At the south end there appears to be the foundation of a Roman house and a spring appears to rise in it or nearby, but enough was not laid bare to give an opinion on it. At some distance from it to the west is the remains of a pavement about one foot below the surface composed of red tesserae about 6 feet long from east to west and about 4 feet wide from north to south. Portions of amphorae and black urns were discovered.[18]

September 13. Mr. Bowler at the brewery, North Hill, has had the Town Wall repaired the length of his premises in Balkon Lane.

September 23. Purchased some fragments of embossed Samian ware found at the Grammar School works.

November 24. The shops closed and business suspended in consequence of the funeral of the Duke of Wellington.

November 29.   Visited the Roman Catholic chapel. Cardinal Wiseman came down purposely to confirm the younger members of the community.

December 14.   A public meeting at the Town Hall to form a Colchester and Essex Archaeological Society.[19] Not many attended... There was exhibited ... the sphinx from the Hospital.[20]

About 8 o'clock in the evening a fire occurred in the Model Room of the foundry, High Street, the property of Mr. Thomas Catchpool... It was three quarters of an hour before water could be obtained to supply the engines.

1853

February 17.   Attended the first meeting of the Essex and Colchester Archaeological Society, held at the Lecture Room, Literary Society, John's Street, when a paper was read by Mr. John Taylor on Roman remains found at West Lodge...

March 3.   Died ... at the advanced age of 97 Mr. George Sansom... The deceased was a wool card maker, for many years the only one of his trade in the Eastern Counties and the last relic of the ancient and once flourishing bay manufacture of this town.

March 22.   The town wall at the bottom of Cheaping field is exposed to view by cutting a trench for a footpath, in doing which the remains of what appears to have been a square tower was exposed to view.

March 29.   Mr. Mattacks, Sen., informs me that the Methodist Reformers have taken the old chapel, St. Helen's Lane ... and that they had the title deeds and other writings belonging to it... This chapel has undergone more changes in respect to the religious tenets preached there than any other place of worship in the town. Erected in the year 1666, it was presbyterian and so continued for more than 150 years. The first change was an Independent form of worship, then a Unitarian, next a Swedenborgian, and at this time used by the reform Methodist... These alterations have arisen in consequence of the foundation deed not stating that it shall be confined to any particular sect.

May 9.   A vessel built for Mr. John Mann on a new principle was launched from the ship yard at the Hythe amidst a great concourse of people.

May 13.   Mr. Smith, brush maker, who travels the country, informs me that there is on Goldhanger marshes, Essex, a field called Red Hills or Red Field; the occupier of it told him that there is a Roman pavement there.

July 8.   The reservoir, top of Balkon Hill, is being cleaned out and the mud and sludge is put in the Roman Guardroom near it.

July 22.   A letter passed through the local post office with the following address one day this week

> Run, Postman, run; the faster, the better
> And to Mr. James Clerk deliver this letter.
> Colchester, Essex, is his abode
> Near the Mill in the Butt Road.

August 4.   The new Grammar School was opened this day. The friends of the pupils, Town Council, Clergymen and other gentlemen met at the Town Hall, walked in procession preceeded by a band of music to the new school, when the Head Master (Dr. Wright) had possession given him by the presentation of a key, after which they adjourned to the Cupps Hotel, where pupils and gentlemen partook of a cold collation.

August 8.   The first stone of St. Mary Magdalen new church laid.

August 9.   Received the freeman's money, 18/–.

1854

March 23.   Last Tuesday the first stone of the new church, Mile-end, was laid, on which occasion a sermon was preached . . . at St. Peters. During the time the congregation was coming out of the above church, some ladies and gentlemen had their pockets picked.

April 29.   "Duck Lane" is re-christened by the name of "North Gate Street", "Dead Lane" is called "St. Peter's Street" and "Sneak Lane" by the euphonious sounding of "Serpentine Walk".

May 9.   Mr Smith, brush maker, Magdalene Street, informs me that a laboring man, stubbing up an alder plantation at Holbrook near Ipswich, Suffolk, found an earthern urn containing nine hundred and fifty one silver coins, which the finder took to London and sold for ten pounds.

June 26.   The church rate in St. Nicholas Parish was polled for this day and lost by a majority of 19. Immediately the poll was struck, the clock was stopped.

1855

January 8.   Went before the Inspector of the Post Office, when the following questions had to be answered: the date of appointment as letter carrier, the names of the principal streets in my delivery, and requested to count the number of letters at each delivery for two days and the average time each takes.

January 9.   Number of letters a.m. delivery 237, exclusive of newspapers; p.m. delivery 89. $2\frac{1}{2}$ hours to deliver a.m.; $1\frac{3}{4}$ hours to deliver p.m.

January 10.   No letters 195, time of delivery $2\frac{1}{4}$ hours.

January 17.   Purchased a bronze ornament . . . found in the field opposite the silk factory, Military road.[21]

February 24.   This day the frost broke up by a thaw commencing after it had lasted nearly six weeks with snow on the ground during that period. The frost was so severe that the river and ponds bore and presented a very animated appearance by the number of skaters and sliders that were on them, in particular Bourne Pond which was a favourite resort.

March 14.   Mr. George Western, one of the overseers at the silk factory, Dead Lane, died suddenly at the Globe Inn, North Street, where he had gone to practise of the hand bells.

March 15.   Mr. Graves, another overseer at the same factory, died suddenly. The two men lived in adjoining houses in the factory yard.

May 3.   Sold my Colchester and Essex collection of mss. books of scraps, cuttings, scarce tracts, etc., to Mr. Acton for £30. I am sorry to part with them, but, as they are of no particular use to me and the money of more service, they are disposed off.

Mr. Smith, fruiterer, North Hill, informs me that he has discovered a tessellated pavement in the garden in his occupation behind the Chaise and Pair, North Hill.

During the course of this and last week petitions to both houses of Parliament against the Maynooth Grant and for closing Public houses all day on Sunday have been carried about for signatures.

June 30. Purchased a base silver coin of Julia Donna, found in some garden, Lexden Rd. Latterly more coins of hers have come into my possession than of any period of the Roman Empire.

July 12. Preparations are being made for the erection of a barracks on the Ordanance field by sinking twenty five wells and otherwise preparing the ground.

July 18. Sent a letter and newspaper to my son Herbert at Singapore.

1856

January 26. This day the depot of the Eleventh Regiment of foot, consisting of about three hundred men, took possession of the new barracks erected on the Ordnance field. These are the first soldiers that have been quartered in barracks in this town since the old barracks was taken down some years since. They were played in from the Railway Station to their lodgings by the fine brass band belonging to the Essex Rifles.

A public meeting was held at the Town Hall yesterday to consider the best means to be adopted to remove St. Runwalds church and the houses in the Middle row, when a committee was appointed to take the matter into consideration. This subject has been mooted and meetings held at different times for the same purpose ever since I can remember.

January 29. This forenoon the Royal Essex Rifles who had been billeted at the different public houses in this town for some months past went into the barracks.

February 5. The Drum Major, accompanied by the drummers and fifers belonging to the East Norfolk Militia, paraded the town and gave notice to the public not to trust the soldiers of that regiment more than one day's pay, as the officers would not be answerable for more than that amount. This is a new feature in the town, but of course in accordance with military etiquet.

March 26. Three letter or Post Office pillars are put down in the Street, one at Plough corner, one near the King's Arms Inn, Crouch Street, the other near North gate, for the reception of letters.

April 10. Attended a meeting of the Essex Archaeological Society held at the School Room, Coggeshall, J. Disney in the chair. . . A paper by the Hon. R. C. Neville, president, on Roman infant burials discovered at Chesterford was read by the Rev. Professor Marsden, then another by the Rev. E. L. Cutts, curate, on Coggeshall Abbey, then a visit was made to the remains of the Abbey, which is a very interesting building and now used as a barn. . . Then to the White Hart Inn, where about twenty clergy and gentry sat down to dinner, after this to the railway, Kelvedon, and so home. The Rev. B. Lodge, of St. Mary Magdalene, Colchester, was kind enough to pay for my dinner.

April 14. Made a return of the number of newspapers and letters delivered by me from the 8th to the 14th of this present month, both inclusive, newspapers 154, letters 2129.

April 19. This evening at a quarter past ten my beloved parent died at Winsley's Alms houses, aged 85 years, where he had been an inmate for ten years. He was the oldest Free burgess of Colchester but one.

April 21. Prince Albert paid this town a visit to inspect the camp. There was a large number of pedestrian and equestrian spectators met at and near the railway station. . .

April 27.   The remains of my beloved father was buried in the same grave as my dear mother at the Baptist Chapel, Eld Lane. This was the last interment at that place previous to its being closed for burials.

May 1.   The cemetry is opened this day for burials.

May 4.   Thanksgiving day to Almighty God for Peace.

May 29.   Those soldiers who had been to the Crimea dined at the public expence in the New Corn Exchange.

June 4.   The West Essex Militia left the camp for Chelmsford to be dis-embodied there, and the other Regiments leave this week.

June 11.   An order has come down to the Post Master here stating that the Letter carriers are to have "a fortnight's holiday in the aggregate in the year at the Revenue expence."

July 19.   The British German Legion – Rifles (Jagers) – came into this town about two thousand strong and are encamped in a canvas camp on the old Barrack ground.[22] The last canvas camp in this town was on Lexden Heath about fifty years ago.

September 9.   Received a box of curiosities from my son Herbert, which he purchased at Whampoa or Hong Kong.

October 30.   A subscription having been made for the removal of Middle Row in the High Street, a commencement was made by taking down the shop adjoining the East end of St. Runwalds Church.

1857

February 17.   Purchased a circular enamelled ornament found at the Grammar School and a first brass coin of Hadrian.

March 3.   A laboring man brought in a gold noble of one of the Henries, weight 96 grains, which he said he found in the channel near the Hythe. In consequence of too much being asked for it, I did not purchase.

[DIARY ENDS]

N

XIV

The Reverend Denys Nelson Yonge, Vicar of Broxted in 1869–85 and of Boreham in 1885–1918, may be compared with the curate of Thaxted of 1759 (See Section III). Yonge is seen to be far busier in the holding of services, and particularly in the church's social missions which in 1759 were almost non-existent. Indeed, to make a selection from the very detailed account of his life left by Yonge is to obscure the full extent of his daily, often hourly, parish commitments, which included frequent services, active supervision of two parish schools, an attempt to hold a young men's evening class, the running of a Benefit Club and, above all, an unending succession of personal visits to parishioners. In other respects the lives of the two Vicars seem very similar. Both are at ease in local polite society, enjoying its company and diversions, and both relish a holiday away from their parishes. They keep strong links with the world of their own boyhood or youth, even if Yonge's connections are sentimental ties with school and university and Cooper's those of continuing Classical scholarship. In neither case does inner spiritual feeling or philosophical reflectiveness find expression in what they write, though the practical benevolence of each is beyond doubt. Whether Cooper grew in spirituality as he rose hierarchically there is no means of judging, but Yonge's diary for 1900 indicates that for him nothing has changed since 1877, except the location of his parish, the addition of snooker and tricycle riding to his daily round, and a somewhat greater participation by the laity in church life.

Yonge's diaries are in the Essex Record Office. They cover the years 1877 and 1890–1919 [D/DU 358] and from them I have selected those for 1877 and for 1900, January and August. Also at Essex Record Office is a dissertation on the diaries by M. M. Boardman entitled 'A Vicar of the Nineteenth Century', which contains useful biographical detail.

The Diary of Rev. D. N. Yonge.

1877

Mon., Jan. 1.   Servants wages £6. Mattins at 11.30, with Holy Communion. In afternoon sermonised at the church. Fine evening, about 20 present.

Tues., Jan. 2.   Mattins at 9.30. In morning read paper and did Magazine for the month. At 12 started with Lotty and walked to Thaxted and back, called on the Symmondses[1] and Watsons, came back by 3.45. Sold pony and carriage for £10 today to Mr. Phillips. Dined at 5.30 and read in evening.

Wed., Jan. 3.   Church at 11.30.

Thurs., Jan. 4.   Mattins at 8.30. To Cherry Green at 11 and waded through a lot of slush. Did Club business. Dined at 2. After dinner planted a tree in churchyard. Tea at 5.30 and sermonised in evening.

Fri., Jan. 5.   Mattins at 11.30, then practised children and took money for club. Dined at 1.15. At 2.30 went out with Lotty. Lord Rosslyn[2] called when I was out. Tea at 5.30 and sermonised.

Sat., Jan. 6.   Mattins at 11.30, but no congregation. Sermonised in evening.

Sun., Jan. 7.   Offertory 2s. od. Fair day and fair attendance.

Mon., Jan. 8.   Up at 7.10. Breakfasted. Embarked in C. Reynolds cart and reached Elsenham by 8.15. Liverpool St. and Waterloo. Reached Torrington at 6.30. Came up in bus which was very full. Found all quite well. Dined at 7. Smoked. Cart 2.0. To Liverpool St. 4s. 4d. To Torrington 18s. 8d. Cab 2.0. Bus 6d.

Thurs., Jan. 11.   Breakfasted at 9.20. Went out hunting in the morning, that is went to see some beagles, had a walk with C. and L. Dined at 2. In the evening to an entertainment of comic singing, Jolly Nash. Very good. Stall ticket 2s. od.

Fri., Jan. 12.   At 4 to the rooms and dropped some coin, but won it back at whist at Palmers, where L. and I went at 7.15.

Fri., Jan. 19.   Expenses at Torrington £1. 2. 0.

Sat., Jan. 20.   Up by 6.15. Breakfast. Said good bye to mother and Fanny. Charlie went as far as London with me, which was jolly. Eventually reached Broxted at 6.10 and found all well and hearty. Dined at 6.30. Fire in bedroom.

Sun., Jan. 21.   Service and school at usual time.

Mon., Jan. 22.   In morning did club accounts and bills and at 11.20 to school for the usual time and then took school pence.

Tues., Jan. 23.   The photograph man came and took views of the interior of the church.[3] To school. After lunch to London for the Xts' dinner, which came off at the Albion, Girdlestone in chair. Whist. Slept at Bedford. Dinner £1.5. Cab 1s. 6d. and 2s. od. Cards 8d.

Fri., Jan. 26.   Walked to Easton Lodge and found the Rosslyns at home. Saw Mrs. Baker on the way; she has lost a son by smallpox.

Sat., Jan. 27.   C. Reynolds drove me to Horham Hall, where we lunched and there was a treat for the children, which they enjoyed much.

Mon., Jan. 29.   Went to school and took classes.

Thurs., Feb. 1.   Went up to Cherry Green and the Bush. Took class at school. Called on sick people.

Fri., Feb. 2.   Did not go out in the afternoon, except to the greenhouse and potted some Pelargoniums.

Mon., Feb. 5. Went up the parish en route to Little Easton where dined with the Tufnells[4] and had a pleasant evening.

Tues., Feb. 6. To S. Green and visited. The cottages at S.G. are being done up and not before they were wanted.

Thurs., Feb. 8. Parliament opened, Queen's weather.

Fri., Feb. 9. Practised for some time, mostly playing the harmonium.

Sat., Feb. 10. Watson came and vaccinated me, also Mary Ann.

Mon., Feb. 12. Mr. S. Scruby called and had a long talk about the strike and asked me to go to the farmers' meeting.[5]

Thurs., Feb. 15. To school at 11.25 and gave the first two classes a drilling. Dined at 1.10, after which went up to Cherry Green[6] and took a class there for an hour.

Mon., Feb. 19. Very Mondayish.

Tues., Feb. 20. Was to have gone to the Farmers' Association meeting, but did not, as the weather was bad.

Thurs., Feb. 22. Started at 8.15 with Molly and Liddy for station. Went to Cambridge with them and saw them off for Hempstead.[7] Came back to Dunmow and was kindly driven by West to High Easter, where we had our Clerical Meeting, Wright and Walker being the only others present. Came home in snow.

Fri., Feb. 23. Very curious being alone.

Mon., Feb. 26. My birthday and am grateful for it. Heard from Mother. Molly gave me a hat, very useful present.

Tues., Feb. 27. Heard from Moll.

Thurs., March 1. Myself getting more "vox et praeterea nihil".[5]

Sun., March 4. Wet day and very few indeed in church. Stove rebelled and smoked the whole place.

Tues., March 6. In the evening read and played backgammon.

Tues., March 13. Chopped up wood all the afternoon till nearly 6. It being G.'s birthday we had a late dinner and drank his health.

Tues., March 20. The boys left Torrington today. Thought of the parting a good deal. Mattins at 8.30. School at 11.25, and then up to Woodgates End and saw [6 names given]. Lunched and walked to Elsenham and arrived in London about 4. Changed hat, drove to the Bedford, went to Waterloo Station, met the boys, dined and smoked together.

Wed., March 21. Breakfast at 9.15, after that some smoking room, then went out and walked to S. Paul's and then to Cannon St. and bought some meat at American Stores. Lunched at Wanderers with C. and G. Annie and Ethel dined with us and we all went to the Gaiety and saw "Artful Card". A. and E. went back by 12 train.

Thurs., March 22. Charlie and Georgy off by the 7.40 train from Charing X. Said good bye dolefully but there was no help for it; they went off in pretty good spirits. Came home by 1. Clerical meeting here at 3 and a fair attendance.

Sat., March 24. Mattins at 8.30. Oxford and Cambridge Race at 8.15. DEAD HEAT.

Thurs., March 29. Cambridge won the double rackets, Oxford the single.

Fri., March 30. Good † Friday. Attendance at church in morning exceeding poor. Not one farmer present.

Sat., March 31.   Easter Eve. Service at 11.30, no one but ourselves being present.

Tues., April 3.   Vestry meeting at 2.0, passed off very well. Election of 2 Churchwardens.

Thurs., April 5.   Dined. Mackarel now in season.

Mon., April 9.   Today we had an outing. We went to Dunmow in a fly and took Freddy with us and we all lunched at the Knockers. Sundry shopping took place and we left at 4. At 5 had a funeral of one Collins from workhouse.

Tues., April 10.   Went up to Cherry Hall and called on John Phillips and took petition to sign, which he did.

Wed., April 11.   Reading Pride and Prejudice.

Fri., April 13.   Tufnell came and lunched. Concert in evening at Dunmow, went in a Fly and supped at Knockers.

Tues., April 17.   Papers now are very warlike and it seems quite a case that Russia and Turkey will soon be at it.

Sun., April 29.   School. 60 present.

Wed., May 2.   Tithe day. Very busy collecting and had about 7 to dinner. Liddy dined also and behaved very well.

Thurs., May 3.   Doing school accounts in the evening.

Tues., May 8.   School inspected by Mr. Rowan. I don't think the children did very well. The arithmetic was very bad.

Wed., May 9.   Went up to Cherry St. to give Holy Communion to Widow Perry but she was too far gone, so prayed by her. Came back by 4 and met the deputation of the A.C.S. Put up sheet for lantern. Began lecture at 7.30. Money collected 14.4.

Fri., May 11.   Heard from Mr. Eyre, who sent a cheque for £50, £25 for church, £25 for self, very good of him indeed.

Mon., May 14.   Left in Reynold's cart for Elsenham and then to Taplow via London. Missed train at Paddington and telegraphed to Ward to meet me at Taplow. Found Mary and W. at dinner. Port wine, etc. W. does not smoke now.

Tues., May 15.   The day was very lovely. Walked around with W. Lunched at 1, after which Mary and I drove to Braywick and she called on the Hibberts. Dined at 6.30 and, it being Mary's birthday, had a great feast.

Thurs., May 17.   It rained the whole way and the whole day so that I got a little wet in Reynold's cart at Takely. Reached home at 1.50.

Fri., May 18.   Went up to Cherry Green and found no school, as s. mistress was laid up.

Mon., May 21.   It being a Bank holyday, took it myself.

Tues., May 22.   Started for Sampford and called at S. Green⁹ on way. The walk was a long one, nearly 9 miles. Had an agreeable evening.

Wed., May 23.   Breakfast at 8 and amused myself as best I could, as Price was engaged with his pupils for some time. Went out with him and saw his fields. Lunched at 1 and walked home. Was very stiff.

Tues., May 29.   Mary confined at 6.30 a.m. She began to feel queer at 2, so I called the nurse and at 4 I went to Thaxted for Watson, he drove me back and at 6.30 the little boy was born, and a fine boy, too, the doctor said. M. doing very well indeed. Wrote 11 letters.

Wed., May 30. Molly had a very good night, and the infant likewise. Kitty came at 6.50 and I was very glad. Silvio won Derby.

Fri., June 1. M. doing first rate. Placida won Oaks.

Wed., June 6. Club taking today, a good many paying up.

Thurs., June 7. Fine day and pleasant walking. Went out to Cherry Green and took Club.

Tues., June 12. Up at 6 and went to S. Albans via Hitchin and Hatfield. The Bp. was enthroned. Over 300 clergy walked in procession from the Town Hall to the Abbey, a grand sight. Town was decorated and all the people took a holiday.

Tues., June 19. Nurse went.

Mon., June 25. Left for Takely Station at 9 en route for Lords, which reached at 12.5 about and found Cambridge going in. They all got out for 134 only. Oxford then went in and, though wickets fell very fast at first, they made 217. Dined and slept at 17 Norfolk Road.

Tues., June 26. Some rain, had hair cut, and at 1.30 went to Lords. Cambridge in their second innings only obtained 127, so that Oxford had only 47 to get to win, which they did without the loss of a wicket.

Wed., June 27. Up by 9 and at 11.30 went with Austin to the Eton and Harrow Club, Park Place, St. James Street. Small it is, but tolerably neat. I went to Liverpool Street by omnibus and reached home by walking at 7.0.

Fri., June 27. St. Peter and therefore Mattins at 11.30 with the Holy Communion. Practice afterwards and Club *pour les enfants*. In afternoon buried the child Dicken who had died of diphtheria.

Wed., July 4. Mary went to Church today and returned thanks for her safe delivery.

Sat., July 7. Mattins at 8.30, Lucy as congregation.

Sun., July 8. Very fine day with very good congregations, especially in the afternoon. Our baby Xtened.

Thurs., July 12. Dined at 1.30, Tufnell coming. Walked back with him and called on a Mr. Rumsey at Easton Lodge and had a game at Lawn Tennis and came remarkably hot.

Fri., July 13. Mr. Davies came today, much to L's gratification. Eton and Harrow match this day.

Wed., July 18. INSPECTION of school by Burn at 10. He was there until 12.45. The children did very much better this time.

Sun., July 22. Exchanged with Tufnell for the whole day. Reached Church at 10.30. Lunched with Grace and Hugh and came back to dinner here and met Tufnell.

Mon., July 23. Left Vicarage at 8.20 for Takely en route for Southwold to stay with W., he being there for the sake of his health. Found W. waiting by the sea, lodging close by. Dined at 6 off soles.

Tues., July 24. Went to bathe after breakfast. Simpson, W's sailor valet, went to look after me while bathing.

Wed., July 25. Went to Mattins at 8. The parson ignored the Saint's Day, which was a pity. Bathed, went out trawling with W., Simpson and another fisherman and caught some soles, was nearly sea sick.

Thurs., July 26. Did nothing much, read Old Sir Douglas, which is a humbugging book.

Fri., July 27. Mattins at 8. Breakfast and then bathed, the sea being very calm. The day in fact was quite perfect. W. was photographed with two of his sea-faring mates. In afternoon walked down to the Gunhill. After dinner had some fishing and caught a salmon trout.

Sat. July 28. Mattins at 8. Left Southwold at 10, reached Takely about 5.10 and Broxted at 5.45 and found all well.

Mon., July 30. To Lt. Easton, where dined with Tufnell and played some cricket.

Wed., Aug. 1. This was our cricket match day at Lt. Easton, Hugh Tufnell's eleven against Capt. from Hatfield. Walked over. Play began at 11.45. Mr. Percy Watlington drove the eleven over in his dray. The upshot was that we licked them easily. I got a brace of 1s.

Thurs., Aug. 2. Mattins at 8.30, Mary, Lucy and I. Cherry Green morning; went up about 10.15, took school and club and saw some people, coming back by 1.15. After dinner went out again and saw people [15 names given] at the Malting. The two Scruby girls came to tea at 6. Croquet, first game this season.

Mon., Aug. 6. Left Broxted for Hempstead at 11.15, Lucy and I in Reynold's cart and the others in [*not given*]. Reached H. at 7.30.

Tues., Aug. 7. Up by 9. We all bathed after breakfast. In afternoon sat out until it rained.

Wed., Aug. 8. Somewhat bilious from the strength of the air. Went down to the beach and paddled Liddy. After dinner some of us drove to Hempstead Rectory.

Thurs., Aug. 9. In afternoon played croquet and took a walk to the lighthouse.

Fri., Aug. 10. Played lawn tennis at 12. In afternoon played lawn tennis again.

Sat., Aug. 11. The usual amusements of seaside.

Sun., Aug. 12. Very wet day. Church at Happisburgh both times – very dull day indeed.

Mon., Aug. 13. Papers came today.

Tues., Aug. 14. No bathing again, as it was too rough.

Wed., Aug. 15. Charlie, Lucy and Liddy went to Stalham in the carriage. Mary went and bathed and so did I. Had a game of lawn tennis.

Thurs., Aug. 16. The carriage with some of us went to Hempstead. Saw the church with Charlie – in a dilapidated condition but capable of restoration. In afternoon had some lawn tennis, but the rain came on and I could not see.

Fri., Aug. 17. Had some croquet. We played till 5.15 and after tea some lawn tennis.

Sat., Aug. 18. Left Happisburgh at 9.15 and was driven by Ducker to N. Walsham and caught the train. Eventually reached Elsenham, walked to Broxted and was very hot. Sermonised.

Sun., Aug. 19. Fair congregation.

Mon., Aug. 20. Left Broxted at 10.40. At Cambridge met the Harts and travelled with them to N. Walsham, took dog cart to Happisburgh and found all well. Wedding day 1872.

Tues., Aug. 21. Rough morning. We were to have gone with the Whites of Stalham to a picnic on the Broad, but it was put off. Some of them went out driving. Croquet in afternoon.

Wed., Aug. 22. The bathing tent was used today for the first time. 3 girls bathed in it, after which Charlie and I took it down, and we bathed. After dinner Moll. and I had a walk to the lighthouse and got our feet wet.

Thurs., Aug. 23. Bathed after breakfast in the tent.

Fri., Aug. 24. St. Bartholemew, but no service here whatever. After dinner Mary and I walked to Eccles Tower along the sand, the carriage taking us from thence to Hempstead. Croquet in the evening.

Sun., Aug. 26. Took Mr. Harris' duty.

Mon., Aug. 27. Gloomy. Did acrostic in John Bull.

Tues., Aug. 28. We were all going to Norwich, but the weather was too bad.

Thurs., Aug. 30. Very fine. At 11 bathed, all the kingdom bathing likewise. Lawn tennis.

Fri., Aug. 31. Walked on the coast with Moll.

Sat., Sept. 1. Left Happisburgh with Johnny in Ducker's cart, the others all having gone on. Left the lot at Norwich and reached home at 3.30. Sermonised and dined.

Sun., Sept. 2. Text afternoon, "The harvest is the end of the world". Offertory 2.0.

Thurs., Sept. 6. Very fine day throughout. Heard from Molly. After breakfast took a lot of cuttings. West called, after which went to Bush. Dined at 2. Wrote to Molly. Called at Moor End and then at the School.

Fri., Sept. 7. Came back across the fields and met a lot of people who had been gleaning.

Mon., Sept. 10. A glorious day for harvesting. Walked to Elsenham and took ticket for Cambridge, where met Moll. and the children, Johnie escorting them so far. Dined at 6. The days close in very fast now.

Wed., Sept. 12. In the afternoon changed our rooms, made the nursery our room and vice versa.

Thurs., Sept. 13. Silvio won the Leger, Lady Golightly (both Lord Falmouth's) coming in second.

Fri., Sept. 14. Lizzy came on a visit and brought a ham and some beautiful butter.

Tues., Sept. 18. Turks are thrashing the Russians like anything at Plevna. Put carpet in the hall and so made it look comfortable.

Thurs., Sept. 20. Parker tuned piano and harmonium. Clerical meeting at Horham Hall.

Fri., Sept. 21. Evensong at 7.30, very few present. Text "Follow me".

Sun., Sept. 23. Fire in the library for tea.

Tues., Sept. 25. Went up to Cherry Green and found they were all gleaning.

Thurs., Sept. 27. HARVEST Thanksgiving. Holy Communion at 10, but only 9 present when there should have been many more. The church looked beautiful. Service at 4. West, Chapel, Hart and the preacher. A dinner party we gave.

Sun., Sept. 29. No children at school yet – long time coming.

Mon., Oct. 1. At Dunmow church for their H.T. They collected £25 for Indian Famine.

Tues., Oct. 2. To school, but only 20 present.

Wed., Oct. 3. Took club money, £8. 13. 0.

Thurs., Oct. 4.   In the afternoon started with Molly for Horham Hall. M. was driven to Thaxted church and I walked. A grand harvest service. Over 30 people at supper afterwards.

Tues., Oct. 9.   Mattins at 10. School at 11.25. Left Boxted at 1.15 and reached Elsenham in time to catch the 2.25. Left Cannon St. by 5.4 and reached Tunbridge Wells by 6.30 and was in time at Sandhurst Lodge for dinner. Found my old friends very well and very glad to see me.

Wed., Oct. 10.   Cold very bad, with sore throat. Up by 9, prayers and breakfast, after which lots of talking. Walked down to the bath place or rather water place, had a glass of water.

Thurs., Oct. 11.   My cold at its height. Down the town with Miss Eyre, and she bought for Molly a beautiful lace collar and cuffs for 16s. Lunched at 1, after which we all drove to Tunbridge and came back through a park.

Fri., Oct. 12.   With Miss Eyre for a walk on the Common. Lunch at 12.15 and then said good bye to them all and walked to the station. Reached Broxted about 5.30 and dined at 7, with plenty to talk about.

Sun., Oct. 14.   Text afternoon "When He beheld the city, He wept over it" (New one).

Tues., Oct. 16.   School at 11.25, there being over 100 present now. In the evening dined with the Rosslyns, they very kindly sending for us and bringing us back. At dinner Mrs. Langtree (a beauty), Count Someone, a pleasant German, Mr. Cooper and Ramsey. We came back by 11.15 and enjoyed it all.

Wed., Oct. 17.   Busy finishing club tickets for distribution. At 3.40 gave out club cards to the different people, but, it being rent day, only children were present generally.

Thurs., Oct. 18.   At 7 to Evensong, the numbers being few and far between. Preached ex tempore and got on fairly.

Sun., Oct. 21.   In evening with Molly to Cherry Green and preached ex tempore. Hard day's work.

Tues., Oct. 23.   Cambridgeshire won by Tonfleur, Belphoebe 2, Hilarious no where.

Wed., Oct. 24.   Went to school and took 3rd class in sums.

Thurs., Oct. 25.   Very wet. Felstead Church re-opened. M. and I walked to Lodge and were picked up by the Wests. Service at 11.30. Bp. preached. Public luncheon, lots of people. Moll. bad. Dined at Wests and M. stayed the night.

Tues., Oct. 30.   Evening school at 7, commencement thereof, and 7 boys turning up.

Wed., Oct. 31.   Evening school at 7.

Fri., Nov. 2.   Tufnell called at 4.30. Late dinner, duck and the like.

Sun., Nov. 4.   Evening Mole Hill Green.[10] "Prodigal Son". Baptised little Claydon.

Tues., Nov. 6.   Some tithe payers paid today, as Mr. Smith was collecting Gt. Tithes. Mr. Maitland sent £5. In afternoon with M. to Malting Evening School. 11 present. Tithe Day. Rate £13.6.5.

Wed., Nov. 7.   Mattins at 11.30. We had a Baptism also, Widow Barker's bastard child, the Turners standing for it, so that is well over.

Tues., Nov. 13.   Mattins at 10. Congregation immense. Night school, 12 being present.

Thurs., Nov. 15.   Mattins at 10. School at 11.25. Dinner at 1. After that to Cherry Green and took the school for 1½ hour. Tea at 5.20 and Night School at 7.15. So did some teaching.

Mon., Nov. 19.   A snug evening with reading.

Tues., Nov. 20.   Kars taken, news came today. Mr. Pridden came over from Cambridge; we like the young man. Evening school at 7, 12 boys.

Wed., Nov. 21.   Went at 11.10 in Marvill's cart to Elsenham station and lunched with the Collins at Wenden.

Fri., Nov. 30.   St. Andrew. Mattins at 11.30 and had a Celebration for a wonder, there being enough.

Sat., Dec. 1.   We went to Dunmow in Ridgewell's brougham and shopped and dined with the Knockers.

Wed., Dec. 5.   The two fanatici, having to leave their houses, are much cast down.

Mon., Dec. 10.   In evening double acrostics.

Tues., Dec. 18.   Left Vicarage in Marvill's trap about 9.15 and went with Molly, Freddy and baby (Jane being late and so missing the train) to Stortford, where did some shopping and came back by 1.

Thurs., Dec. 20.   Children busy helping at decorations between school hours.

Mon., Dec. 24.   Very busy all day, putting up decorations. The Wests lunched here. After lunch went at it again. Buried Enough Diken. Evensong at 4.30 and went on decorating until 5.45. Wests did chancel, Mary nave, Miss Scruby's font and West window.

Tues., Dec. 25.   Cold and seasonable. Most miserable congregations indeed; never saw such a thing. Dined at 1.15. Mrs. Pryor and servants sent dinner to R. Baker, etc. Evensong at 3.

Wed., Dec. 26.   Mattins at 10, Molly and I being the congregation. Lunched at 1, after which walked to Cherry Street. Dined late, on Xmas turkey for a change.

Thurs., Dec. 27.   Church at 10, Moll. and I. After that read and wrote somewhat. Tea at 5.30 and read. Choirs' supper.

Fri., Dec. 28.   M.'s birthday. She had a lot of letters and a present or two, but the bulk of them are to arrive later on. Tea and supper and drank M.'s health. Snow and much rain.

Sat., Dec. 29.   Afternoon loafed about.

Mon., Dec. 31.   Last of the Mohicans. Another passed. "Haec via ducit ad urbem". Perge puer.[11] Magazine. Visited Laverick, Samford, Green.

1900

Mon., Jan. 1.   This diary is not quite the same sort as my last. However, it will do as well. Early celebration at 8. Club day at 11 or so. Very foggy. After dinner called on Mrs. Tyrell who had influenza, had tea there, came back by 5.

Tues., Jan. 2.   Dark, dull and dreary
              Far from bright and cheery.
Influenza here, there and everywhere. Doing magazine for two hours. After dinner went out and saw some people, all the Haslewoods to wit, to wit, to woo. Evensong at 5. Mrs. Peppitt and Miss Hobbs came to supper.

Wed., Jan. 3.   I rather like the paper of this new diary, as it is of better quality.

War news rather better. Writing magazine. In afternoon went out and saw some people.

> Influenza sore
> Long time they bore.

Thurs., Jan. 4.   Dull day, no letters of any importance. Mattins at 10. Doing accounts, offertory and others. After dinner Mary had mothers, but only 5 turned up, as there [are] many laid up with sickness. M. and I dined at Boreham House,[12] went and returned in brougham. Snooker.

Fri., Jan. 5.   Mattins at 10 and a dullish day. Did not go out very far in the morning, but wrote accounts. Dined at 1 and in afternoon stayed in, except that I called on Mrs. Crow. No practice, Mrs. Lewin being ill and Knight not having returned.

Sat., Jan. 6.   No one turned up at Early Celebration.

Sun., Jan. 7.   At H.C. only 20.

Mon., Jan. 8.   Roads muddy after so much rain. Writing in morning. Lunched at 1. Did very little, as was Mondayish. Evensong at 5.

Tues., Jan. 9.   Bright day, with sun. School at 9.25. Mattins at 10 and up the parish at 11.15, came down by 1.10. In afternoon Mary had Mothers' Union, 14. Evensong 5. Church meeting at 7. Repulse of the Boers from attack on Ladysmith.

Wed., Jan. 10.   Mrs. Wells gave school children a tea and magic lantern in school room from 4 to 7.

Thurs., Jan. 11.   School at 9.25. Writing and then visiting. A great number of people are ill. After dinner buried little twin Middleditch, then visited. Evensong at 5. Mary had mothers' meeting, but only 7.

Fri., Jan. 12.   Litany with children at 9.15, but they were very much out of tune. After dinner buried Wilkinson. N.B. 3 funerals in 3 following days. Visited. Evensong. Practice in S. Room.

Sat., Jan. 13.   Visiting on tricycle. Denys, mi., came at 3.30. Lots of people influ.

Sun. Jan. 14.   10 at Early C.

Mon., Jan. 15.   Rain and dirty roads. Club Day. Went down to Mill and paid Mrs. Threadgold reserve pay. C.E.T.S. meeting at 7. Magic lantern in school, attendance limited.

Tues., Jan. 16.   School, Mattins and Writing.

Wed., Jan. 17.   To WR School and closed it for 10 days owing to whooping cough and influenza. After dinner Horace left for school in Wombell's cart.

Thurs., Jan. 18.   To lunch at B. House with Mary.

Fri., Jan. 19.   Intercession at 11.15, but too many were the people who came. SLACK, SLACK, Slack. Paid in some shoe club money. Mary went to Chelmsford by Moore.[13] Mrs. C. Gepp and children had tea.

Sun., Jan. 21.   People are slack
> When pain in back.

Bad attendance at H.C. Guild meeting.

Mon., Jan. 22.   S.P.G. meeting. Wombell drove me to Station. After business walked to S.P.C.K. with Dale, then to Sheffington, called on D.W.Y. and saw his employers, who gave me sherry.

"Coughing in a shady street
  Was a well known Vicar.
  Sherry gave they him, a treat,
  And it was good liquor."

Lunch at restaurant 9d. Down by 4.18.
  Wed., Jan. 24.   Dull day – sic omnes.
    Letters, letters,
    Letters, letters.
At 7.30 general meeting Cottage Garden.
  Thurs., Jan. 25.   No one at early Celebration except ourselves. The ways of
so called Church people are inexplicable.
  Fri., Jan. 26.   "Club money from the post for Hare
    to pay his Club bill, which is fair,
    But coals are dear, will dearer be,
    Which fact is rather hard on me."

  Sun., Jan. 28.   The Rev. Lewis preached to a good congregation. School at
10. Children's service at 3. Evensong at 6.30. Snow in evening.
  Mon., Jan. 29.   Buller re-crossed Tugela, the Kop being found untenable.
At 6.30 Annual Club Tea, 18 being present. Got away about 9.10.
  Tues., Jan. 30.   Evensong with a huge congregation!
  Wed., Jan. 31.   At 12 Intercession Service for War.
  Wed., Aug. 1.   This day was wholly given to Leatherhead. Isabel and I went
to Speech day. Much rain between 10.30 and 1.30. Horace met us at L. Station.
Then we had the inevitable lunch at a nice public place, Institute to wit.
Chapel at 2.30, very good singing. Prizes distributed by Bp. of Winchester,
Horace got one for book-keeping, Macaulay, very handsome. Came back 5.31
and caught 7.15 at L. St.
  Thurs., Aug. 2.   Isabel and Horace to Chelmsford. H's. new bicycle very
smart indeed.
  Fri., Aug. 3.   Boreas, or rather Notus, favoured us with something very
like a gale.
  Sat., Aug. 4.   Ventus agit nimbos et tempestas furiosa
    Poma parum miserans obruit ante diem.[14]
Lots of apples blown down, some bushels. Sermon-writing. In afternoon girl
Baffe came and played tennis. Philip came from Aldershot, bronzed by sun.
  Sun., Aug. 5.   32 at H.C. Isabel and Horace supped at B. House.
  Mon., Aug. 6.   Bank Holiday and what a sell,
    Disappointments who can tell?
    "Nothing to do", aye, there's the rub.
    Nothing to do, we'll go to the pub.
    Our sons and daughter did not go,
    Neither their father nor their Mo.
    When rain cleared up at half past five,
    They all played golf, as I'm alive,
    Quite cheery, though they might have sworn.
    To use bad language all would scorn.
    Mary and I to Boreham House to dinner.
    This is quite true or I'm a grievous sinner.

Tues., Aug. 7.   School opened after Bank Holiday.

Wed., Aug. 8.   After breakfast Mattins and then some writing. After dinner went out on tricycle, came back at 5 for evensong. Lemaire's boys came to play.

Thurs., Aug. 9.   Isabel and Horace went to Chelmsford at 10.30 for shopping purposes.

Fri., Aug. 10.   Horace and I thought of going to Leyton to see Essex v. Lancashire, but the weather was unpropitious. Isabel and Horace to Boreham House for Evelyn Baffe's birthday – 16.

Sat., Aug. 11.   Tea in the garden.

Sun., Aug. 12.   Mary CD with headache.

Mon., Aug. 13.   Splendid weather for harvest. S. Barnabas' boys at tea. We all had dinner at B. House, a splendid evening with moon on the waters.

Tues., Aug. 14.   Beautiful day. Mattins after school. After dinner went to Hulton's garden party on tricycle, Mary and Isabel in Haslewood's trap.

Thurs., Aug. 16.   Horace and I went to Leyton for cricket match, Essex v. Warwickshire. We got there at 12.40. Warwickshire were in the whole day, getting wads of runs. Freddy and Philip joined us.

Fri., Aug. 17.   School broke up at 12 for harvest holiday. Gave away prizes.

Sat., Aug. 18.   All the boys came down.

Sun., Aug. 19.   12 at H.C.

Mon., Aug. 20.   Twice fourteen years ago today
        I married my Mary.
    Unselfish, good, she's ever been
        And never once contrary.
    If our Fred. should seek a wife
        And wed a lovely Sairey,
    She never could be half so sweet
        As my own sweetest Mary.

Tues., Aug. 21.   Mary and Isabel to Jacksons' garden party. Mary had a lift home in the Luards' carriage. Dinner at 7.45. Whist.

Wed., Aug. 22.   Intercession for War at 12.

Thurs., Aug. 23.   Horrida tempestas caelum contraxit.[15]

Thunderstorm at 10, while we were at Mattins and afterwards a young whirlwind turned over hen houses.

Dum per agros vastos dira ruina ruit.[16]

We all went to see the havoc. Evensong at 5 and the usual occupations.

Fri., Aug. 24.   Mary, Isabel, Horace and I went over to the Royds for luncheon to meet the John Yonges. Carriage met us and brought us back. Croquet, etc. . . Cigars. Away by 5.30. Practice in dining room at 7 p.m.

Mon., Aug. 27.   Club day. Evensong κτλ.[17]

Tues., Aug. 28.   Horace went to Lt. Waltham to see Tancock about W.R. School and Board of Education and about his teaching Horace. F. and P. came to stay a week. Whist at 8.45.

Wed., Aug. 29.   Mr. and Miss Scott came to tennis. Whist in evening.

Thurs., Aug. 30.   At 3 District Visitors' meeting. At 7.30 we gave a supper to returned soldiers.

Fri., Aug. 31.   8, Mattins and Litany. At 11 went to Chelmsford on tricycle, hair cut and shaved. Came back to lunch. Evensong at 5 and Choir practice Vicarage 7 p.m. Baptised a Bone.

NOTES

I

1. Maldon's Parliamentary politics were complicated. The best analysis of them is by Namier and Brooke, *The House of Commons*, 1754–90 (1964), I, 280–1.

The chief candidates at Maldon, mentioned by Crosier, are the following:

Bullock, John (1731–1809), of Faulkbourne Hall, near Witham, represented Maldon 1754–74, Steyning 1780–4, Essex 1784–1809. Director of East India Co. Though a Whig, he was supported for the Maldon seat by his neighbour Strutt and other Essex Tories, but after his election he soon moved over to the Whigs.

Gascoyne, Bamber (1725–91), of Bifrons, Barking. M.P. for Maldon 1761–3, later M.P. for Midhurst, Weobley, Truro, Bossiney. Son of a brewer, attended Felsted School and Queen's College, Oxford. Elected at Maldon with the help of Strutt and, though defeated by Huske in 1763 to his own great resentment, he maintained a very active interest in the borough's politics. (For other references to him, see also the index of this book.)

Henniker, John (1724–1803), of Stratford House, West Ham, and of Newton Hall, Dunmow. M.P. for Sudbury 1761–8 and Dover 1774–84. Director of London Assurance Co., importer of masts from Norway and Russia, shipowner and shipbuilder. Sheriff of Essex 1757–8. In 1768 he was persuaded by Strutt and Gascoyne to stand for Maldon, but was unsuccessful despite his having paid £800 to win some 50 voters living in London.

Huske, John (1724–73), M.P. for Maldon 1763–73. Born New Hampshire, moved to England in 1748. Allegedly won Maldon by demagogy. In Parliament spoke as an expert on American affairs.

Nassau, Hon. Richard Savage (1723–80), son of 3rd Earl of Rochford. M.P. for Colchester 1747–54 and for Maldon 1774–80.

Rainsford, Charles (1728–1809), M.P. for Maldon 1772–74, afterwards for Bere Alston and Newport. Son of a Maldon alderman. Brought in as a stop-gap to hold the Maldon seat until Lord Rochford's nephew was ready to take it.

Waltham, Lord; Drigue Billers Olmius (1746–87), 2nd Baron Waltham. M.P. for Weymouth 1768–74 and for Maldon 1784–7. Son of deputy-governor of Bank of England. He inherited New Hall, Boreham, from his father.

2. At Colchester.

3. Copperas nodules were gathered from the cliffs at several points in the Tendring Hundred, including Walton. From the nodules was made green copperas or green vitriol for the manufacture of black dyes and black ink. For details see *Victoria County History of Essex*, II (1907), 411–2.

4. Maldon's Whig leader. See also index.

5. Presumably because, with the suspension of Maldon's borough charter, there were no properly appointed borough Justices.

6. A Chelmsford artist and playwright. See *Essex Review*, VIII, 135–8.

7. So called because situated on Cromwell Hill, Maldon. The last pump erected is still to be seen in 1971.

8. Over the River Blackwater at Wickham Mills in the parish of Wickham Bishops.

9. Copt Hall, near Epping.

10. Mistley Hall. The church referred to was probably the one consecrated in 1735. Crosier saw it only a year before it was re-built by Robert Adam.

11. At Witham.

12. Langford is a parish adjacent to Maldon.

13. Of Boreham House.

14. Crosier does not give the date; it was 1768.

15. Evidently because in the 1763 election the Maldon Corporation used its influence to help Huske to defeat Gascoyne by a large majority.

16. Potman Marsh on the North of the river near Fullbridge, where Maldon cricket ground was situated.

17. A water-mill at Woodham Walter, about two miles from Maldon.

18. The salt works were probably situated at Heybridge at this time. They were later moved to the riverside at Maldon, where the business is still conducted. Crosier leaves blank the name of the port from which came the rock salt used in the process; it was probably Liverpool that he had in mind.

19. Wanstead House, built in 1715 by Colen Campbell for Sir Richard Child.

20. Henry Bate (1745–1824), clergyman and journalist. He was nicknamed 'The Fighting Parson' because of his duelling propensities. In 1784 he assumed the name of Dudley to comply with the terms of a relative's will and in 1813 was made a baronet. In his early career he was rector of North Fambridge, Essex, editor of the *Morning Post*, founder of the *Morning Herald*, and author of comic operas. In 1781 he bought the advowson of Bradwell-on-Sea for £1,500, apparently became curate of the parish, farmed the glebe, reclaimed much coastal land, created a large estate and rebuilt his house, Bradwell Lodge. In 1797, on the death of the incumbent, he presented himself to the living, was refused institution by the bishop on the grounds of simony and then found that the right of presentation had lapsed to the Crown, to his own considerable financial loss.

21. Dr. Nicholas Wakeham, Dean of Bocking, had been Captain of Eton and Fellow of King's College, Cambridge. He came from a West Country farming family, and the three hunting horns, shown on his arms, proclaim his sporting interests.

22. Probably this was a sitting of County Justices, held in Maldon because there were no Borough courts existing at the time owing to the suspension of Maldon's charter.

23. Golding Constable, the painter's father, had left Flatford Mill and built this three-storey brick house at East Bergholt. At the time of Crosier's visit John Constable was 9 years old.

24. A ferry over the River Crouch some 8 miles south of Maldon.

25. Pattiswick, a village two miles west of Coggeshall.

26. Galleywood Common, near Chelmsford.

27. At Lt. Easton, 2 miles N.W. of Dunmow.

28. Edward Bright (1721–50), a Maldon shopkeeper, weighed about 42 stone, was 5 feet 9 inches tall and measured 6 feet 11 inches round the belly.

29. A village one mile S.E. of Rochford.

II

1. Sudbury Wool Hall.

2. The Braintree rural area was one of the minor centres of hop-growing in Essex.

3. Ruggles had installed a wool-mill, a revolving box within which the wool was cleaned and loosened by being tumbled about. It was probably worked by horse-power and it certainly reduced labour costs by superseding the lengthy process of beating the wool on hurdles. It is not known if the incendiarist was caught, but opposition to wool-mills proved unavailing and they were soon in use in Essex textile towns.

4. This was a remarkable labour dispute, both because of its duration and because of the able, determined way in which the 500 strikers presented and supported their case. Their efforts proved unsuccessful, however. The waste, referred to here, consisted of the thrums, the ends left on the loom after weaving and hitherto regarded as the weaver's perquisite.

5. The rowing or roughing mill had been introduced into Essex some ten years previously. It raised the nap on the cloth by means of revolving cylinders covered with teazles and worked by horses.

6. These food riots were widespread in Essex. See also p. 65.

7. This firm handled the export of cloth for a number of Essex firms. See also pp. 82–9

8. The owner of Gosfield Hall.

9. Four farms had been bought for Guy's Hospital in about 1725 when the Lumley estate was sold to pay the family's debts.

10. A number of Essex parishes tried to provide free or cheap bread in 1795 when food prices suddenly rose. These schemes were soon abandoned in favour of the so-called Speenhamland system of giving labourers allowances from the Poor Rate to bring their income up to an agreed minimum.

11. Stourbridge Fair, Cambridge, see p. 80.

12. Probably the earliest silk factory at Bocking.

13. This entry is struck out, because the sale was postponed.

III

1. Heckford lived opposite the Church porch in a house now called Clarance House. An inscription on the floor of the church nave records the heavy child mortality in his family.

2. The Maynards lived at Easton Lodge, a few miles from Thaxted.

3. The Bowling-Green was an inn at Dunmow, long since closed.

4. Romantic presumably because of the ruins of Tilty Abbey.

5. Probably Waltons. See N. Pevsner, *Buildings of England, Essex* (2nd edn., 1965), 71.

6. 'How comes it, Maecenas, that nobody lives contented with that place in life which his reason has chosen or chance has set before him?' The quotation is from the opening of the first poem in Horace's first book of *Satires*.

7. 'I prefer that your father be Thersites, provided that you yourself be like Achilles and take up Vulcan's arms, rather than that Achilles be your father and that you should resemble Thersites'. In the Iliad (II, 121 foll.) Thersites is shown as ugly, low-born and seditious. Vulcan, or Hephaistos, made for Achilles the arms with which he went forth to his famous fight with Hector.

8. Probably being grown for seed, a branch of agriculture already being developed at Coggeshall and later to become very prominent there.

9. Viticulture was probably a survival from the time of Coggeshall's Cistercian Abbey.

10. 'What their shoulders are fit to carry and what they refuse.'

11. Situated opposite the place where today stands Colchester's Albert Hall at the west end of the High Street.

IV

1. The correct spelling was Western. The Western family occupied Felix Hall for almost a century.

2. Galleywood Races, held just outside Chelmsford.

O

3. The Assembly Room of this inn, formerly one of the most important in the town, still stands in a courtyard off the West side of Head Street, Colchester.

V

1. Captain Adams of Warley Place.

2. During the 1772 food shortage (see also p. 45) the labourers tried to enforce the sale of food at pre-shortage prices.

3. Lord Rochford at St. Osyth Priory.

4. Wivenhoe sea-water baths had been started in about 1750 by a local doctor, whose assistant became their proprietor in 1756. In 1777 they were taken over by the landlord of the Anchor inn, the Munnings referred to in the letter of Aug 14, 1778.

5. Captain Harvey was owner of the Repulse, one of the country's largest revenue ships. During hostilities with France it chased a smuggling cutter too close to the shore near Calais, ran aground and was captured. It was then equipped as a French privateer, only to be re-captured by the English, but the crew spent 13 months in a Calais prison.

6. Probably Bamber Gascoyne (see p. 199).

VI

1. Holland Brook.

2. The building is now a geriatric hospital, Heath Hospital, Tendring.

VII

1. This firm handled the export of cloth for a number of Essex firms. (See also p. 46.)

2. A firm of carriers used by several Essex clothiers.

3. Stourbridge Fair, Cambridge. See Introduction to this section.

4. The Bull Inn, Leadenhall Street, terminus for several Essex carriers.

5. A Coggeshall clothier, to whom Boggis was probably supplying wool, contained in pack cloths. The newsman referred to was probably the distributor of the local weekly papers, the *Chelmsford Chronicle* and the *Ipswich Journal*.

6. Probably groups of domestic spinners who spun worsted yarn from longer wool, but possibly groups of spinners living in distant villages (see Introduction).

7. Hinxton in Cambridgeshire.

8. The Rose and Crown, Ashdon.

9. Evidently Boggis' employee, who managed the firm's spinners.

10. The letter is addressed to the parish vestry. Belchamp Walter and Helions Bumpstead are villages in N.W. Essex.

11. Probably a Norwich or Norfolk clothier or flock manufacturer, who bought some of Boggis' thrums or waste.

12. A family friend living in London.

13. The new Shire Hall of 1792, designed by John Johnson, County Surveyor, which still stands at Chelmsford.

14. A Cambridgeshire village.

15. It is not clear for what purpose this meeting was called, but Kelvedon had been used previously as the meeting place for Essex clothiers, when they wished to discuss matters affecting their common interests.

VIII

1. Harwich sea-water baths, which included a warm bath, had by this time been in existence for half a century.

2. Owner of Wivenhoe Hall.

3. A bridge about a mile and a half up the Roman River, a tributary of the Colne.

4. An inn in the centre of Fingringhoe.

5. A Wivenhoe maltster and brewer.

6. Probably the Wivenhoe Association against Horsethieves and Housebreakers, founded in 1784, but possibly just a local club.

7. A Lodge of Freemasons.

8. At Wivenhoe Park.

IX

1. Charles Keymer. His son, Carter's benefactor, was Thomas Keymer (ex. inf. Mr. J. Bensusan Butt).

2. William Tufnell, elected in 1806.

3. Colchester Philosophical Society, founded in 1820.

4. Entitled 'Lectures on Taste'.

X

1. A Spitalfields firm, which between 1827 and 1836 had a silk-throwing works in Back Lane, Coggeshall, and also employed domestic weavers on serges.

2. The Royal Mortuary in Military Road, once part of the barracks erected in Colchester during the Napoleonic Wars, was subsequently used as a silk factory.

3. This workhouse, built in 1714 in Church Street, had been maintained by Witham parish until, under the New Poor Law of 1834, it was temporarily used as one of the institutions of the new Witham Union of parishes. It was soon superseded by the building still standing at Witham on the North side of the Chelmsford road.

4. The Rev. Joseph Herrick was Minister of East Stockwell Street Congregational Chapel, Colchester. In 1843 he was ejected for a short period, but was quickly reinstated. (See also pp. 167–70.)

5. Now St. John's Street.

6. A Liberal landowner, then living at East Donyland Hall, near Colchester.

7. Probably a Friendly Society.

8. Earlier a leader of the Colchester Chartists.

9. Later to be proprietor of the town's leading engineering firm.

10. Colchester's Liberal leader over many years.

XI

1. *Pigott's Directories*, 1827–35, give the following information about Asplin and his friends:

> Jonas Asplin, M.D., Prittlewell.
> Mr. Charles Asplin, Lt. Wakering Hall.
> Rev. Wm. Ramsden, Lt. Wakering.
> Mr. Wm. D'Aranda, Southend.
> J. B. Scratton, Esq., Milton Hall, Southend.
> Robert Scratton, Esq., High St., Southend.
> Charles Miller, surgeon, Wakering.
> Michael Sheeby, surgeon, Southend.
> John Watson, surgeon, Southend.
> Christopher Parsons, The Lawn, Southchurch.
> Captain Scallon, Prittlewell.

2. An inn in Southend.

3. In his *Foulness* (Essex Record Office Publications, No. 55 (1970), 41) J. R. Smith writes of the communications between the island and the mainland prior to the opening of the military road in 1922, that 'access was by ferry, or at low water from Wakering Stairs along the Broomway. The Broomway is an ancient trackway which runs for a distance of six miles across the Maplin Sands, following the contour of the land about a quarter of a mile from the shore . . . when it was in regular use the Broomway must surely have been the most dangerous road in England, for the Maplins, a continuation of the Foulness Sands, are a vast area of almost level sand, and once the sea has reached that level, miles out, it floods over the rest like a mill race'. Mr. Smith's book also contains maps and photographs of Foulness.

4. This election was the worst in Maldon's long record of electoral corruption. T. B. Lennard, Whig country gentleman and eldest son of the owner of Belhus, Aveley, challenged the Tory coalition of the Hon. George Winn, of Warley Lodge, and Quintin Dick, a millionaire. Each of the three used bribery on an immense scale, spending between them some £50,000. Dick's tavern bills alone came to £4,000. Of the electorate of 3,113 only a tenth part came from Maldon, the remainder, like Asplin, being from other parts of Essex, or from London and even more distant places. Dick's cynical reliance on his money seems to have lost him the votes of moderate Tories like Asplin, who preferred the Essex man, Lennard, despite his being the county's Whig leader. Though he omits to record the fact, Asplin voted for Lennard as well as for Winn.

5. The school referred to was probably Prittlewell Free School, a charity school founded in 1727 and later combined with the National, or Church, School.

6. The Foulness Commission, established in 1800, was responsible for the island's protection against flooding from the sea (Smith, *op. cit.*, 27–8).

7. Possibly Milton Hamlet.

8. A small island lying between Wakering Stairs and Foulness.

9. This work, carried out by Francis Bannister, owner of Rushley Island, was successful in obtaining a copious supply of fresh water, hitherto totally lacking in the neighbourhood. Within a few years his example had been followed on the adjacent islands.

XII

1. Elizabeth Fry, the diarist's famous grandmother, lived at Upton Place, Upton Lane, West Ham.

2. Warley Barracks, built in 1805 to house 2,000 cavalry were sold in 1842 to the East India Company to accommodate troops in transit to India. (See also p. 178.)

3. Presumably Brentwood.

4. The church of St. Thomas, a chapel of ease to Romford, erected at Noak Hill by Sir Thomas Neave of Dagnam Park, as requested by his wife before her death in 1835.

XIII

1. The site referred to was the important Trinobantian centre just outside modern Colchester, containing a Roman-Celtic temple, a theatre of Classical type and extensive ranges of portico (see M. R. Hull, *Roman Colchester* (1958), 259–70).

2. If Wire identified the seal correctly, it was the one fixed to a bale of baize cloth by the officials of the Colchester Dutch Corporation who had enjoyed the

right to inspect this kind of cloth from the Corporation's establishment in Elizabeth's reign until its dissolution in 1728.

3. The siege referred to is that of 1648, when Parliamentary forces under Fairfax besieged Colchester, which had been occupied by Royalist rebels.

4. A fellow-radical of Wire's in earlier years, Clubb was still the foremost Chartist leader of the town.

5. Vincent had been the Chartist leader whose imprisonment in Monmouth gaol provoked the march of the Monmouthshire miners to Newport in 1839, the so-called Newport Rising. Vincent had now become a lecturer for the Liberal supporters of electoral reform. J. B. Harvey was the latter's leader in Colchester.

6. Son of a painter, Dunthorne had been a friend and associate of John Constable.

7. Shrub End Church.

8. Opened in 1843, these schools were built on to the structure of Culver Street Methodist Church, now demolished.

9. The area referred to is the site of Camulodunum, the Belgic town established here some 40 years before the Roman occupation. There were also extensive pottery kilns in the vicinity in Roman times.

10. A tract of 1648 on the Siege of Colchester.

11. Wire here refers to the earthern walls and ditches defending Belgic Camulodunum, which are still visible in several places.

12. Balkerne Gate, still substantially surviving, was the main gate into the Roman town. It was situated in the west wall.

13. Hythe Bridge, for instance, had collapsed on 1 April, 1839, soon after a local M.P. had called it 'elegant, substantial and in every way commodious'.

14. Named after the mythical saint of woolcombers, it had been one of the inns most frequented by clothworkers before the industry's collapse.

15. Colchester had been famous for its candied eringo since about 1600. Made from the sea holly, *eryngium maritimum*, it was valued as a sweet and as an aphrodisiac. The recipe, which was secret, had been passed down in the way described by Wire.

16. A distillery near the site of the present Public Library.

17. The clergy feared that funds would be diverted from their current building programme.

18. The drain and the 'house' are discussed in detail in Hull, *Roman Colchester*, 85 foll.

19. Now the Essex Archaeological Society.

20. The Sphinx may be seen in Colchester Castle Museum.

21. There were two silk factories in Colchester, one situated in the former Mortuary of the Napoleonic War barracks in Military Road, and the other in Dead Lane, now St. Peter Street.

22. After service in the Crimean War, 5,000 men of this force eventually arrived at Colchester. Their presence in the town in such numbers caused some apprehension, especially as a few of them had previously been involved in a fight with British soldiers at Aldershot, but their good behaviour, romantic appearance and the concerts given by their bands won them considerable popularity in Colchester.

XIV

1. The Rev. G. E. Symmonds, M.A., J.P., Vicar of Thaxted.

2. The Rosslyns were evidently living at Easton Lodge, Lt. Easton, though Miss Maynard was its owner.

3. The church had been extensively repaired a few months previously at a cost of £2,200.

4. The Rev. G. C. Tufnell, M.A., was Rector of Lt. Easton.

5. S. Scruby was a farmer on Broxted Hill. Though Joseph Arch's National Agricultural Labourers' Union had elsewhere declined since its initial success of 1872–4, in Essex it still retained a wide influence. A strike at Gt. Sampford in February, 1877, seems to have been supported in other villages in the neighbourhood, including Broxted where the farmers locked out Union members and joined the Farmers' Defence Association, set up at Dunmow in retaliation. The Union was not crushed, although its Broxted members may have suffered some victimisation if they included in their number the 'fanatici' referred to by Yonge in his entry of 5 Dec., 1877. Branches of the Union survived and Joseph Arch was very well supported at a rally in Thaxted in 1878.

6. A detached hamlet, officially called Chawreth Green, where in 1848 an infant school had been built at Viscount Maynard's expense.

7. Not Hempstead in Essex, but Hempstead in Norfolk which, like Stalham and Happisburgh, referred to by Yonge here, lie S.E. of N. Walsham.

8. 'A mere voice and nothing else.'

9. Probably Suckstead Green between Broxted and Thaxted.

10. Between Broxted and Takely.

11. ' "This way leads to the city" So press on, lad.'

12. Situated south of the Witham–Chelmsford road, built in 1728 and occupied in 1900 by Lt.-Col. J. L. Tufnell-Tyrell. (See Pevsner, *Buildings of England, Essex* (2nd edn., 1965), 83.)

13. Moores of Kelvedon ran a carriers' business, then some 60 years old, and were shortly to establish a motor bus service.

14. 'The wind drives the storm clouds, and a savage tempest pitilessly hurls down the apples before dawn.'

15. 'A harsh storm has brought a frown to the heavens.'

16. 'While through broad fields terrible destruction sweeps.'

17. Abbreviation of καὶ τὰ λοιπά, the Greek for *et cetera*.

PLATE I

SIR HENRY BATE DUDLEY (1745–1824)
(See page 200)

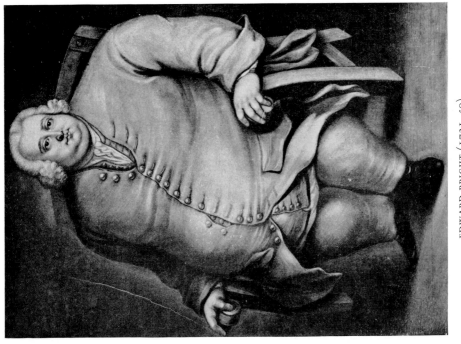

EDWARD BRIGHT (1721–50)
(See page 36)

PLATE II

WILLIAM WIRE (1804–57)
(See Chapter XIII)

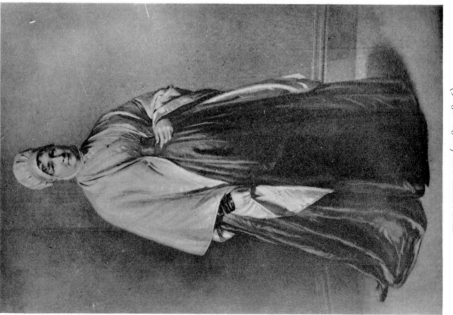

ELIZABETH FRY (1780–1846)
(See Chapter XII)

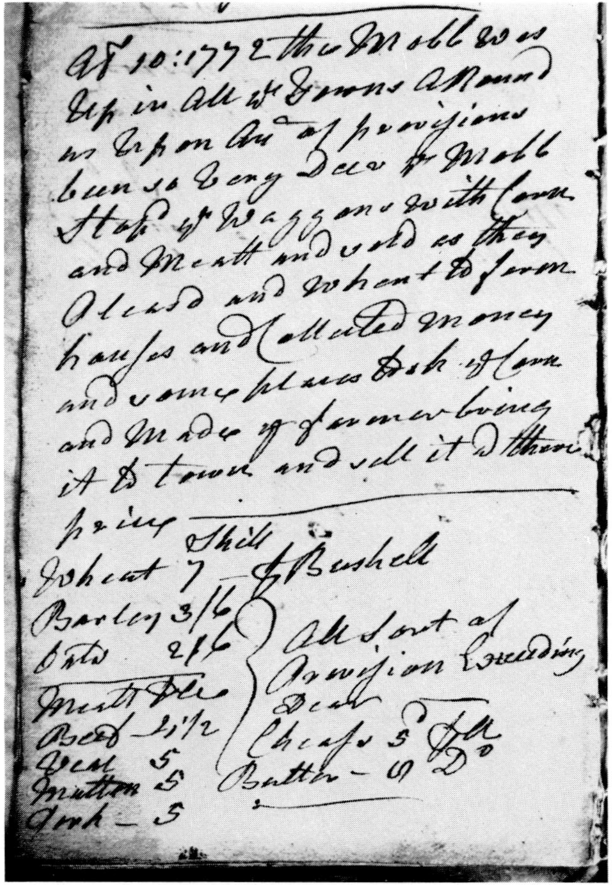
Ap 10: 1772 the Mobb was
Up in All the Towns A Round
us Upon Acc of provisions
been so Very Dear the Mobb
Stop the Waggons with Corn
and Meatt and sold as they
Pleased and Wheat to from
houses and Collected money
and some places Brok the Corn
and Made the farmer bring
it to town and sell it at their
price

Wheat 7 Shill the Bushell
Barley 3/6
Oats 2/6
Meatt the lb
Beef 2 1/2
Veal 5
Mutton 5
Pork 5

All sort of
provision Exceeding
Dear
Cheese 5 the lb
Butter 9 Do

'PARTUKLER THINGS' NOTED BY
JOSEPH SAVILL IN APRIL, 1772
(*See page 41*)

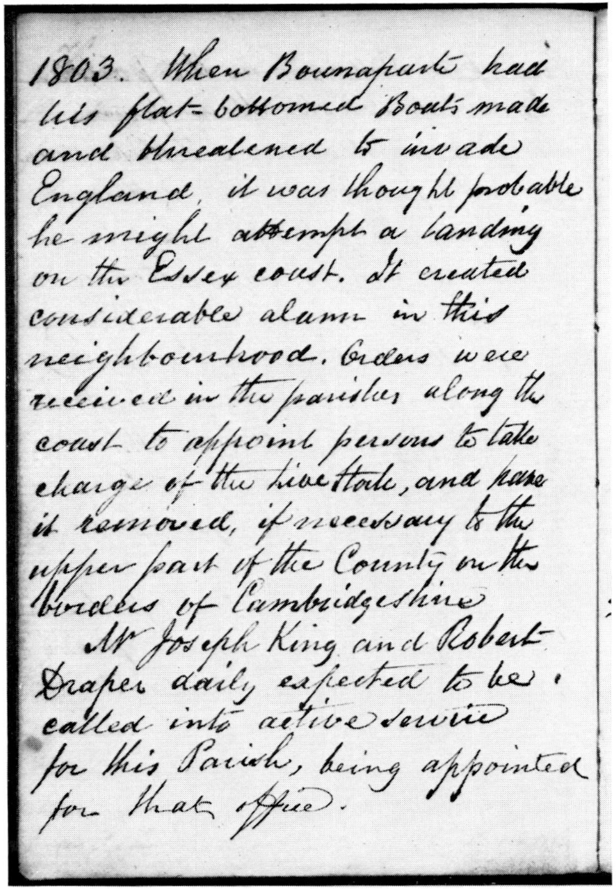
1803. When Bounaparte had
his flat-bottomed Boats made
and threatened to invade
England, it was thought probable
he might attempt a landing
on the Essex coast. It created
considerable alarm in this
neighbourhood. Orders were
received in the parishes along the
coast to appoint persons to take
charge of the Live Stock, and have
it removed, if necessary to the
upper part of the County on the
borders of Cambridgeshire
Mr Joseph King and Robert
Draper daily expected to be
called into active service
for this Parish, being appointed
for that office.

CHARLES HICKS RECALLS THE THREAT
OF INVASION IN 1803
(*See page 71*)

PLATE IV

EASTON LODGE DESCRIBED BY THE REV. WILLIAM COOPER
AND VISITED BY THE REV. D. N. YONGE
(See Chapters III and XIV)

WIVENHOE PARK, THE HOME OF MARY REBOW
(See Chapter V)

PLATE V

LITTLE WAKERING HALL, ONCE THE HOME OF THE
ASPLIN FAMILY
(See Chapter XI)

BOREHAM HOUSE AS IT WAS KNOWN TO THE REV. D. N. YONGE
(See Chapter XIV)

PLATE VI

THE OLD WORKHOUSE, TENDRING
A parish workhouse, replaced by Tendring Union Workhouse in 1838 (see page 77)

MIDDLE ROW, COLCHESTER HIGH STREET, IN THE 19TH CENTURY
(See page 185)

PLATE VII

GATHERING COPPERAS ON THE SHORE AT DOVERCOURT IN THE 18TH CENTURY

(See page 6)

A PROSPECT OF WIVENHOE WELL KNOWN TO JOSEPH PAGE

(See Chapter VIII)

PLATE VIII

SOUTHEND (OF THE PARISH OF PRITTLEWEL) AS IT WAS KNOWN TO
DR. JOHN ASPLIN IN THE 1820S

(See Chapter XI)

INDEX

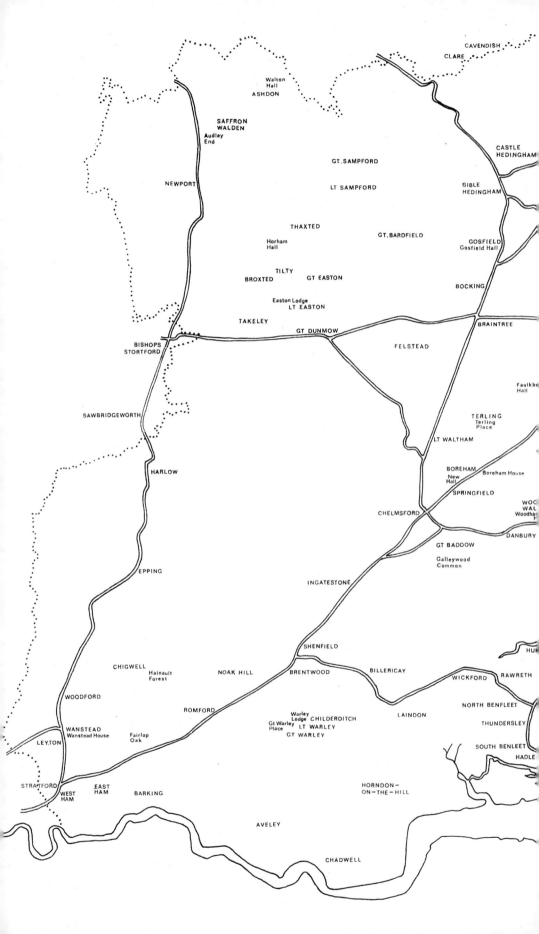